THE UNITED STATES AND TURKEY

With contributions by

Morton Abramowitz

Henri J. Barkey

Cengiz Çandar

Omer Celik

Yalım Eralp

Ercan Kumcu

Philip Robins

M. James Wilkinson

THE UNITED STATES AND TURKEY
ALLIES IN NEED

Morton Abramowitz, Editor

A Century Foundation Book

The Century Foundation Press ◆ New York

The Century Foundation, formerly the Twentieth Century Fund, sponsors and supervises timely analyses of economic policy, foreign affairs, and domestic political issues. Not-for-profit and nonpartisan, it was founded in 1919 and endowed by Edward A. Filene.

LIBRARY OF CONGRESS CATALOGING-IN-PUBLICATION DATA

The United States and Turkey : allies in need / Morton Abramowitz, editor.
        p. cm.
Includes bibiliographical refrences and index.
    ISBN 0-87078-479-X (pbk. : alk. paper)
    1.   United States--Foreign relations--Turkey.   2.   Turkey--Foreign relations--
United States.   3.   United States--Foreign relations--2001-
4.   September 11 Terrorist Attacks, 2001--Influence.   5.   War on Terrorism,
2001---Diplomatic history.   6.   Turkey--Politics and government--1980-
I. Abramowitz, Morton, 1933- II. Title.
    E183.8.T8U537 2003
    327.730561'09'0511--dc21

                                                                           2003001164

Design and photoillustration: Claude V. Goodwin
Manufactured in the United States of America.

Foreword

Two years ago, The Century Foundation sponsored a volume of essays that explored both internal political developments in Turkey and that nation's complex relationship with the United States. Senior fellow Morton Abramowitz, former American ambassador to Turkey, guided the development of the project and edited the resulting volume. At the time of that publication, Turkey was not in the front rank of American interests. Indeed, the summer of 2000 was a period of less than intense interest in foreign policy generally. The presidential election that year, for example, provoked few meaningful exchanges on foreign affairs or national security. Both candidates had things to say, of course, but it was apparent that neither thought such comments would have much, if any, impact on the outcome of the election. As predicted in the earlier volume, given the breadth and salience of America's impact on the world, such a situation was likely to be temporary. Still, no one anticipated that the unhappy events set in motion since September 11, 2001, would be the cause of such a sharp and compelling shift in the priorities of both American officials and the public. National security, terrorism, and statecraft are now at the top of the list of national concerns. The Bush administration's focus on overturning the regime in Iraq, in particular, has sparked new attention to all the countries in the Middle East, especially Turkey.

As reflected in the earlier volume, the political situation in Turkey has been complex and the cause of some dismay for the past decade, although during the past year there have been a number of startling developments. As of this writing, the United States is applying increasing pressure on its longtime ally to play a much stronger supporting role than it did in 1991 in another coalition organized for a conflict with Iraq—this time in a war that would be a sure flashpoint for governments throughout the Islamic world. Moreover, Turkey's larger relationship with the West has been further complicated by the latest setback in its efforts to secure a firm date for membership talks with the European Union. At the same time, Turkey has a new and untried government headed by the Justice and Development Party, a party with strong Islamist roots.

Like the earlier volume, this set of essays has been written by individuals with great expertise who bring deep knowledge and experience as well as important and fresh insights to the issues they discuss. Again, like the book published in 2000, this work is not comprehensive in the sense of addressing all of the questions that might be of interest to an American or a Turkish audience. It does, however, cover many of the most important matters, including political Islam, the Kurdish issue, the critical Cyprus question, Turkey's EU dilemma, the Iraq problem, and the increasingly complex U.S.-Turkish relationship. For both policymakers and citizens, staying abreast of the best thinking about Turkey is obviously of vital importance. While the authors make no claims to certainty about the future, taken together, these essays do offer a rich menu of information and analysis about this fascinating and critical American ally.

This volume is part of a broad Century Foundation program examining American foreign policy in the post–cold war era. It complements work we have supported on specific regions such as Karl Meyer's forthcoming book *The Dust of Empire: The Race for Mastery in the Asian Heartland* and the report of our task force on Russia, done in collaboration with the Stanley Foundation, as well as explorations of the larger issues involved in foreign policymaking by Henry Nau, Walter Russell Mead, and Robert Art, an analysis of American intelligence policy and national security by Gregory Treverton, and our major, ongoing examination of the issues involved in homeland security. Indeed, through these and many more projects, we have been attempting to contribute to the debates raised by the sweeping reorientation of American interests since the end of the Soviet regime.

Once again, we are indebted to Mort Abramowitz for his leadership in making this book a reality. On behalf of the Trustees of The Century Foundation, I thank all the contributors for their timely and important work.

RICHARD C. LEONE, *President*
The Century Foundation
January 2003

CONTENTS

Foreword *by Richard C. Leone*   v

Acknowledgments   viii

1. Introduction: The United States and Turkey:
    New Opportunities, Old Problems
    Morton Abramowitz   1

2. The Unfinished Struggle for Economic Stability
    Ercan Kumcu   31

3. Turkey and the Fate of Political Islam
    Omer Celik   61

4. Turkey and the Kurds: Approaching a Modus Vivendi?
    Philip Robins   85

5. An Insider's View of Turkey's Foreign Policy
    and Its American Connection
    Yalım Eralp   109

6. The Post–September 11 United States through
    Turkish Lenses
    Cengiz Çandar   145

7. The Cyprus Problem: The Last Act
    M. James Wilkinson   173

8. The Endless Pursuit: Improving U.S.–Turkish Relations
    Henri J. Barkey   207

9. Afterword: Turkey's 2002 Elections: A Political Earthquake
    and Its Aftermath
    Cengiz Çandar   251

Notes   257

Index   277

About the Contributors   289

ACKNOWLEDGMENTS

The authors want to thank The Century Foundation for its encouragement and support for this book. The editorial staff was superb in helping prepare the book for publication and putting up with all sorts of problems involved in the final product because of the significant changes in Turkey in late 2002. The editor is particularly grateful to his assistants, Wouter Vandersypen of The Century Foundation and Zeynep Orhun, for their dedicated work with the authors and their manuscripts.

Chapter One

Introduction
The United States and Turkey: New Opportunities, Old Problems

Morton Abramowitz

Why This Book?

A reader of our last set of essays on Turkey—*Turkey's Transformation and American Policy*—might well ask, Why are you doing another set after only two years? Did you get it all wrong? Forget something? Have there been radical changes in Turkey or its relations with the United States? The sponsor of this book, The Century Foundation, certainly asked these questions.

There are a number of reasons for this second book of essays. While countries rarely change overnight, major changes have taken place in Turkey that we did not predict, although we expressed concern about persistent domestic political frailties and growing economic uncertainties. The year 1999 was one of promise. By 2002, Turkey was in something of a shambles. Turkey's economic crisis started in 2000, and in 2001 the country fell into a deep depression that apparently has begun to lift after more than a year. The large jump in both unemployment and prices produced enormous pain for millions of Turks. For the eighteenth time, Turkey became a ward of the international community; to date it has had available over $31 billion from the International Monetary Fund (IMF), making Turkey the fund's largest recipient. The long economic crisis severely damaged Turkish foreign policy, aggravating particularly its already doubtful desirability as a European Union (EU) member.

With an international gun to its head, Turkey's desperate coalition government passed some twenty pieces of major financial and economic reform legislation required by the IMF to get the funds. The legislation will not lead to economic nirvana, but it will significantly improve the ways both the Turkish public and private sectors do their business. It has already done so. Reexamining basic questions of what happened to Turkey's economy and whether Turkey can grow on a steady basis without recurring crises is in order.

September 11 produced another major change: a concerted American international effort against terrorism and "rogue states" having or intending to acquire weapons of mass destruction, notably Turkey's neighbors Iran and Iraq. A large part of the U.S. agenda of the 1990s with Turkey—the attention to internal shortcomings—has been shunted to the rear. Once again, the focus has become Turkey as a strategically vital country. Indeed, strategic considerations, many Turks believe, were a major factor in why the U.S. government went along with the IMF bailout, even after the Bush administration publicly declared its abhorrence of such economic rescues.

Rising to the top of the American agenda has been Turkey's cooperation in counterterrorism. War in Afghanistan created interest in Turkey's providing forces for peacekeeping in Kabul and replacing Great Britain in leading the international security forces. Iraq, of course, arouses the greatest American interest in Turkey because of the need for its cooperation in any effort to get rid of U.S. enemy number one, Saddam Hussein. Indeed, in 2002 Iraq sometimes seemed the only preoccupation in Turkish–American relations. Working out an arrangement for Turkey's support for a war it most vociferously does not want has become America's highest priority in Turkish policy.

Does Turkey's enhanced strategic importance require American policymakers to alter the U.S. relationship with Turkey in terms of continuing and increasing assistance? To take a different stance on issues particularly important to Turkey such as Cyprus, where the Turkish position gets no support from any government, including the United States? On the Cyprus issue, it seems bizarre to many American conservatives for the United States simply to accept tiny Greek

Cyprus's admission to the EU at the expense of giant Turkey's exclusion, possibly producing political instability in Turkey and conceivably, if improbably, affecting Turkey's ability to cooperate with the United States in the Middle East militarily. Should Turkey use this crucial time to seek a better bargain from the United States? A tougher stance in Ankara, however, is complicated by Turkey's dependence on the United States for support in the IMF and for advanced weaponry.

Finally, fundamental change in the workings of the Turkish state has speeded up because of the economic crisis. How far and how quickly Turkey will go in establishing political stability, lowering limits on political freedom and public expression, reducing vast corruption in government, and diminishing military involvement in political life are unclear. The November election may be one of those great watersheds I keep looking for in Turkish politics, completely changing the political party scene by bringing a party to power with strong Islamist roots. That can have profound internal and external implications or turn out to be a large but momentary blip.

Change has been propelled mostly by disaster and external forces—prolonged political and economic failure, IMF demands for economic reform, and EU requirements for political reform if Turkey wants to join Europe. A fierce struggle within the Turkish elite has been going on for the past few years over the EU and the internal changes needed to win admittance. The outcome will affect the course of Turkish life for decades to come. This struggle contributed to the sudden implosion of the Ecevit government in the summer of 2002 and new elections in November. That implosion also permitted the Turkish parliament to enact suddenly and surprisingly an impressive package of reforms—long stalled in the government coalition—meeting many of the EU's Copenhagen requirements for membership. Ultimately incorporating Muslim Turkey into the EU—should it occur—will be one of the world's seminal events.

The passage of time also offers opportunity for reflection, constructive criticism, and even, alas, changes in view. A book with a focus on policy must not be mesmerized—difficult as that may be—by the unfolding of the incredible events invariably served up in Turkey. We had to try to put events in Turkey in a context that would not be overwhelmed by the turbulence of Turkish politics, to distinguish what is ephemeral from what is not. That factor also influenced our thinking on the selection of subjects.

We also felt subjects had to be looked at from a fresh perspective and that we must not simply bring the first volume's essays up to date. Political Islam deserved its own chapter, particularly after September 11 and for its impact on Turkey's internal stability and possible membership negotiations with the EU. We also wanted a greater Turkish perspective: a chapter, for example, dealing with Turkey's approach to foreign policy and particularly toward the United States. Four of the seven authors are Turks, including two with much policymaking experience, and a fifth, a Turkish-American with State Department experience.

This volume retains something of the first's idiosyncratic character. We chose to focus on subjects central to understanding the present U.S.–Turkey relationship. We left out discussion of many specific foreign policy issues. As we did with our first volume, the authors met in Istanbul in the late spring of 2002 and went over in detail every draft essay. Both volumes complement each other and, taken together, present a more rounded, better informed view of the policy context of Turkish–American relations over the past decade.

One thing has not changed in producing a second book. As we moved toward our finish, once again major new developments—this time the fall of the Ecevit coalition, parliamentary passage of reform legislation, and the scheduling of new parliamentary elections—took place in quick succession, forcing us to scurry around and reexamine our basically completed handiwork. Turkey always shows a wonderful capacity to surprise. We await with eagerness and some trepidation for this book the results of the November elections.

CONTINUING INTERNAL WOES

Producing a book of essays on today's Turkey sometimes seems a folly given the roller coaster Turkey has been on for the past ten years or so; you are likely to find yourself always behind the curve. Nevertheless, most of the underlying difficulties have not changed much. The following key interrelated issues continue to roil Turkey's domestic scene: political fragmentation and governmental instability; the inability to produce new political leaders; military intrusion in political life; the fate of religious political parties; the difficulties of better integrating

Turkey's large Kurdish population; and financial crises, depression, and undulant growth.

Most Turks agree that these are issues they must overcome. They have been vigorously arguing about them for the past decade. On some, substantial progress has been made in the past few years; on others, little has changed. Progress has been less the work of internal reformers or popular pressures and more the demands of two international institutions: the IMF and the EU. Without the foreign hand, Turkey does not seem able to sort out its internal difficulties.

To the surprise of many Turks, the coalition government of Bulent Ecevit lasted three years and might well have lasted to the required 2004 elections but for the deterioration of Ecevit's health. It was held together not by strong programs and clear goals—it could not be because of its very disparate nature—but essentially by failure: it produced a massive, lengthy depression. This failure, combined with an old man's relentless determination despite ill health, convinced the coalition to hang on, hoping that recovery would occur before 2004 to permit the three parties to overcome their unpopularity and return, if not to power, at least to parliament until the EU issue blew the coalition apart. Economic crisis did produce one long-term dividend: bowing to necessity, the coalition carried out—with little enthusiasm given its short-term economically contractive nature—an IMF economic stabilization and reform program, which so far has prevented the country from imploding.

Politically and economically, the past decade has been a wasted one in many respects. In fact, the biggest impediment to increasing Turkish prospects for EU membership has probably been the decade's persistent economic turmoil and lack of growth, although other factors, such as religion or immigration, get the most attention in Turkey. The country has failed to attract foreign investment. Had Turkey's numerous governments successfully managed economic affairs and produced a steady, significant level of growth, the ability of the EU to continue to fend off Turkey, to not take the country too seriously, and to treat it cavalierly would have been harder, if not impossible. Turkey unfortunately does not have too much goodwill among the governments or peoples of Europe to fall back on. Nor can Turkey's people take much comfort from the fact that per capita income in 2001 was lower than in 1991 and that some 60 percent of the country has fallen below the poverty level. Income inequalities remain as bad as those almost anywhere else in the world.

TURKEY WILL NOT BE FIXED UNTIL ITS ECONOMY GETS FIXED. Its turbulent economic ride has not precluded a great measure of globalization and the establishment of a vigorous modern sector. It has permitted its military establishment to expand its capabilities vastly and pursue a long internal war. Impressive infrastructure has been built. But the decade also has included periodic crises and great human suffering such as we see today. The major causes of these crises have been the financial and economic policies of the Turkish government, which have their roots in the weaknesses of government coalitions and the political system. Excessive government spending has been central to Turkey's continuing inflation and its inability to maintain a stable economy. The debt burden is enormous—almost equal to its Gross National Product at the end of 1991—which the IMF steps in periodically to control; the profits of many firms, including very large ones, come less from commerce and more from interest on government debt. Government, particularly the banking system, has been the principal source of corruption, and many informed Turkish businessmen assert that corruption has mushroomed since the time of Turgut Özal. Corruption is a genuine public preoccupation. The subject produced an incredible public spat between the president and the prime minister in 2001 that sent the Turkish lira into a tailspin and turned out to be the final straw precipitating the current depression.

The latest economic crisis has been the deepest and longest-lasting since World War II. Recovery seems to have begun and progress has been made in financial stabilization under the IMF stand-by. The current IMF stabilization program followed immediately on one that "failed miserably." Most important and embarrassing for the coalition government, they had to import a prominent Turkish economist at the World Bank, who had been away from his country for twenty-five years, to take charge of the economy. Without Kemal Dervis it is doubtful that Turkey would have received so much IMF funding and been able to carry out a serious reform program. The IMF-dictated programs have produced, inter alia, a floating exchange rate, a long-sought separation of the central bank from government control, the consolidation of state banks and the elimination of weak private banks, controls on government spending making it difficult for politicians to spend at will, and more transparency and accountability in the system.

In this volume, former central bank deputy director Ercan Kumcu reviews in depth the travail Turkey has gone through over the past three years, with an eye as to whether crises are likely to recur with such frequency. In his view, bad economic management by the government, faulty IMF policy, and the coalition's political weakness produced and accentuated the crisis. He acknowledges the benefit of recent reforms, but strong resolve and less fragmented government, he feels, are needed to enact further fundamental and politically difficult reforms such as seriously downsizing the government and expanding the tax base. Unlike leading Turkish government officials, he is not sanguine that the measures so far enacted, however restrictive, will be sufficient to prevent bad financial behavior by Turkey's politicians and weak coalition governments. The current stabilization program, he argues, has been flawed by its failure to find ways to encourage growth. The inability of the country to grow over the past few years in turn will make further reform far more difficult politically.

POLITICAL PARTY REFORM IN TURKEY HAS BEEN NOTABLE MOSTLY FOR ITS CONTINUING ABSENCE. The lack of democracy in political parties has allowed leaders to remain almost indefinitely in power, whether they are successful or not in winning elections. Only the passage of time produces change. Few politicians challenge their party leaders and survive. That is why Ecevit and Suleyman Demirel—mostly considered to be failures as leaders—have kept appearing and reappearing for more than thirty years. Young emerging political stars like Cem Boyner in the 1990s and Mehmet Ali Bayar in 2002 are invariably portrayed as white knights riding to Turkey's rescue with their sudden appearance on the political scene, hailed and to a great extent created by a Turkish media desperate for new faces in politics. But quickly the new knight burns himself out and is forgotten. Only Kemal Dervis, parachuting into Turkish politics in 2002, has had some continuing resonance on the political scene because of his formidable abilities, his excellent reputation, and above all his major contributions to Turkey. But even his political appeal has faded in the election campaign.

All this has furthered the fragmentation of the political system and the continuing decline of the center parties and the rise of religious and nationalist parties. Governments end up as a mélange, with one or another party usually repudiating many of the past positions they have publicly espoused and unable to carry out effective programs. Dervis's efforts in 2002 to unite the left before the November elections failed, but he may have helped the political landscape by joining with the Republican People's Party (CHP) and making it once again a serious party and a possible contender to the Justice and Development (AK)

Party emerging from the November elections as Turkey's leading party. Interestingly enough, the November elections could eliminate or reduce the fragmentation (for awhile, at least) with one or two parties dominating the parliament and perhaps one or two others barely meeting the 10 percent barrier. In looking at Turkish politics, it sometimes seems that Turkey has a unique and infinite ability to repeatedly immolate itself in a reasonably democratic manner and always arise phoenix-like from the wreckage. The capacity of the Turkish electorate to endure successive bad coalition governments and bad policies in those areas affecting their most basic interests has never failed to amaze me. Conceivably that patience will end with the upcoming elections.

How much Turkey's political miasma can be attributed to the military and its periodic intrusions—overtly or quietly—into Turkey's political life to remedy the deficiencies of governments and political parties can be and is much argued. Turkey is the only state in Europe where such interventions occur. Secular and democratic Turks like to have it both ways: they want more democracy and strong civilian leadership, but they are mostly pleased—openly or, more likely, secretly— to have the military around should disorder or Islamism rear their heads or mainstream political parties falter. And, except for an increasing number in the media, the elite do not protest when the military conveys a strong perspective about the dangers from Islamist political parties. The religious parties see the military as their principal scourge, but they are careful not to go after it frontally, believing that would be electoral and/or judicial folly.

For its part, the military would prefer to stay out of politics; there are no Turkish pashas on horseback. It is easy to understand the military's despair about civilian governments. In the continuing political crisis of 2002, the military appears to have been very restrained. Whatever the apparent conflict within the military over the internal changes needed to meet the EU's Copenhagen criteria, it did not intervene to prevent the parliamentary passage in August 2002 of a reform package limiting the death penalty, allowing Kurdish to be used in education and in the media, and reducing limits on free expression. On the other hand, there is no doubt that, for the military, the Islamist and Kurdish issues remain central problems to the existence and territorial integrity of modern Turkey. Winning in these realms is not a one-time proposition for the military, and how the new reform legislation is implemented remains to be seen. In responding to perceived threats from political Islam, the military seeks firmness—which, it believes, governments frequently are not willing to show because Islam as religion has become a popular political vehicle for candidates. The EU, however, is less charitable about the Turkish military's role in political life. It professes itself unprepared to allow Turkey to begin membership negotiations when the military continues to be involved in political life on the basis of the unique and continuing threats to Turkey and its unity. This issue with the EU is far from resolved.

ON TWO NEURALGIC POLITICAL ISSUES—POLITICAL ISLAM AND KURDS—THERE HAS BEEN CONSIDERABLE CHANGE, ALTHOUGH NOT ALL TURKS WOULD AGREE. On the first, the overthrow in 1997 of the coalition government led by Islamist Necmettin Erbakan and his Welfare Party inflicted a grave blow to Islamist aspirations. The Erbakan-led Islamist movement soon found itself increasingly marginalized, particularly once its leader was banned from political life in 1998 for five years. An emerging new, more modern wing of the party saw that the still-dominant Erbakan, banned or not, was an albatross. Hopes for attaining power depended heavily on much greater tolerance from Turkey's secular leadership, particularly the military; that would be impossible with Erbakan in effective control of the party. This wing broke with Erbakan in 2001 and established the AK Party. The AK Party has tried to make peace with the secularists and proclaims loud and strong that it wants to be part of the broad prevailing Turkish political consensus. It has publicly adopted a more democratic, more nationalist, less one-dimensional religious posture. Their party headquarters usually shows a young, mostly secular face. Party leaders have indicated continuity in foreign policy and reached out to American conservatives and Jewish groups to show they are the real thing and not the old fundamentalist bogey. The AK Party's present leader, Recip Tayyip Erdogan, the most popular political leader in Turkey today, frequently asserts that his party is a center-right party, not a religious one. His party has consistently led in the polling during 2002 by a large margin. Erbakan's new party incarnation—now called Saadet or Felicity Party—has dwindled in significance.

Omer Celik, a journalist and now a winning AK Party parliamentarian, provides a brief history of the political Islam movement in Turkey in this volume. He points out the special conditions in Turkey that, for the past fifty years, helped shape a radically different political Islam ethos than in Muslim countries of the Middle East, one without violent predispositions and ultimately willing to put aside traditional political-religious goals. He describes how political Islam in Turkey frequently changed its spots, taking on different postures—for example, rightist or nationalist—at different periods in Turkey's political evolution in a continuing effort to advance beyond its small number of devotees. In this way it succeeded in making itself more politically respectable, attracting wider voter attention and enabling it to better survive, and ultimately come to power through elections. Celik believes that the overthrow of Erbakan was a decisive event for political Islam in Turkey, putting an effective finish to true Islamist parties in Turkey and to Erbakan as the central Islamist politician after forty years. He characterizes the AK Party as a center-right party suffused with an Islamic consciousness but without the aim of promoting a political system dominated by Islam and particularly Islamic law.

Even if this change is in fact genuine, many, but not all, secularists are skeptical of the AK Party's rhetoric, its dedication to democracy, or its acceptance of the Turkish political consensus. They do not trust Erdogan and his colleagues. They fear that, should the AK Party attain power, the rhetoric will change; that after a decent interval it will focus on enlarging religion's role in public life and whittling away Turkey's secular nature. There are in fact serious disconnects between the interviews Erdogan gives to the mainstream Turkish and Western media and, I am told, how he sometimes speaks to the faithful. Kurdish political leaders often characterize the AK Party as pro-Ataturk in Ankara, pro-Kurdish in Bitlis (the southeast where most of Turkey's Kurds live), and pro-Islamist in the heavily religious Konya. AK Party's candidate list has also aroused some concern in secular circles.

In September 2000, Erdogan was tasting the prospects of power. But his dream was rudely interrupted when, after a long court battle, he was barred from running for parliament. Whatever its political impact on the elections, it is not clear who will lead the party in parliament and become its first prime minister should it attain power. The party has taken in adherents from all walks of life and keeping it together and singing the same tune, including its more religious members, may not be easy. After the elections the party will make every effort to find a way to permit Erdogan to take a seat in parliament. Certainly the military still is deeply skeptical of the AK Party. It could be proscribed after the election, but more likely the military will first watch closely its performance should it form a government. Erdogan still has a tough road to travel to convince secularists that the leopard has changed its spots.

THE "KURDISH ISSUE" WAS FOR YEARS TURKEY'S MOST VIOLENT, PAINFUL, AND COSTLY PROBLEM. It has been radically transformed. While occasional skirmishes occur and the Turkish military continues to monitor PKK activities carefully in northern Iraq, casualties have basically ceased and the issue gets far less public notice. PKK leader Abdullah Ocalan remains alone on his island but no longer faces the death penalty. His political future is over, yet he remains the leader of the movement. Nevertheless, the Southeast, the locus of the fighting, continues to be a terrible sore, much of its population displaced and the bulk of its people still enthralled to poverty. Plenty of talk is still heard of government intent to transform the area economically, but there is little evidence of any serious effort. Depression and a lack of urgency have taken their toll. The specter of Kurdish separatism, however, remains, not from the PKK but from the Iraqi Kurds. The most immediate concern—and it could indeed become a big one—is the emergence of a Kurdish entity from the possible disintegration of Iraq or a serious loosening of centralized power in Baghdad after an American military destruction of the Saddam Hussein regime. Most of Turkey is increasingly concerned by such a possibility.

Despite the decline of the PKK, the Kurdish issue internally does not go away. Indeed, in a sense the whole country for two years has been hung up on Kurdish issues—all related less to concerns over dealing with Kurdish grievances and more to meeting the EU's Copenhagen political requirements so that Turkey's membership negotiations with the EU might begin. Part of the debate has been on abolishing the death penalty, which turned into an anti-abolition political effort led by the Nationalist Action Party to play on the emotional public interest in executing Ocalan for his responsibility for the death of thousands of Turks in the war against the PKK. Many Turks have wanted to pursue the execution of Ocalan to the bitter end, despite this being a barrier to negotiations with the EU. A similar debate has gone on over education and broadcasting in Kurdish. On these issues, a broad element of Turks, including many in the military, have been opposed to any loosening of existing restrictions, still seeing such a development as the start of the slippery slope toward Kurdish secession. The inability to resolve this debate politically hindered Turkey's EU fortunes, but in August 2002 the parliament passed the long-sought reform legislation cited above. Another, less vocal debate has been going on over whether to proscribe the leading Kurdish political party once again, this time renamed HADEP (the People's Democratic Party)

and most recently changed to DEHAP (the Democratic People's Party).
Not surprisingly, the judicial system banned the party leader from
running for parliament.

In short, Turks have treated the Kurdish issue for the past few
years as a constricted one and show little sense of urgency about the
growth of serious dissatisfactions among Kurds or about meeting
the common needs found in other democratic countries of ethnically
diverse populations. This is not surprising. Turks are increasingly tired
of the issue. They feel they have won the war against terrorism, and
now legislation has been passed giving Kurds more rights. Turks have
expressed contempt for the PKK's transformation into a political party
and refuse to have anything to do with its new politicians. They resist
a general amnesty for PKK members. The question of actual implementation of the recent legislative reform measures awaits a new government.

In his chapter, Philip Robins discusses the Kurdish issue in detail.
He believes there has been movement in a positive direction by both
Kurds and Turks to diminishing hostility, but there is still a long way to
go and many uncertainties. The Turkish govenment, he feels, should
be pursuing change more aggressively, taking advantage of the vastly
altered Kurdish situation and the significant moderation of Kurdish
demands. Turkey is missing a good opportunity to diminish Kurdish
grievances further with little threat to the country. He also thinks that
Turkey fails to perceive the depth of the EU's common values, even if
Europe is reticent about speaking out openly and sharply on the
Kurdish issue. EU unhappiness with Turkish treatment of the Kurds,
even with the new legislation, could adversely impact and at a minimum delay the process of Turkish integration into Europe, which in
turn could harm Turkey's democratic liberalization process. The
Kurdish issue is not dead and could arise more starkly from the activities of militant Kurds in Europe and, most importantly, from developments in northern Iraq.

IS THE EU IN TURKEY'S FUTURE?

Whatever the importance of Turkey's role in the Caucasus and Central
Asia, however useful its relations with Israel or troublesome its continuing problems with Greece, despite the likelihood of an American

war on Iraq and its economic and political spillover to Turkey, the most important issue for Turkey this decade is clear: can Turkey seriously proceed toward EU membership negotiations. The answer to this question, vital for Turkey and its economy and of great importance to the world, remains uncertain.

In Turkey, EU admission is a foreign policy issue, a domestic political issue, and at bottom an existential issue. It promises profound changes in Turkish life, even though many Turks do not realize that. Simply proceeding to negotiations will require major alterations in Turkey's management of internal affairs and enormous advances in cleaning up its persistent economic difficulties. It will likely also require a settlement in Cyprus, another fiercely neuralgic issue in Turkey. That is an enormous amount to put on Turkey's plate at this time of weakness and uncertainty in the political system, when the nature, strength, and direction of the next government are uncertain. Whatever Turkey does, it is the EU that will make the final determination and that could depend on the domestic politics of key countries.

The Turkish elite has been split on joining the EU, but by all polling the public is supportive. Much of the exuberance for the EU is in the cities, not the countryside. By and large, the public believes that membership is about economics pure and simple: that integration into Europe will lead to prosperity. Major elements of the elite, including the military, however, have been divided over how dangerous to Turkey's stability are the internal changes required by the EU. The upcoming national elections may be a referendum on the EU for the politicians of Istanbul, but it is not why the AK Party, which strongly supports EU admission, has advanced its fortunes. They are running on the economy and voter resentment at the way the country has been governed.

Turks have another dilemma, which EU opponents like the Nationalist Action Party are quick to point out: making the changes necessary for membership talks to begin will still not necessarily lead to that negotiation or ultimately to membership. Many Turks remain deeply skeptical that the EU will in the end accept Turkey, and the conservative electoral advance this year in a number of European states has reinforced those doubts. Similarly, on the Cyprus issue, those skeptical of abandoning Rauf Denktash will be reinforced by the fear of political retribution for "selling Cyprus" without any certainty that it will produce negotiations on admission. While the reform legislation passed in August 2002 has helped move Turkish membership negotiations

along, many question whether it will be enough to get the EU leaders
to offer Turkey a date for such negotiations at the Copenhagen summit
in December 2002. If, on the other hand, there is also a Cyprus settlement or real progress toward one, it would be much more difficult for
the EU not to give Turkey a date.

The debate over the EU in Turkey, however, has not advanced
to the point, given the uncertainties, that Turks are seriously considering either alternatives to EU accession or the posture that should be
adopted if EU negotiations are seriously delayed. Indeed, they may
have become collectively delusional in their expectation that they will
and should be offered membership talks. Occasionally a prominent
Turk throws out the notion of the United States as some sort of alternative to the EU. That idea gets an endorsement from some American
conservatives, but so far a new American–Turkish relationship has not
become a serious part of the Turkish debate. Conceivably it could
become the fallback if Turkey's EU efforts are perceived as failed or
moribund. Some senior Turkish officials argue that 2002 is not as crucial a year for the EU's future as its proponents make out, that Turkey
does not have to hurry to try to get into the EU and should make the
required internal changes at its own pace. The anti-EU school seems to
believe that Turkey is sufficiently large and strong to make it on its
own, or even that the EU will in the end come around to Turkey's terms.

The Cyprus issue has become an integral part of the EU debate
and is now perhaps the biggest fly in Turkey's EU ointment. For many
years, the Cyprus dispute has been the principal difficulty in Turkey–
Greece relations, rocking along in seemingly endless negotiations for
a settlement. Indeed, mention the Cyprus issue to almost anyone in
the State Department let alone to the wider public and eyes glaze over.
The issue, however, took on a new cast when the Republic of Cyprus
began serious negotiations with the EU for membership. In 2002 it
became urgent, as Cyprus certainly has met all EU membership
requirements and will be offered membership at the December 2002
summit in Copenhagen. The EU has warned Turkey not only that
Cyprus will be offered membership whether or not the two Cypriot
parties reach a settlement but also that Turkey's EU membership
prospects will be affected by failure to reach a settlement.

This was a gauntlet thrown down to Turkey. The Ecevit government responded in a tough way, declaring that the EU stance is unacceptable and warning that it would annex the northern portion of
Cyprus if the EU offers membership to Greek Cyprus on behalf of the

entire island. That is unlikely and would certainly put a damper on Turkey's admission prospects. Indeed, if the EU goes ahead with offering membership to Greek Cyprus, many Turks doubt that Turkey will ever enter the EU without a Cyprus settlement, since the two Greek states could hold Turkish admission hostage to a settlement.

Something of a game of chicken has gotten under way, and the Cyprus issue has been effectively turned into a much broader one: the future of Turkey, its basic stability, and, some fear, even its orientation. The EU Commission recommended in October not to offer membership negotiations to Turkey. Conceivably, EU leaders at the summit in December could reverse that, and face much pressure to do so, but it is unlikely without real progress on Cyprus, and possibly not even then.

We are probably witnessing, as James Wilkinson points out in his chapter, "the last act" of the Cyprus drama as we have known it for twenty-five years. Either the two aged leaders, Rauf Denktash and Glafcos Clerides—adversaries for nearly a half a century and once again in face-to-face negotiations since January 2002—will work out a settlement or show progress toward a settlement, or one of the parties will blink, or we will witness something of a diplomatic disaster. For most of the past year, crisis loomed on the horizon. The Cypriot leaders had made little or no progress on key issues, Turkey was backed into a corner, and the Greek Cypriots could sit tight waiting to see if the EU pressure would move Ankara.

In November, however, UN Secretary General Kofi Annan threw all the old cards up in the air with a bold new set of proposals. The nub of his new package, compared to what has been on the table up to now, seems to be a trade-off that would give Turkish Cypriots more devolved power in the new Cyprus, but also displace a very large number of Turkish Cypriots—perhaps 40,000 or more—to accommodate the return of real estate to Greek Cypriots. The UN document, at 150-plus pages, addresses the panoply of issues from constitution to a South African-style reconciliation commission and undoubtedly conceals an army of devils in its details. Both sides will probably accept it as a basis for discussion, but it could take some time to see whether the new balance of benefits bring closure.

Revising the bottom line on Cyprus will not be easy for the new Turkish government, but it seems far more willing to break with the past. Erdogan's positive references to the Belgian model confirm that he is open to the kind of structure proposed in Annan's plan, and he could count on strong support from the business community and much of the media if he shifted Turkey to a more flexible position across the board. The pro-EU sector of the elite knows Denktash has little credibility on the international scene, and they do not like the notion that Turkey's fate can be determined by 150,000 Turkish Cypriots. On the other side of the coin, conservative elements are loathe to make more concessions on Cyprus, and the Foreign Ministry was quick to try to temper the AK Party's budding enthusiasm for an early agreement based on the Belgian experience. Moreover, the passage of the EU reform package has raised the psychological stakes over Cyprus. Many Turks feel they have met the EU's basic requirements and are resentful that the EU still holds the Cyprus gun to their heads.

We can all cross our fingers and hope the Annan Plan leads to the promised land of a new Cyprus. History suggests the odds are against it, but times have radically changed and so have some key players on the Turkish side while Denktash has been weakened; the parties may find reconciliation is now more in their interest than ever before.

Washington's deep concern to garner Turkish support for American policy on Iraq will continue to mitigate strongly against any U.S. intervention on Cyprus negotiations, since to do so would necessarily risk uncertain outcomes. The Annan initiative takes the pressure off a more direct U.S. involvement as long as it remains viable, but there are no guarantees. On the other hand, Washington is eager to facilitate Turkish cooperation on Iraq and will press the EU hard on an admission date for Turkey. Wilkinson would prefer to see a more proactive Washington role in the negotiation to improve the chances of early agreement. The danger Wilkinson fears is that a breakdown could quickly become irreversible. If the Annan Plan begins to falter, he stresses the need for Washington to mount a rescue operation on short notice by convoking Cypriot, Greek, and Turkish leaders along with EU and UN representatives. Washington cannot expect to impose a solution, but it can work for a transition that keeps the EU option open for Turkish Cyprus and minimizes the damage to Turkish relations with the West if (Greek) Cyprus enters the EU before a settlement.

Three authors—Cengiz Candar, Yalim Eralp, and Henri Barkey—all agree that integration into the EU is the most crucial issue for Turkey today. All three believe from their national perspectives that Turkey's entrance into the EU is in the profound interest of Turkey. They also believe that the changes the EU process accelerates will greatly transform Turkey and meet important U.S. interests in the country in the long run. They want all obstacles to EU membership, including Cyprus, to be swept away and Turkey to meet all the criteria necessary to advance to membership talks, although they are cognizant of the EU's ambivalence toward Turkey, as well as Turkish political difficulties in responding to EU concerns. Eralp, like many Turkish internationalists, is deeply troubled by the inability of the Turkish leadership to grasp the nettle and overcome Turkey's obstacles to membership. He remains dubious that the traditional government parties will do the things necessary to permit the start of serious membership negotiations. Eralp believes, as does Barkey to a lesser extent, that if the Turkish EU effort fails or falters, the United States cannot really serve as a substitute, although in that event the United States has an important role to play in helping preserve Turkey's internal stability and external position. For Barkey, only a Turkey in the EU offers a genuinely desirable basis for a long-term U.S.–Turkish "strategic partnership."

For over a decade, the United States has strongly supported Turkey's admission into the EU diplomatically. This has been a no-brainer. The United States has always wanted Turkey firmly anchored to the West; admission to the EU is the easiest and lowest-cost way politically and economically for the United States to encourage it. If it became a member, Turkey would become the economic ward of the EU if need be, not of the United States. There are differences within the United States on Turkey's EU dilemma. One school, more often than not a conservative one, would like to see Turkey in the EU but considers the problem as mostly a European one: that EU countries for cultural, religious, and economic reasons do not really want seventy million more Muslims, that they simply do not want to extend Europe to the borders of troublesome countries like Iran and Iraq. Furthermore, the costs of integrating low-income Turkey into the EU would be enormous. For good reasons, this school asserts, the EU has done little to prepare Turkey for possible membership and has dealt with Turkey during the pre-accession period very differently than the other candidate countries. This school sees EU members as troubled and divided over Turkey's possible membership by every indication, with few seriously arguing for Turkey's entrance.

A second group—even more dedicated to Turkey's admission—shares many doubts about the EU's genuine interest in Turkey as a member and recognizes Turkey's dilemma that it could carry out politically difficult internal reforms and still not get into the EU. Nevertheless, it also focuses on Turkey's need now to clean up its domestic problems by agreeing to and seriously implementing the Copenhagen criteria and other necessary measures, making it clear to Europe that Turkey shares the former's fundamental political and moral values. This school sees membership pressures as enormously important in strengthening Turkey's democratic institutions now.

On the issue of Cyprus—so vital to Turkey's EU prospects—the first group has been in no hurry to pressure the Turks, although it is not unmindful of the domestic political imperatives in the United States. The second school believes it is up to Turkey to get Denktash to make the necessary compromises and reach an accommodation to further Turkey's EU admission efforts. This school sees no other practical alternative given the international community's total opposition to the Turkish position. It argues that the environment surrounding the Cyprus issue has radically changed from the 1960s and 1970s and that Denktash is behind the times, even behind his own fellow Cypriots, a great number of whom are eager to join the EU.

ONCE AGAIN, IRAQ

The United States has many interests in Turkey and the Turkish–American agenda has expanded enormously over the past decade, from the North Atlantic Treaty Organization (NATO) and the Balkans to the Caucasus, Central Asia, and Afghanistan to the Middle East and energy. These are all matters of great importance to both countries. A stable, secular, democratic Turkey allied to the West remains the most fundamental American long-term interest for the country. Today's Turkish–American dialogue takes place in the atmosphere of a strong relationship nurtured in the 1990s and drawn even closer as a result of Turkey's recent dependence on the United States for economic support and Turkish help to the United States after September 11. Even the Turkish military, which Cengiz Candar finds has always harbored a deep ambivalence toward the United States, has come around largely to bury if not forget the abrasions of the past—including the 1964 Johnson letter and the 1974 embargo, which so embittered them.

But the times are not quiet, and despite the vastly increased interactions three issues have come to dominate the agenda between the two countries and will likely continue to do so for the foreseeable future, if not longer. Two have already been discussed: economic recovery with the aid of the IMF and Turkey's possible integration into the EU, including the resolution in one way or another of the Cyprus problem. The third is Iraq and the likelihood of an American effort to bring down the Saddam Hussein regime.

Both the Turkish public and its principal decision makers—the Turkish military—are united in their distaste for an American military attack on Iraq. The country's leaders argue against it and wish the notion would go away. As one senior Turkish official put it, therapy is needed on Iraq, not surgery. But Iraq is not an issue that has produced, at least thus far, a real cleavage between the two countries (it has led to a rise in anti-Americanism), in part because Turks know that if the United States decides to attack, Turkey cannot stop it. America remains Turkey's best friend and certainly Turkey does not want to break with the United States, particularly given its new dependence on the United States to keep IMF funds coming, the uncertainties of their EU aspirations, and the vital defense relationship. Turkish military cooperation would be further facilitated if any military effort against Iraq had UN approval. It is hard to believe that in the end the Turks would not cooperate with the United States if war takes place, with or without UN blessing. Instead, Iraq has become for Turkey more a problem of how to make the best of it or prevent bad things from happening, or, as Barkey points out, a bargaining issue to try to get the United States to meet pressing Turkish concerns.

The visit of Deputy Secretary of Defense Paul Wolfowitz to Turkey in July 2002 provided a major manifestation of Turkey's attitude toward an American attack—the expression of reluctance coupled with the need to elicit from the Americans reassurances and ways to minimize Turkish concerns. The content of any agreement on Turkey's help in Iraq is not likely to be resolved until the United States actually makes the decision to go to war.

For the United States, the use of Turkish bases for bombing, logistics, and search and rescue operations is the most essential need, as it was during the Gulf War. On that score, the Turks can be expected to respond favorably to an American request. Beyond that, much depends on American military strategy and the help in basing it gets elsewhere in the region. Two other possible requests would cause the Turkish government greater difficulty and certainly arouse even more popular displeasure: the stationing of American ground forces in Turkey and their later insertion into Iraq, and the arming and training of Iraqi Kurdish forces.

Turkish bottom lines have been made clear: no creation of a Kurdish state, probably including a federal one in the aftermath of the departure of the Saddam Hussein regime; continued IMF funding as necessary; and sizable economic assistance in the event of shocks to Turkey's parlous economy. The Turks have expressed serious concerns about the difficulty of managing such shocks and continuously remind Americans of the costs to Turkey of eleven years of sanctions on Iraq. On the first point, the U.S. government reassures Turkey almost daily of its firm support for a unified Iraq and its opposition to any Kurdish state as well as the need to protect the interests of the Turkomans of Iraq, including the oil area of Kirkuk. The Turks do not trust the Iraqi Kurdish leadership, whatever the latter's continuing statements on the need to keep Iraq intact. Some Turkish forces have long been in northern Iraq to fight PKK remnants, but also for intelligence purposes, and as a deterrent both to Iraqi Kurd independence and refugee flight. The Turks watch with apprehension the growing cooperation between Kurdish factions, the deepening American deliberations with the Kurds, and the drawing up of a constitution for the Kurdish area of northern Iraq. They keep expressing their concerns publicly and privately, fearing the uncertainties in Iraq once Saddam Hussein departs.

On the economic side, the United States almost certainly will agree to continue IMF support as needed and short-term direct assistance. Based on past experience and much lesser expected international financial support to the United States than during the Gulf War, the United States will likely be cautious in providing large-scale, long-term bilateral aid. The U.S. government has argued that, once Saddam Hussein is ousted, Turkey will benefit enormously from the end of sanctions, large-scale Iraqi construction—an industry Turkey is well acquainted with—and the reestablishment of traditional economic ties.

Turks also worry (less vocally in the government) about a possible declining American interest in the final political outcome in Iraq once Saddam's rule is over. They are skeptical about the depth of U.S. knowledge of Iraq and do not share American regard for the effectiveness of the external Iraqi opposition. They also know it is hard to predict, in spite of U.S. protestations, how Saddam will leave the scene and the political possibilities for the Kurds his departure would open up in Baghdad. That is why it is quite possible, unlike during the Gulf War, that Turkey will intervene in northern Iraq with its own forces, however much Turkish leaders probably prefer not getting involved and not creating problems with Iran. Some Turks even urge that Turkish forces enter Iraq at the beginning of hostilities to prevent Iraqi Kurds from fleeing to Turkey. The situation in postwar Baghdad will be crucial to determining the possibility of forming a serious, stable government to run a united country and to the Turkish response.

It is hard to say what the U.S.–Turkish relationship would have looked like without the Iraq issue, since Turkey was essential during the past eleven years to the United States "keeping Saddam Hussein in his box" and protecting the Kurds. What will the U.S.–Turkey relationship look like after the fall of Saddam Hussein? That of course depends on many factors, external and internal, most importantly on how Saddam Hussein's rule ends, what happens in Iraq, the role of the United States in postwar Iraq, and the impact of the war on the entire area. It may take some time to sort out after hostilities, but the United States obviously would prefer to avoid any occupation of the country. Once the overwhelming, immediate U.S. interest in Iraq is diminished, Turks will wonder about the depth of continuing ties. Despite U.S. promises about building a united democratic Iraq, Turks will watch closely the evolving situation there and how long U.S. forces remain in the country. Whatever the cynicism of some Turks about the United States, it is reasonable to expect the continuation of a very close American relationship with Turkey because of the ongoing joint involvement in Iraq, the basic stability a Western-oriented Turkey brings to the Middle East, and the uncertainties of life in the area. In addition, the U.S. needs military bases to be used in the war on terror in the Middle East and central Asia. Washington may want to obtain greater use of Turkish bases for that purpose. One, moreover, cannot preclude Iran coming into U.S. crosshairs if the destruction of the Saddam Hussein regime is quick and successful. That would generate a new and vastly difficult problem in American relations with Turkey.

WHERE SHOULD THE UNITED STATES GO FROM HERE?

Within the small numbers of persons in and out of the U.S. government that are deeply interested in U.S.–Turkey relations, there is a constant search for ways to deepen this relationship and to develop a coherent long-term strategy toward Turkey. One term frequently gets bandied about in this effort and has been much used in recent years by both U.S. and Turkish officials: a strategic partnership. The United States, of course, has had something of a strategic partnership with Turkey for a long time—in NATO, in the Gulf War, and perhaps soon in another war with Iraq. Some of this has been less partnership and more the United States dragging Turkey along as a partner. Nevertheless, because of Turkey's size, location, strength, orientation, and its involvement in so many places of interest to the United States, there is almost a natural American interest in deepening close working arrangements on many common concerns. Turkey would certainly seem important in many ways, for example, to continuing U.S. involvement in the Caucasus and Central Asia. A stable, secular, democratic Turkey in an unstable area of the world has been and will remain the most basic common strategic goal of both countries. In his chapter, Barkey speculates on ways of deepening a strategic partnership and relating any approach to the complications raised by whether or not Turkey makes its way into the EU.

Despite the rhetoric of senior officials, the United States has never shown much interest in pursuing this concept except when trouble arises, as it has twice in Iraq. After the Gulf War, President Turgut Özal spoke of a strategic relationship with the United States in the Middle East. What he meant was never clarified, and the first Bush administration never showed any interest. Nor does it appear that there is much interest so far in the present Bush administration except as relates to Iraq. Why has there been so little interest other than rhetoric in times of trouble by various American governments in the concept of strategic partnership? Perhaps because they do not believe that there is really much to these words, and the benefits, a specific contingency aside, are not worth the possible costs and complications. Nor is it really clear what the Turks are interested in by that term beyond increased textile quotas and more investments, although they would want to continue a defense relationship with the United States under almost any circumstances, including Turkey's entrance into the EU.

The answer to this question probably lies in Turkey's internal troubles and the unwillingness of any administration to get too deeply enmeshed with Turkey. Short-term worries drive out long-term uncertain benefits, even of a strategic character. And one has only to look at the situation in Turkey today to grasp the concern. The Turkish political system has been in virtual shambles for a year. The country has been utterly dependent on relief from the international community, for how much longer no one can safely predict. Turkey's huge debt narrows its ability to grow and the margin to make more economic policy mistakes. The country remains divided on some basic issues and made a decision on one aspect of them—the reform legislation necessary to advance Turkey's prospects with the EU—essentially by accident.

Turkey always seems to be at a crucial juncture, whatever the year is. Despite its fragmented politics and opportunistic government coalitions, key decisions do get made and the country moves on to another crucial juncture. Turkey in 2002 is at another such juncture—a big one even for Turkey—and some very fundamental decisions cannot be avoided. These decisions also have to be made by an entirely new government, which itself may present a problem because of the likely strong position of the AK Party. The new government must decide Cyprus, Turkey's future with the EU, its relations with the IMF, and its role in an Iraq war and its aftermath. That is an enormous platter for an untried government.

It appears at this writing in late October that the AK Party will emerge as the country's leading party, with quite possibly a parliamentary majority. Indeed, one unexpected result from the election is that political fragmentation could well be significantly reduced and the new parliament will have at best only a small number of parties. The three coalition parties all are expected to be thrown out. The advent of the AK Party to power will be a domestic and international question mark. Aside from its Islamist origin, many will point to the absence of an economic program and the party's lack of experience in running a government. However, to be fair, the experienced parties hardly have done an impressive job. Moreover, AK Party leaders are noticeably wary about repeating Erbakan's early mistakes in seeming to depart from Turkey's traditional foreign policy when he became prime minister in 1996.

There have been different approaches by American governments to dealing with Turkey's internal problems. The Clinton administration, as Henri Barkey points out in detail, put great stress on these problems, believing they are the crux of Turkey's incessant political and economic difficulties and that they needed to be confronted if long-term stability were to be achieved. The administration spent much effort, publicly and privately, urging Turkish governments to address human rights abuses, Kurdish issues, and other democratic deficits.

But it imposed no conditionality. The administration also saw the EU as the principal vehicle for inducing domestic political reform and lobbied strenuously to advance Turkey's efforts ultimately to join Europe.

The Bush administration came in strongly supportive of Turkey at senior levels. It is aware of Turkey's internal difficulties but has been reluctant to criticize Turkey publicly since it is an ally and friend. The administration believes Turkey does have special internal circumstances that require well-intentioned foreigners to be cautious in criticism, and in any event the domestic shortcomings will be remedied over time given Turkey's advanced democratic circumstances. The United States should not harp on these problems to avoid increasing domestic instability, undermining our friends, and possibly endangering the benefits Turkey provides the United States. The need for Turkish support in Iraq has strengthened this perspective and also contributed to the stepped up American activism in pushing Turkey's EU candidacy.

Given present circumstances and uncertainties about the new government, it is hard for both countries to take a long-term perspective and to plan the pursuit of longer-term goals. It is rather more compelling for both countries to be candid about the uncertainties of the present situation, to prevent bad things from happening, to avoid acrimony, and to pursue realistic objectives in close cooperation.

I would close with the following observations and recommendations:

- If the AK Party, as expected, leads the new government, the United States will face a new situation. It will have to get used to very different and often new faces in leading positions. Unlike 1997, when Islamist Necmettin Erbakan led a coalition government and the U.S. government did its business mostly with his coalition partners and the military, it will have to deal directly with Erdogan, the new prime minister, and their colleagues. That should be not too difficult since the party is saying all sorts of reassuring things about the promotion of democracy and human rights, the urgency of getting a date for EU membership negotiations, and continuing the main lines of Turkish foreign policy. On the other hand, the new government will be called on to define quickly their approach to critical issues such as Cyprus, Iraq, and the IMF. Showing flexibility on Cyprus could be hard since flexibility has not been the main line of Turkish policy; it would be an impressive departure from orthodoxy. Most important within Turkey is how the new government handles the economy, particularly its dealings with the IMF. They inherit serious limitations in this arena. Until AK Party policies diverge from their rhetoric, the United States should make it clear that it is prepared to work closely with them and to continue to support strongly such essential objectives as restoring economic growth, Turkey's bid for membership talks with the EU, and domestic political reform. At the start of what may turn out to be a genuine new era in Turkey, the United States certainly does not want to roil the waters.

+ Any Turkish government must recognize that it is not likely to get into the EU on its own terms. The EU shows few signs of looking at the Turkish admission issue geo-strategically. If Turkey wants to start membership negotiations it will most likely have to meet the political criteria the EU requires of all members. It very likely also means, fair or unfair, reaching a negotiated solution to the Cyprus problem or at least significant progress. Conceivably the EU could be generous on the first point, as Turks feel they should since they passed the reform legislation under great difficulty. Such generosity is uncertain but less likely unless Turkey deals with the Cyprus issue. Despite increased pressure from the United States, the EU is more likely to take the stance that Turkey is not yet an acceptable candidate for membership but still hold open the door. Turkey will probably have to bring its aspirations more in line with its current situation. I do not know how the new Turkish government will handle the Cyprus issue, but the government may have to scurry to prepare the public for bad news on EU talks if there is no progress on Cyprus. It also will have to find ways of not turning Cyprus into a permanent bone of contention with the EU.

+ The handling of an Iraq war will be a difficult one under the best of circumstances for both countries. The United States will want close Turkish cooperation. The biggest problems between the two countries may well occur in the aftermath of war. The United States must not forget that it has a long-term stake in Turkey in addition to short-term needs. It particularly must remember that after Saddam Hussein is finished. That means the U.S. government must make it clear that the United States is ready to stay in Iraq for as long as it takes to produce a functioning, satisfactory government. It means also a balancing of Kurdish and Turkish needs, which can best be met by a decent central government in Iraq—not an easy proposition by any shot. The United States could be faced with the Kurds, exuberant with Saddam's departure and seeing chaos and uncertainty in Baghdad, trying to establish an independent state. Both countries need to avoid a Turkish seizure of northern Iraq and the uncertain consequences such a development would produce in the area. Sizable economic aid to Turkey could help a lot.

♦   The United States cannot step back from the EU issue. Seeing Turkey in the EU is a matter of great importance for both countries and indeed for the world. However difficult, the United States must continue to weigh in strongly with the EU on starting membership talks with Turkey and must do its best publicly and privately to encourage Turkey to make the necessary internal changes to allow talks to begin, regardless of what is happening on Iraq. Realistically, the United States cannot substitute for the EU, although it can certainly help Turkey alleviate the shock of the EU failure to set a date for membership talks.

♦   All this also requires the United States to do its best to prevent a Cyprus disaster. If the Annan Plan founders, the United States, as James Wilkinson proposes, should forcefully intervene, bring all the concerned parties to Washington, and try to hammer out a solution. Failing that, it needs to pursue a policy that minimizes the damage to Turkey should (Greek) Cyprus enter the EU before a negotiated settlement.

♦   The United States should continue to support IMF financing for Turkey's economic stabilization and reform program. That program—despite its unpopularity in Turkey—is essential to Turkey's internal health and to building its standing as a negotiating partner with the EU. However, the United States should make it clear to the Turkish government that it will not continue to support further bailouts without continuing commitment to the implementation of the economic reform program and a similar commitment to EU integration.

♦ A strategic partnership is a worthy objective and the United States should not want to do things that may make it difficult to realize in later years, particularly with the uncertainties in the Middle East and central Asia associated with the war on terror. Still, life right now is too uncertain, the agenda is too full, and U.S.–Turkey cooperation in any event has been close. Thus, we can safely leave that subject to be discussed another day, particularly if Turkey's EU effort falters.

A Brief Postscript

The essays in this volume, including this introduction, were completed in late August and updated and revised in late October. As I wrote above, you can always find yourself behind the curve in writing about contemporary events in Turkey. These essays were going through their final stage of publishing when another political earthquake hit Turkey. The magnitude of the AK Party victory was a stunner and may herald a period of radical change in Turkey; they have the votes. There is presently much excitement, vigor, and openness in Ankara, elements that have been missing since the early days of Özal. Erdogan keeps saying that "from now on, nothing will be the same in Turkey." And much of Turkey wants to move away from some long-standing political shadows.

While all the essays remain essentially as they were before the election with one exception, we simply could not avoid reflecting something of this seismic political event for Turkey. Cengiz Candar was asked to write a separate, brief analysis of the elections and its implications for Turkey, which concludes the book. Henri Barkey also added a postscript to his essay evaluating the implications of an AK Party government for the United States. James Wilkinson revised his essay to take account of the election but mainly because of the new and creative way Kofi Annan shuffled the Cyprus issue negotiating deck in November. The secretary-general's proposal seemed to open up a more promising opportunity for progress on that chronically neuralgic problem, and Erdogan's early positive pronouncements on the package encouraged optimism for an ultimate compromise, a commodity in rare supply when it comes to a Cyprus resolution. Wilkinson's revisions also required a revision of the Cyprus portion only of this introductory essay.

The AK Party victory, the activism of Erdogan and the new government, and their message of radical and rapid domestic change
sparked enthusiasm in most quarters in Turkey, including the once
hostile media, and much attention in Europe. Erdogan quickly took
off to deliver the new message, not to Iran and Libya as Erbakan did in
becoming prime minister in 1996, but rather to Athens and all other EU
capitals. He repeatedly announced Turkey's determination to acquire
a date for membership talks at the EU Council meeting in December
2002 and the new government's dedication to secularism, the promotion of democracy, and the end of torture and other offenses
against human rights and thereby to genuinely satisfy the EU's
Copenhagen requirements. Much to the dismay of the foreign ministry
he avowed recognition that failure to resolve the Cyprus issue did
indeed affect Turkey's chances of getting a membership date, that
Kofi Annan's plan offered a good basis for negotiations, and that compromise was necessary.

However well the new government is playing in Turkey and the
West and the domestic and foreign encomiums about the advent of a
genuine Muslim democracy, its future will be determined by its ability
to meet the enormous challenges facing it now or over the near-term
horizon. It must organize its disparate ranks and put together a government that can function effectively and manage relations with the
military. It must find a way of getting Erdogan into the parliament and
end the potential internal party problems caused by his not being
prime minister. It has to make a decision on the new Cyprus negotiating package, and clearly wants to eliminate the Cyprus stumbling block
to the EU, a step that could involve the government in a domestic political crisis early on. Erdogan has personally pulled out all the stops to
get a membership negotiating date from the EU, but unless the EU at
its Copenhagen meeting in December offers Turkey a specific date for
membership talks or a creative alternative short of that, he may find
himself having to handle a politically painful response to the EU decision. The government will have to manage the demands of the faithful on social and educational issues such as the head-scarf against the
efforts of recalcitrant secularists to find some issue to turn the military
against them. It will have to carry on negotiations with the United
States over Iraq, an issue it is uncomfortable with, even while it indicates a desire to cooperate with the United States. Most important, the
AK government will have to do something about the basic reason it

received such a large electoral mandate—the poor state of the economy. And its margin for getting serious growth going and gaining changes in the IMF standby for immediate social improvements will be limited. Turkish optimism is presently great, as Cengiz Candar notes in his Afterword, but I am not sure it is enough to get by on.

In short, the biggest difficulty for the new government will not likely come from its Islamist roots and its problems with secularists, although that should not be minimized. The military are quiet and recognize that the AK Party received a political mandate far beyond Erbakan's in 1996. They also recognize that this is not an Erbakan government. The AK Party has gone a considerable way in winning support from the articulate public as not only an acceptable new phenomenon in Turkish politics but also as an engine of fundamental change, much of which they would welcome. How long public support lasts remains to be seen. It is more likely to be its ability to manage the country, to show the public that there are tangible benefits to its stewardship, and that it is a vast improvement over what went before that will determine its staying power. But even if the new government is slow in reviving the economy without serious inflation, it still could score lots of points with the Turkish people if it takes serious action on corruption, a deep and persistent public preoccupation, and on establishing a better rule of law and less judicial favoritism for the well connected. All that would be no mean feat and could occasion a pronounced backlash.

Lastly, a word about the United States. Whatever the misgivings about the election results the U.S. government, of course, has to be pleased about the new government's rhetoric and avowed policy line. It is what the United States has advocated for years and if rhetoric turns to results, Turkey would indeed, as Henri Barkey points out, offer an impressive model to the whole Muslim world. The U.S. government has also clearly decided that the best way to ensure that deeds follow words is to work closely with the new government and to sympathetically urge them to carry out their new policies without backsliding, including on its flexible position on the Annan plan for Cyprus. The United States has also gone strongly to bat with EU countries urging them to take a geo-strategic perspective, at this crucial moment when we might be soon at war with a Muslim country, to bind Muslim Turkey to the West by giving Turkey a date for membership talks this December, and end any notion of a Christian/Muslim divide in the world. President Bush himself has picked up the phone to lobby. And as Iraq hostilities seem closer, the Bush administration is talking more and more about a sizeable aid package for Turkey. All this seems very sensible indeed at a critical moment.

November 20, 2002

Chapter Two

The Unfinished Struggle for Economic Stability

Ercan Kumcu[1]

Faced with one of the worst economic crises in its history following the two oil shocks of the 1970s, Turkey achieved remarkable progress in transforming its economy in the 1980s. It moved from a closed market based on import substitution to an open, export-led growth economy. Radical structural reforms were made in areas of foreign trade, the financial sector, and foreign exchange. The foreign trade regime was liberalized with competitive foreign exchange rates, import quotas and price controls were lifted, the financial system was deregulated, and restrictions on international capital movements were completely eliminated.

Since then, Turkey's economic performance has been mixed. Following this first giant step, Turkey has struggled to turn the final corner (former prime minister Turgut Özal's euphemism for succeeding in the new Turkey)[2] in the late 1980s and the 1990s. Although successive governments have attempted to restructure the economy through several International Monetary Fund (IMF)–sponsored stabilization programs, Turkey has instead spent the better part of the 1990s to the present running from crisis to crisis. What went wrong?

In retrospect, the structural reforms implemented in the 1980s were certainly bold, but not enough to pave the way to sustainable growth and price stability. The ultimate goal of growth and low inflation remained just out of reach for Turkey, for two interrelated reasons:

◆ *Lack of discipline in public finance.* While undertaking difficult structural reforms in most areas of the economy, Turkey has consistently neglected to establish the necessary discipline in public sector finance. Successive governments have always spent more than they had. Reforms to regulate expenditures and tax collection were either overlooked or went unimplemented. Confronted with an unacceptable but sustainable high rate of inflation and highly undulant economic growth, the financial balance of the public sector has gradually deteriorated over the past twenty-five years.

◆ *Political fragmentation and the inability to coordinate the political calendar with the economic calendar.* Attempts to stabilize the economy inevitably failed because successive two- or three-party coalition governments lacked the will, the cohesion, or sufficient political or public support to cope with the adverse political consequences of structural reforms necessary to bring about economic stability—that is, additional unemployment in the short run and significant reductions in government subsidies. During most of the 1990s, a decade of unstable coalition governments, leaders followed politically popular policies rather than policies of economic stabilization (see Table 2.1).

This chapter examines Turkey's unfinished journey to economic stability in the form of steady growth and stable prices. Special attention is paid to Turkey's 2000 program with the IMF, which outlined in detail the economic reforms that Turkey must undertake to gain economic stability. The chapter also deals with the effects of the external and internal economic and political shocks on Turkey's reform plans—namely the 1998 Russian crisis, the devastating 1999 earthquake, and the two domestic crises in late 2000 and early 2001 that derailed the year 2000 IMF-backed stabilization program.

The effect of these events on the Turkish economy show how tenuous Turkey's political and economic situation has become. Whereas a stronger, more stable economy would probably have been able to shrug off these external shocks, Turkey spiraled out of control. In spite

TABLE 2.1. RECENT ECONOMIC AND POLITICAL HISTORY

YEARS	IMF PROGRAM	SIGNIFICANT EVENT	PSBR/GNP RATIO[1]	INFLATION[2] (%)	POLITICAL SITUATION
1980	Yes	Economic crisis	8.8	107	Military rule
1983	Yes	Return to democratic rule	5.3	31	Majority government
1985	Yes	End of the IMF program	3.6	40	Majority government
1987	No	Banned political parties returned	6.1	39	Majority government
1989	No	Populist measures started	5.3	64	Majority government
1994	Yes	Financial crisis	7.9	121	Two-party coalition
1998	Staff Monitoring Agreement	Russian crisis	9.5	64	Three-party coalition
1999	Staff Monitoring Agreement	Earthquake	16.2	52	Three-party and minority government
2000	Yes	Financial crisis— November	12.5	39	Three-party government after elections
2001	Yes	Financial crisis— February	15.9	89	Three-party coalition
2002	Yes	A new program with the IMF			Three-party coalition

[1] Public sector borrowing requirement/gross national product, indicating the stance of fiscal policy.
[2] Computed with consumer price index, end of the year.
Source: Data compiled by author; PSBR/GNP is from Turkish Department of the Treasury and inflation rate is from the State Institute of Statistics.

of these stumbles, international sympathy, coupled with Turkey's geopolitical importance, has made the international community and particularly the United States more willing to bail Turkey out. Nevertheless, the costs of these shocks could have been smaller if both parties—the IMF and the Turkish government—had shown more flexibility. Indeed, in large part, the government and the IMF are to blame for Turkey's crash landing into the last recession of 2002.

The chapter concludes with an analysis of the conditions necessary for successful implementation of the most recent standby 2002 agreement with the IMF. For the program to succeed, two preconditions must be met: the economic calendar cannot be held hostage to the political calendar, and the stabilization program must create an environment for short-term economic growth without causing further harm to the financial position of the public sector. Failure to meet these conditions will likely undermine what has already been achieved to date, resulting in a greater loss in the economy and a more costly recuperation. Failure to stabilize the economy will also continue to jeopardize Turkey's bid for European Union (EU) membership.

AN INCOMPLETE TRANSFORMATION

In the late 1970s, battered by two global oil shocks, Turkey faced a devastating economic situation. Economic activity came to a standstill, production plunged, and inflation skyrocketed. A severe foreign exchange shortfall coupled with shortages of goods, both imported and domestically produced, called for a complete overhaul in economic management. The 1970s also marked the beginning of Turkey's almost epic battle against inflation. For the past thirty years, Turkey has been struggling with double-digit inflation averaging around 60 percent annually. From time to time attempts have been made to reduce the inflation rate to single digits. All attempts have failed. On the other hand, Turkey did succeed in containing the rate of inflation below 100 percent. Unlike countries such as those in Latin America, Israel, and the former socialist countries, Turkey has not experienced hyperinflation. Yet, inflation remained very high and, as defined by most economics textbooks, ultimately at an unsustainable level.

POLITICAL WILL TO CHANGE: TURGUT ÖZAL'S ERA

The first attempt to fundamentally tackle the growing list of Turkey's economic woes began in 1980, with the launch of an adjustment and stabilization program supported by the IMF and the World Bank. The program emphasized export-led growth. Following a substantial devaluation of the currency, trade was liberalized: import taxes were substantially lowered, import quotas were lifted, and significant incentives for exports were granted. The fixed exchange rate regime was abandoned. Instead, Turkey established a managed peg, which allowed the central bank to adjust exchange rates daily, closely following the rate of inflation. Substantial portions of short-term public debt abroad were rescheduled with support from the IMF, which gave the government more breathing room. Government subsidies in all areas were reduced; for State Economic Enterprises (SEEs), pricing rules were changed to eliminate subsidies. Price controls on both imported and domestically produced goods were lifted entirely. The depressed banking sector was brought back to life by allowing banks to set their interest rates freely for both deposits and lending.

The economy responded to these measures immediately. Growth in real output resumed modestly, while inflation declined from more than 100 percent to 25 percent in a few years. Exports to neighboring countries grew first, later expanding to Organization for Economic Cooperation and Development (OECD) countries in parallel with growing imports. The volume of trade approached 30 percent of gross national product (GNP), a doubling within the first four years of the program, with only a modest trade deficit.[3]

Soon after the program was launched, the military came to power. Ruling from 1980 to 1983, the military ended domestic political quarrels and allowed the government to make difficult decisions. However, it was the return to civilian government that catalyzed reform. Turgut Özal, elected as prime minister in 1983, had the vision and determination to liberalize the economy more profoundly. Importantly, Özal's party's absolute majority allowed him to push tough decisions through parliament. The import regime was completely liberalized, eliminating all quotas. The list of goods that were allowed to be imported was replaced by a short list of goods for which import permission was needed. This list included only weapons, drugs, and ammunition.

The foreign exchange rate regime was further liberalized, allowing banks to hold positions in foreign exchange. Residents in Turkey, both individuals and corporations, were also allowed to open foreign exchange deposits with Turkish banks.[4] International capital movements remained restricted until 1989. In 1985, the government started borrowing in financial markets for the first time by issuing government papers at auction. In 1986, an interbank money market was established and the central bank started conducting open market operations in both government papers and the interbank money market.[5]

In parallel with financial market liberalization, monetary policy was made quite flexible, but not necessarily independent. The independence of monetary policy could not be achieved because of the unsustainable nature of the public sector borrowing requirements over the years—similar to the experience of most emerging market economies. The central bank's independence was limited in the sense that it had to focus only on keeping inflation in check; it had no ability to influence economic growth through monetary management.

The standby arrangement with the IMF was completed in mid-1985, a rare example of a Turkish government successfully completing a standby arrangement.[6] At the time, the economy grew at more than 4 percent, while inflation still fluctuated in the range of 40 to 50 percent. The level of determination to implement reforms during this period should not be underestimated. Essentially, what distinguished the 1980 stabilization program (implemented between 1980 and 1985) and the reforms from 1985 to 1987 from all of the previous fourteen programs supported by the IMF (as well as those implemented in later years) was this determination to implement the reform program and to secure international support.

LIBERALIZATION WITHOUT INFRASTRUCTURE

In 1987, a national referendum allowed politicians who had been banned from political life by the military regime to reenter politics. In the 1987 general elections, Özal's party maintained its absolute majority in the parliament, albeit with declining public support. These elections turned out to be a significant juncture; Özal's government became increasingly populist as its public support deteriorated.

In response to declining public support in local elections in 1989, in which Özal's party lost in large cities, generous increases in wages and salaries of public employees were granted. In essence, Özal sacrificed financial discipline for public support through nominal subsidies to different segments of the economy. The increase in real wages in the public sector was soon followed in the private sector. Except for the introduction of value-added taxes in 1985, nothing was done to improve the fiscal imbalances. The government was unable to enlarge the tax base and had to rely on increases in tax rates to reduce public sector deficits. At the same time, the unregistered economy grew as people strove to evade taxes.

Consecutive governments had to rely on loose fiscal policies to bridge the short-term adverse consequences of their economic reforms and of changes in the institutional framework. They had to borrow directly from the central bank or rely on the inflow of international capital to supplement the international reserves of the central bank. For the past twenty-five years the Turkish economy simply has learned to live with an irresponsible fiscal policy. Hence, they have not yet been successful in bringing down the rate of inflation to single digits.

Remarkably, Özal did continue to liberalize the economy on other fronts. Although some of these reforms were bold and correct, they were not necessarily timely for lack of an appropriate technical infrastructure. Most notably:

* In 1988, interest rates on banks' deposits were freed, allowing banks to determine their own deposit and lending rates. This was before a proper regulatory and supervisory framework in the banking sector was established. Although interest rate liberalization did not lead to major dislocation in the financial system outside of an initial rise in deposit interest rates, some later problems in the banking sector can be attributed to the premature liberalization of interest rates.

* In 1989, the government lifted all restrictions on capital account transactions, declaring the Turkish lira "convertible" as described in Article VIII of the IMF's Article of Agreement. Again, the decision was premature: it made capital flows volatile, instantaneous, and potentially huge. The government should have first reduced its budget deficits and limited the exposure of banks to external shocks by establishing a proper supervisory and regulatory environment. Surprisingly, however, no major adverse development occurred because of the premature liberalization of capital flows. In fact, the move enabled Turkey to better deal with its high inflation,

as the capital inflows helped maintain and finance otherwise unsustainable public sector deficits. Moreover, in later years, as pointed out in the next section, relative economic stability and growth in Turkey could only be achieved by a substantial inflow of foreign capital. Still, recent severe problems in the banking sector can be attributed to too great an exposure to foreign exchange rate changes by banks for lack of a proper supervisory and regulatory environment.

High inflation diminished people's faith in the lira as a savings instrument. Foreign exchange deposits eventually comprised nearly half of total deposits in the banking sector because of severe currency substitution. With completely liberalized financial markets, capital flows moved in and out depending on the public's choice between domestic currency and foreign currencies. As a result, any change in expectation about inflation or economic growth started to have a strong impact on macroeconomic balances.

All these far-reaching economic reforms were a partial attempt to transform Turkey into a free market economy. Foreign exchange crises were no longer characterized by acute shortages of foreign exchange as in the 1970s but by an uncontrollable fall in the value of the lira in foreign exchange markets. Concern was no longer with quantity but with price. Because of the continued budget deficits and high inflation combined with free capital flows, further reforms were essential.[7]

THE BUDGET RUNS AMOK[8]

During the 1980s, public sector financial balances not only gradually deteriorated, but new extrabudgetary funds—mechanisms designed to loosen the budget constraint outside parliamentary supervision—contributed to fiscal irresponsibility. More than two hundred extrabudgetary funds were instituted, which allowed government revenues to be earmarked for certain expenditures: "budgets outside the budget." While in principle a fund's expenditures were limited by its revenues, most funds were allowed to borrow and run substantial deficits over the years, especially those involved in the government's investment programs.

Public sector finance thus gradually lost its transparency. The government budget abandoned its role as an indicator of fiscal policy.

Budget appropriations approved by the parliament at the beginning of the year were no indication of how fiscal policy would be implemented. In most years in the 1990s, actual expenditures exceeded budget appropriations by more than 10 percent, and in some years 30 percent (see Table 2.2). Huge budget deficits were camouflaged by higher deficits of extrabudgetary funds or by financing expenditures by the public banks (duty losses) without registering them in the budget.

The most striking deterioration in public finance took place in the 1990s during a period of consecutive coalition governments. Both budget deficits and public deficits outside the budget, including SEEs, extrabudgetary funds, and subsidies financed through public banks, soared during this decade. Consecutive governments were unable to limit the deficits and had to continue attracting foreign cash by keeping domestic interest rates high. During most of the 1990s, real interest rates remained unsustainably high (see Table 2.3). Of course, high real interest rates in turn further exacerbated public sector deficits, creating a vicious cycle. Public debts were continually rolled over, while the accumulating cost of the high interest rates snowballed.

Seemingly counterintuitively, the Turkish economy was able to grow. With free capital movements, successive governments had relied on both substantial private sector savings and short-term capital inflows to finance the budget deficit. In other words, the government had to borrow heavily from abroad and at home to finance the gap. But as long as there was a large enough inflow of capital from abroad, there was money to invest. One can therefore discern a clear correlation between capital inflows and economic growth (see Figure 2.1).

When the government was reluctant to pay the necessary high real interest rates, the economy went into crisis, as was the case in 1994.[9] In periods such as 1995–97, when governments accepted to live with high real interest rates, the economy achieved remarkable growth.[10] However, Turkey did not attract foreign direct investment in comparable magnitude to that of most emerging market economies during the 1990s, due mostly to the uncertainty created by high inflation.[11] (Political instability and the legal framework have also been limiting factors.) Hence, growth could only be achieved through borrowing large amounts of international funds at very high real interest rates, sufficient to cover both economic and political risk. Not surprisingly, Turkey's international rating came down from BBB at the end of 1993 to B by the end of 1994 and has remained at that level since then.

TABLE 2.2. BUDGET APPROPRIATIONS AND REALIZATIONS (TRILLION TURKISH LIRA)

	1993	1994	1995	1996	1997	1998	1999	2000
TOTAL EXPENDITURES								
Appropriation	397	819	1,331	3,511	6,256	14,792	27,161	46,739
Realization	508	958	1,809	4,114	8,364	16,194	28,668	49,439
Difference (%)	27.9	16.9	35.9	17.2	33.7	9.5	5.5	5.8
CURRENT EXPENDITURES								
Appropriation	177	323	551	1,046	2,125	4,457	7,964	13,044
Realization	211	376	683	1,356	2,942	5,450	9,144	14,722
Difference (%)	19.1	16.4	23.9	29.6	38.4	22.3	14.8	12.9
INVESTMENTS								
Appropriation	46	85	85	239	495	1,000	1,346	2,369
Realization	65	87	120	288	711	1,260	1,781	3,103
Difference (%)	41.1	3.6	41.1	20.5	43.6	26.0	32.3	31.0
TRANSFERS								
Appropriation	174	411	695	2,515	4,232	10,433	19,618	34,507
Realization	232	495	1,006	2,852	5,607	10,848	20,131	35,544
Difference (%)	33.2	20.2	44.7	13.4	32.5	4.0	2.6	3.0

Source: Central Bank of Turkey, *Annual Report 2000–2001*, from table based on statistics from the Turkish Ministry of Finance and the Treasury.

TABLE 2.3. REAL INTEREST RATES ON GOVERNMENT BORROWING IN THE 1990S

Year	Interest rates (equivalent in U.S. $)	Year	Interest rates (equivalent in U.S. $)
1990	−4.8	1996	52.3
1991	19.9	1997	56.1
1992	44.3	1998	91.5
1993	−46.6	1999	112.9
1994	236.5	2000	4.5
1995	65.8		

Note: This table is derived from monthly averages of compounded yearly interest rates prevailing in government auctions of different maturities in each month. Average interest rates in Turkish lira in each month are discounted with the realized percentage change in the Turkish-lira/U.S.-dollar rate within the next twelve months. Negative rates in 1990 and 1993 were due to a faster than expected rate of depreciation of the Turkish lira during the Gulf War and the 1994 crisis, respectively.

Source: Treasury, Central Bank of Turkey, and the State Institute of Statistics.

FIGURE 2.1 CAPITAL FLOWS AND INDUSTRIAL PRODUCTION INDEX (ANNUAL)

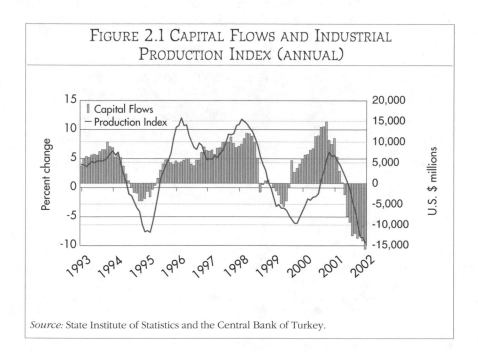

Source: State Institute of Statistics and the Central Bank of Turkey.

The deterioration of public finances and its reliance on short-term capital inflows made Turkey vulnerable to external economic shocks (see Table 2.4). Interestingly, during the 1997 Asian crisis the Turkish economy experienced only temporary adverse effects. Fairly flexible exchange rate management by the central bank coupled with an appropriate interest rate policy insulated the Turkish economy from this crisis. Most short-term foreign capital probably left the Turkish market (roughly U.S. $6 billion), but the central bank's foreign exchange reserves were more than sufficient to cover the outflow of foreign capital. Financial markets calmed down rapidly following a temporary slowdown in economic activity. The fact that international financial markets initially interpreted the crisis in Asia as a regional one also helped emerging markets in other areas, including Turkey.

The 1998 crisis in Russia was a completely different story. Even though similar foreign exchange and interest rate policies were in place, the Russian crisis hit Turkey's economy because foreign investors perceived that its geographical proximity to Russia was important and because of the existence of substantial "unrecorded" trade volume—the so-called suitcase trade—between Turkey and Russia. Real interest rates rose substantially without stopping the outflow of short-term foreign capital. As in the Asian crisis, probably almost all short-term foreign capital left the country (again roughly

TABLE 2.4. SAVINGS IN PRIVATE AND PUBLIC SECTORS, 1980–99 (%)

	1980–89	1990–99
Average propensity to save		
Private sector	14	25
Public sector		46
Net savings/income		
Private sector	1	5
Public sector	–17	–78

Note: Average propensity to save is the percentage of income saved. Net savings are the difference between savings and investments.
Source: State Planning Organization, Annual economic programs by the State Institute of Statistics.

$6 billion, which had come in after the Asian crisis). Once more, the central bank's foreign exchange reserves were more than sufficient to cover the outflow of capital. But the perceived risks for the Turkish economy rose significantly in the eyes of both domestic and foreign investors. Domestic demand plummeted. As a result, output declined drastically in the second half of 1998 and continued to decline throughout 1999, while both inflation and real interest rates rose.

Following a sharp rise in real interest rates and a substantial reduction in capital inflows to emerging markets, the Russian crisis made it almost impossible for the government to manage both internal and external debt. Economic activity declined by 6.1 percent in 1999, while real interest rates reached over 40 percent in a period where public expenditures also rose. The Turkish economy was in dire straits. However, the political climate was not conducive for Turkey to enter a program with the IMF involving bold structural change. The government was a minority coalition supported by a social democratic party. Nevertheless, work on a stabilization program that would likely be supported by the IMF did commence during that period. However, the implementation of the program was held up again by the government's reluctance to pay the political cost of enacting painful, but necessary, structural reforms.

Given Turkey's inability to tackle difficult reforms in the past, specific structural reforms were now laid out in a staff monitoring agreement with the IMF as a precondition for a standby agreement. However, economic difficulties in the second half of 1998 and not-too-bright prospects for the future eventually led to a political crisis, making early elections inevitable. It was evident that public sector debt had become unmanageable; national income was declining, real interest rates were rising, and the public sector borrowing requirement was accelerating in the absence of a comprehensive fiscal retrenchment program. A decision was made to hold early elections in the spring of 1999.

BACK TO PLAN A: THE YEAR 2000
ECONOMIC PROGRAM[12]

The incongruous three-party coalition that came to power after the 1999 national elections provided a better environment for structural reforms in that it represented broad sections of the society—a party from the center right, one from the center left, and the nationalists (conservative right). The new government presumably had five years to fix the economy, when the next elections would take place. Politicians realized that they had to act quickly on the economy. The government's prime goal was to dismantle the mechanisms that had allowed extrabudgetary financing while at the same time tackling already stubborn inflationary expectations by using a preannounced exchange rate as a nominal anchor for inflation. In this case, the fluctuation in exchange rates would be parallel to the targeted rate of inflation and thus inflationary expectations would be anchored by preannounced exchange rates, and changes in prices would come in line with targeted levels of inflation over time. Yet, lingering doubts remained in business circles, the financial community, and the general public as to whether the coalition would be able to agree on the necessary structural reforms after a decade of periodic crises.

A series of events took place in the second half of 1999 that radically changed Turkey's economic and political climate. First, a disastrous earthquake in mid-August strengthened national solidarity, while simultaneously making the economic situation even more fragile. The whole world was watching Turkey, and friendly countries and international organizations rushed to help. Because of the earthquake, there was even a thaw in Turkey's normally strained relations with Greece. The Organisation for Security and Co-operation in Europe (OSCE) summit, held in Istanbul toward the end of the year, put Turkey at the forefront of world public attention. During this summit, President Bill Clinton stayed in the country for about a week, visiting earthquake victims and boosting morale with a string of supportive statements. Second, the EU Helsinki summit in December officially declared Turkey a candidate for full EU membership, an important step toward integrating Turkey with the rest of Europe. These developments renewed the pressure from international circles on Turkey to try seriously to implement a lasting stability program, essential if Turkey was ever to make it into the EU.[13] The developments in 1999 also provided a positive mood within Turkey, which was necessary for a new stabilization effort.

A program supported by the IMF was necessary to secure the confidence of international investors and accelerate adjustment. Keeping in mind its past experiences in Turkey, the IMF preconditioned official support under a standby arrangement on a series of measures:

- A new banking law was enacted in June 1999, establishing the Banking Regulatory and Supervisory Authority (BRSA), a new, independent body free from political interference. Later, another banking law empowered the government to swiftly assume control of commercial banks with financial difficulties.

- The social security law was changed to raise the retirement age of people newly entering the system from fifty-five to sixty, and also increased contributions.

- In an effort to improve the competitive environment in the banking sector, the Savings Deposit Insurance Fund (SDIF) assumed control of banks with weak financial positions. This was a pre-emptive measure aimed at preventing the negative effects on the banking sector of the intended drop in inflation from being compounded by weak banks.

- Constitutional amendments were enacted to allow for international arbitration in license transfer agreements. The aim of this measure was to speed up privatization by attracting foreign investors to privatization contracts containing license transfer agreements.

- The central bank announced a radical exchange rate policy at the beginning of 2000. It committed itself to keep the exchange rate at a preannounced level, so that the Turkish lira would depreciate in line with the targeted rate of inflation. Monetary policy was made passive; the central bank could provide Turkish lira only by purchasing foreign exchange.

- If the targeted rate of inflation of 20 percent by the end of 2000 was realized, the treasury would have had to pay very high real interest on domestic borrowing since the cost of borrowing would then exceed that in the preprogram era by 100 percent. To prevent this, a retroactive tax was levied on the interest on treasury bonds and bills due in 2000 and after.

- The 2000 budget had some discipline. The budget deficit would not grow relative to national income and all expenditures would be inflated consistent only with the targeted rate of inflation.

ANATOMY OF THE 1999 IMF PROGRAM

The 1999 IMF program had a scope of three years. At the end of the first year, inflation was scheduled to decline from around 60 percent to 20 percent; the end of the second year would see inflation of 10 percent, and the third year was to end with single-digit inflation. The targets were ambitious, but technically not unfeasible (see Table 2.5).

The program was built on three interconnected pillars. The first was an effort to bring down the public deficit. Proposed measures included the application of a tight budget, reducing the deficit of SEEs, and a more rational policy of agricultural subsidies.

The second pillar consisted of structural reforms and the completion of privatization; all reforms were designed to permanently reduce the public sector deficit and to provide additional revenues. This meant privatizing the production and distribution of electricity, revising the social security system—including the establishment of private pension schemes—closing down extrabudgetary funds, and a restructuring plan for public banks to guard against political influence. In short, the aim was to remove financially disruptive and not very transparent tools from the grasp of politicians.

The third policy pillar could be applied successfully only if the first two pillars were implemented. When this was the case, the central bank would predetermine the foreign exchange rate and increase it in line with a *targeted* level of inflation. Thus, the exchange rate would rise very slowly compared to past inflation, serving as a "nominal anchor" and bringing down inflation expectations. A slower rate of decline in actual inflation than the targeted path would certainly make

TABLE 2.5. THE PROGRAM AND REALIZATIONS

	2000	2001	2002
GNP growth (%)	5–5.5 (6.1)	5–6 (–9.3)	5–6
Inflation (%)	25 (33)	10–12 (92)	5–7
Current account balance (% of GNP)	–2 (–5)	–1 or 2 (+2)	–1 or 2
Primary balance (% of GNP)	3.7 (4)	3.7 (5.5)	3.7

Note: Figures in parentheses show the realizations.
Source: "Turkey: The Letter of Intent," December 9, 1999, http://www.imf.org.

it more difficult for the central bank to keep the exchange rates on the predetermined path. Along with the first two pillars, the exchange rate policy would impose a limit on net domestic assets of the central bank—an indicator of how much liquidity the central bank gives to the market through credit; in other words, it would limit how much the central bank could lend to the government so that foreign exchange rate policy would be sustainable. According to the program, the central bank could fine-tune liquidity in the market only through buying or selling foreign exchange, no longer through providing credit to the government. Changing the offered interest rates was the only tool for the central bank to determine whether the market would sell or demand foreign exchange. In other words, under the program, exchange rates were to be managed while interest rates would fluctuate for the first eighteen months.

THE PROGRAM IS OFF AND RUNNING

The general public's confidence in the central bank's ability to maintain a declared foreign exchange rate was unquestioned. Market confidence brought nominal interest rates down from around 90 percent to 50 percent and later to 30 percent. Interestingly, real interest rates remained negative for most of the year 2000 in terms of both expected and realized inflation rates (see Table 2.2).

Initially, the government too seemed confident in the steps it took. It courageously made difficult decisions. Commitments regarding tobacco subsidies and support prices for grain were all realized. Domestic prices of agricultural products in dollar terms were scheduled to approach international prices in a few years, and most were to take place in the first year. While past reform efforts always failed because of governmental indecision (in particular regarding agricultural support policies), the new economic stability program appeared to be implemented successfully and decisively during the first half of the year 2000.

The vigorous application of the exchange rate policy, the boldness displayed regarding the implementation of structural reforms, and the discipline imposed on domestic prices by increased imports were the main factors behind the downward trend in inflation. The parliament worked hard until its summer recess and all scheduled laws were passed on time.

HEADING FOR TROUBLE

In the second half of 2000, the government lost the political determination and decisiveness it had shown in the first half of the year; a case of "reform fatigue" in the government developed, in part because some of the further reforms were not politically popular. The sale of the national telecommunications company (Türk Telekom), which had become the flag bearer of the privatization program, became a subject for disagreement and the sale of Turkish Airlines was delayed. In addition, although authorized by the parliament, government ministers would not sign the decree to close the maligned extrabudgetary funds.

In addition to stopping further reforms, the government did not respond timely to a new problem: the current account deficit. A "wealth effect," created as a result of the rapid drop in interest rates, energized domestic consumption and imports took off. By mid-2000, it was clear that the current account deficit would be much higher than expected by the end of the year. Although the current account deficit did not create any immediate financial complications because of the increase in Turkey's international borrowing capabilities, it was clear that policies aimed at controlling domestic demand needed to be implemented. In spite of warnings from the IMF, the government ignored the problem; policies to control the growth of domestic demand were blocked following the severe recession in 1999.

When the IMF delegation came to Turkey in August for the third review of the standby arrangement and discovered that promised reforms had not been enacted (that is, further privatization and the closure of extrabudgetary funds were both on hold), it decided to postpone the third review of the program and combine it with the fourth, scheduled for December. In fact, the coalition government's "reform fatigue" was manifest for all to see. Nevertheless, the IMF refrained from publicly criticizing the government.

In September, the BRSA board officially assumed its responsibilities. The BRSA was a new, hence unknown, institution. As the treasury was in charge of the banking sector before, the BRSA was anxiously awaited. The BRSA's views on unnecessary and/or "against-the-regulations" risks taken by banks to boost profits greatly concerned the banking sector. The concerns of the banking sector multiplied as the BRSA gave markets the impression of inflexibility. The same uncompromising attitude was also displayed with the immediate implementation of the banking sector reforms supported by the World

Bank regarding the reduction in limits on foreign exchange risks and capital adequacy rules. In short, the BRSA behaved as though it would solve forty years' worth of accumulated problems in the banking sector in forty days, ignoring the fact that financial balances in the sector were quite tenuous.

HOW TO MAKE THE PERFECT CRISIS

CRISIS MODE: NOVEMBER 2000

The delays in programmed reforms, the current account deficit, and the uncompromising stance of the BRSA began to unravel financial markets. As the end of the year approached, banks tried to close their open positions in foreign exchange to make their balance sheets look better. The banks' demand for foreign exchange naturally boosted demand for Turkish lira and interest rates rose. Higher interest rates increased risks for the banks that held treasury bonds in large amounts, as the increase in interest rates meant that the value of the bonds held by the banks dropped.

The central bank, sticking to its net domestic assets target (an indicator of liquidity), did not provide liquidity to counter the rising interest rates. Banks known to have invested heavily in treasury bonds were de facto being discriminated against. It became increasingly difficult for these banks to find credit in interbank money markets, and the drop in available liquidity pushed interest rates even higher. The first reaction to the soaring interest rates came from foreign investors holding treasury bills (that is, short-term treasury bonds); believing that they would not be able to sell their bonds later on, they started to withdraw from the market. As they converted bonds into cash, they pushed interest rates even higher while at the same time increasing demand for foreign exchange. The total value of foreign holdings that was eventually withdrawn from the financial market was only between $2.5 and $3 billion. At this stage, too, the central bank maintained its position as a spectator. Despite the rising interest rates, there was no inflow of foreign exchange into the system—a development contrary to what was foreseen by the program. Instead, investors were taking their money out of the Turkish economy as the perceived risk increased.

In addition, "structured finance deals," for which treasury bonds were used as guarantees against foreign exchange borrowing from abroad, threw banks into hardship. The progressive loss of value of treasury bonds made them unacceptable as guarantees for credit obtained from abroad, and thus outstanding short-term foreign credits could not be rolled over and had to be paid off. Banks, forced to pay off their foreign credits, in turn further boosted demand for foreign exchange.

By the time the IMF finally permitted the central bank to relieve the credit crunch by injecting a limited amount of Turkish lira into the market, this liquidity was turned immediately into foreign exchange. Attempting to maintain the exchange rate regime previously announced, the central bank was prompted to describe the situation as a "currency attack." The IMF too had an important part in this interpretation of events.[14]

However, the situation was far from being a currency attack, as there was no significant change in the choice of portfolio allocations of residents. It was simply foreign investors pulling out of the Turkish market, limited to at most $6 to $8 billion. Just like in Thailand in 1997, this was in the first place a liquidity crisis. For fear of having to sell all of its foreign currency reserves, the immediate reaction of the central bank was to cut off its supply of liquidity to the market—a reversal of a policy only a few days old.

In short, help provided by the central bank was "too little too late." In fact, the central bank should have injected sufficient liquidity to ease the credit crunch and reduce the uncertainty in financial markets. Instead, interest rates in the thousands were observed in the overnight market. The interest sensitivity of demand for financial assets virtually disappeared. The crisis of November 2000 was exacerbated by a "misinterpretation of events," the underlying causes of which were "mismanagement" by financial authorities.

The interpretation of these developments as a currency attack, supported by the IMF, resulted in policy responses in Turkey similar to those applied in Southeast Asia and Latin America. Turkey made new pledges and a new agreement was signed with the IMF as a supplement to the standby arrangement. Under the Supplemental Reserve Facility, the IMF provided an additional $7.5 billion to Turkey. Around the same time Turkey received the first installment of $1.1 billion, along with $600 million related to the third and fourth installments of the standby arrangement, the World Bank announced that it would provide $5 billion to Turkey over three years under its Country Assistance

Strategy program. This news temporarily reduced anxiety in financial markets. However, sustainability of the stabilization program became a subject of debate in financial circles.

CRISIS MODE REVISITED: FEBRUARY 2001

Throughout January, the central bank provided more liquidity than the original specified target, and interest rates began to drop to 100 percent. Unbeknownst to the public, the central bank, encouraged by the decline in interest rates mainly due to "good news" of continuing support from the IMF, started consultations with the IMF to bring down the upper limit on the net domestic assets item, reducing its capacity to provide liquidity. In the wake of the November crisis this upper limit was slated to take effect in June 2001, but its introduction was stepped up to the end of February in an effort to reestablish the pre-November criteria on the central bank's balance sheet. Although this decision had no visible effect on the markets, it severely restricted the central bank's ability to reduce interest rates further, if and when necessary. It would have made much more sense to loosen up liquidity, as long as the extra liquidity did not create pressure making it difficult to maintain the predetermined exchange rate regime to permit interest rates to decline close to pre-November crisis levels. Such a strategy could have been relatively easy to implement, as the central bank had record high foreign exchange reserves of over $28 billion at the time.

In this atmosphere, a quarrel between the president and the prime minister in the National Security Council on February 19, 2001, over the government's reluctance to fight corruption became headline news. The prime minister publicly called the disagreement a "state crisis," sending markets, still recovering from their November battle scars, into turmoil once again. As foreign investors tried to pull out of the market, banks started buying foreign exchange to guard themselves against any political ramifications. Meanwhile, the treasury was preparing for the largest internal debt redemption in its history. In an auction to roll over its domestic debt, the treasury reduced the maturity of its internal borrowing, yet there was still insufficient demand. Having sold $7.5 billion to the markets the day before, the central bank decided not to provide Turkish lira liquidity by buying foreign exchange. Turkish banks had barely enough cash to pay foreign investors who were pulling out of Turkish markets and almost had to default. Interest rates again shot up to the thousands in a few days. As in November, the central bank refused to provide additional liquidity to the market, exacerbating the crisis.

The situation was again defined as a currency attack rather than a liquidity crisis, while, in fact, it was a case where foreign investors were pulling out and domestic residents were relatively calm. Again, the crisis was the result of mismanagement.

THE MESS

As a result of these events, financial markets were paralyzed and the payments system collapsed. At this point, to avoid depleting its foreign exchange reserves, the central bank decided to ration its foreign exchange sales to the market. Thus, one of the most comprehensive stability programs in the country's history—the managed exchange rate regime based on preannouncing the daily rates—was abandoned. The value of the Turkish lira was left to float; the dollar shot up from 685,000 Turkish lira to over 1,000,000 the following day.

There was no confidence left in the financial system. In fact, a genuine currency attack started after the Turkish lira was allowed to float freely. Banks on the one hand, and the public on the other, began to turn to foreign exchange. Fears that foreign exchange might be scarce in the future and the uncertainty about its price relative to the lira brought the demand for foreign exchange to unprecedented levels in a few days. Dollarization increased in the economy, and the uncertainty in foreign exchange prices cut domestic demand severely. The payment system grew increasingly paralyzed, and foreign financial sources dried up. Turkey was forced to pay back large parts of its short-term debts, both public and private, and letters of guarantee given by Turkish banks were not accepted abroad. The economy came to a halt, deepening the crisis nationwide.

The sudden and unexpected drop in the volume of domestic demand made it necessary for companies to resort to "leave with pay" for workers. In some sectors, factories closed. Austerity measures by those companies that could still operate increased unemployment further. After two major crises the government had lost all its credibility, and there was no short, easy way out of the mess. Economic expectations degenerated to the point that it was difficult to guess what would happen the next day, let alone the next week.

The banking sector collapsed. The number of banks taken over by SDIF reached nineteen, representing roughly 15 percent of the assets of the banking sector and 20 percent in number. The cost of restructuring the economy ended up being very high. Fortunately, international support was available again to stabilize the situation and to continue the reform of the Turkish economy.

In analyzing the root causes of the crisis, one thing that cannot be denied is the importance of the domestic and international loss of confidence that resulted from the delays and unwillingness on the part of the Turkish government to deliver the structural reforms promised in the stability program. Nevertheless, with the financial markets' uneasiness having turned into crisis, the wisdom of the IMF's uncompromising position regarding the parameters of the stability program, and its pressure on the government and the central bank that "foreign exchange reserves should be protected under all conditions," is debatable.[15] A smoother and more flexible monetary policy might have enabled the Turkish economy to carry on with its stability program without aggravating the existing crisis. All that was needed was to eliminate the pressures that would lead to sharp changes in exchange rates; that is, to sell foreign exchange. After all, Turkey successfully engineered "a foreign exchange crisis" by acting as if foreign exchange reserves were scarce at a time when its international reserves were at a record high, exceeding $28 billion.[16]

One may argue that a freely floating exchange rate regime would be more desirable than a sort of managed-float or fixed exchange rate regime in that floating rates would absorb external shocks and maintain a competitive export sector. However, at the time Turkey moved to a freely floating exchange rate regime, shocks were not external nor was the export sector uncompetitive. On the contrary, very high volatility in exchange rates became a domestically originated shock on financial markets, with a high degree of currency substitution as well on the real sector. Since the introduction of a freely floating exchange rate regime, the demand for Turkish lira has steadily deteriorated due to high volatility in exchange rates mainly caused by speculative moves.

It is interesting to note that what was probably one of the most severe economic crises in the history of Turkey did not have any dire political implications for the government's time in office. Despite the total lack of public confidence, the government was able to remain in power. But it was required to appoint an outsider—Kemal Derviş, a former World Bank official—to run the economy. His takeover as the minister of state in charge of the economy greatly boosted morale and domestic and international confidence. However, abandoning the "controlled exchange rate, free interest rate" policy for a "controlled interest rate, free exchange rate" policy replaced one factor of uncertainty in the economy with another.

A New Program, Cleaning up the Mess

With Turkey on the brink of default, the IMF, again with support from the United States and the European Union, agreed to continue the IMF program in May 2001, but with significant revisions. The IMF's pledge of financial support was increased from $11 billion to $19 billion, in return for a renewed commitment by the Turkish government to pursue a more ambitious reform program than the previous one. The fact that the nonpartisan Derviş was to oversee the implementation of the new program provided some reassurance for international supporters. After losing considerable political capital due to back-to-back crises, the three-party coalition government had little choice but to implement the IMF proposal if it wanted to remain in power.

The new program was no longer designed to reduce inflation to single digits in the near future but rather to control the damage to the economy. With tight fiscal and monetary policies and a freely floating exchange rate regime, restructuring the banking system had priority. Work started immediately with the public banks. As a result of the two crises, the accumulated bad debt of public banks plus the large amount of loans to the government made bank reform very costly.[17] Of the three major public banks, one was closed (Emlakbank) and the other two (Ziraat and Halk) came under the management of a common board of directors mandated to restructure their balance sheets, reduce the numbers of branches and employees, and eventually privatize them.

Although the restructuring of public banks was originally planned for the year 2000, the government's reluctance delayed the program. The restructuring work began with the government's debt payments to these banks, which amounted to more than $20 billion. The government itself provided some additional capital. Public banks became more liquid and ceased to be the cause of high interest rates in money markets. As a result, an important source of market distortion was eliminated. New legislation made certain that public banks would no longer be a little-transparent way to finance government deficits. Along with their downsizing, public banks were virtually withdrawn from the banking sector in that their credits declined significantly in an effort to restructure their balance sheets.

The treasury also funded banks taken over by SDIF against their losses so that these banks likewise would cease to be a source of distortion in money markets. Of the nineteen banks under SDIF, only four were sold to the private sector and two to foreigners, one was kept for the management of assets, and the remaining banks were dissolved.

The floating exchange rate regime continued to be a major source of uncertainty in the economy in 2001. After a sharp depreciation of the Turkish lira by about 50 percent in real terms in the fall of 2001, the parity came down to predevaluation levels in real terms.[18] In other words, the devaluation of the Turkish lira in real terms disappeared, making domestically produced goods as expensive as they were before. Exchange rates were determined not by economic fundamentals but by "news" affecting expectations about political and economic stability. Today, a year after the crisis, the situation remains the same. The very high volatility of exchange rates not only adversely affected the rate of inflation and inflationary expectations, but it also caused a dramatic decline in domestic demand. As a result, it is estimated that GNP fell by around 10 percent in 2001. The rate of inflation reached 92 percent, exceeding the revised program target of 58 percent.[19]

Throughout the year, domestic debt sustainability became another source of uncertainty; the reported domestic debt reached over 80 percent of GNP in 2001 from 40 percent in the previous year. The debt swap, exchanging lira-denominated debt in return for foreign-exchange-denominated debt in June 2001, did not make a substantial difference in the future prospects of debt sustainability. On the contrary, the debt swap initially contributed to a speedy devaluation of the currency, making it hard to pay back foreign-denominated debt.

A higher than expected rate of inflation coupled with a very severe recession in the economy in 2001 kept the "crisis atmosphere" alive, leading to relatively high interest rates, while the government still had difficulty borrowing both domestically and internationally. In effect, the Turkish economy was in need of new credit to avoid the risk of default in the coming years. At that point, the September 11 tragedy in the United States changed the picture. Initially, one expected that, following the September 11 events, economic conditions would further deteriorate as a result of declining international trade and tourism revenues. But because of its increased strategic significance for its allies, Turkey was able to secure crucial financial support for the year 2002 from the IMF as part of a completely new standby arrangement. The previous program ended as "incomplete."

A New Standby Arrangement

Even though Turkey failed spectacularly on the economic front, both at the end of 2000 and in the beginning of 2001, Western financial support continued. Additional credit came quickly in November 2000 in the form of the IMF's Supplementary Reserve Facility and in May 2001 through enhancement of the standby arrangement initiated at the beginning of 2000. As noted, the September 11 tragedy underlined Turkey's political and military importance; economic support from the West was renewed in 2002.

The new 2002 standby arrangement with the IMF involved financial support of more than $16 billion, with a net inflow of additional funds from the IMF of $9 billion. The arrangement continued to enforce tight fiscal and monetary policies with a freely floating exchange rate regime; it aimed for a primary surplus in the budget equivalent to 6.5 percent of GNP. In addition, a marked reduction in public sector employment both in the central government and in SEEs was envisioned. Similar to the previous program, the rate of inflation was targeted to go down to 10 percent in three years, while economic growth should resume and reach 5 percent next year and thereafter (see Table 2.6). In my view, however, with a freely floating exchange rate regime, the inherent volatility in exchange rates will make it difficult for growth to exceed 3 percent.

Along with the usual macroeconomic targets, the 2002 program is more specific in establishing "good governance rules" in that it requires further improvements in public sector procurements and in the rules governing public sector borrowing, both internationally and domestically. In short, the intention is to disassociate daily politics from the running of the economy. Hence, government interventions in the

TABLE 2.6. THE PROGRAM IN 2002

	2002	2003	2004
GNP growth (%)	3	5	5
Inflation (%)	35	20	12
Current account balance (% of GNP)	–2	–1	–1
Primary balance (% of GNP)	6.5	6.5	6.5

Source: "Turkey: The Letter of Intent," January 28, 2002, http://www.imf.org.

economy would be minimized and, where appropriate, the rules of intervention would be transparent and economically viable. With this in mind, several independent boards have been established, ranging from a board for public tenders to a board for energy regulations. In addition, the central bank's law has been modified, making the bank operationally an independent institution from the government.

TURKEY'S UNCERTAIN ECONOMIC FUTURE

Over the past two decades, Turkey has initiated probably the most comprehensive and far-reaching of economic and political programs. However, further economic initiatives are essential to stabilize the economy and to create the right conditions for sustained economic growth and price stability. Failure to implement reforms would once again give the European Union an excuse to postpone Turkey's accession—this time a good one. Unfortunately, Turkey seems to move in the right direction only when there are no alternatives. Even the current economic stabilization plan was a product of one that failed miserably; without radical structural changes in the IMF program, Turkey would no longer have been able to service its external and domestic debt.

The current program takes into account possible external and internal shocks and tries to ensure that an adequate level of international reserves is maintained through a floating exchange rate regime. Sharp movements in exchange rates, as contemplated by those who designed the program, will also act as a disciplinary factor in case politicians relax policy implementation. Despite these inbuilt buffers, however, it is clear that strong political resolve is needed to enact the remaining difficult and politically unpopular reforms, particularly downsizing the central government and its agencies and enlarging the tax base.[20]

Politics could easily torpedo any hope of successful implementation. In the political climate of 2002, no one party or even two parties have received sufficient votes to form a majority government in the parliament. Politics is currently fairly divided, which raises doubts as to whether the politicians have the required coherence and decisiveness to make economic and political reforms work. After all, these reforms reduce the power of politicians to affect the daily life of some people for their own, short-term, political benefit. Politicians are being asked to marginalize themselves. This is the only way the political calendar and economic calendar can be separated.[21]

Since 1999, the three parties in the coalition have stayed together out of fear of new elections. Although the outgoing government has undertaken some far-reaching structural reforms over the past year, its record is seen as mediocre due to a severe recession and rising unemployment. Each day, as elections loomed closer, politicians became increasingly reluctant to make concessions for which they would reap the benefits only in the long run. The new elections now scheduled for November 3, instead of the first half of 2004, effectively suspended all reforms. Economic reforms, however important, will have to wait. A new element has entered the economic scene.

Previous stabilization programs have lacked public support as politicians failed to adequately explain the programs due to their short-term horizons. Further structural reforms also will have little support in public opinion, as most require an outright reduction in public sector employment. At a time when the economy is already in a severe recession, the private sector will be unable to absorb the workers leaving the public sector. In addition, the downsizing of public banks coupled with a severe crisis in the banking sector as a whole already contributes to rising unemployment. Unemployment, above 10 percent in 2001, will continue to rise in the near future.

The current program also limits the power to manage macroeconomic imbalances, which creates uncertainty regarding exchange rates and makes it difficult to improve inflationary expectations. Even when market forces hold exchange rates relatively stable—as observed most of this year—the lack of an explicit mechanism to stabilize the foreign exchange market adversely affects domestic demand. In fact, the economic cycle is currently indexed to movements in exchange rates. Real appreciation of the Turkish lira stimulates growth, while even nominal depreciation of a few percentage points brings economic slowdown. Thus, growth may not resume—support from international organizations backed by the United States and the EU is not in itself sufficient to guarantee it—and is unlikely to reach 3 percent, as targeted by the program. Under these circumstances, inflationary expectations will take a long time to decline to the targeted level, while the economy will remain stagnant until the public is convinced that inflation is declining faster than their expectations. During the process, Turkey may have to go through a prolonged and severe recession.

The lack of economic growth renders balancing the budget more difficult, and the ratio of public debt over national income will not soon improve, even with some austerity measures. For that matter, it seems that limits have been reached in terms of both one-time expenditure cuts and tax increases. In addition, as the government's revenues are adversely affected by an economic contraction, the government would need to cut spending dramatically if it wanted to balance the budget. This in turn would further exacerbate the economic recession.

Under these circumstances, it would make more sense to encourage growth and not to worry about the ratio of national income over public debt. As it is, the stabilization program will not reach its targets because of the inability of the government to reduce public sector deficits faster than the decline in national income. It seems that the ratio of public debt over national income can only substantially improve if the economy is allowed to grow. In addition, without a reasonable level of growth, continuous financial support from international organizations will be required to make the debt dynamics sustainable. The present program fails to address this important issue.

The failure to improve the economy—that is, to promote growth and lower inflation—made the government not only hesitant to reform the economy further, but also to go ahead with the political reforms that are necessary for entering the European Union. The political reform process is already difficult and involves different parts of the society, including the military. Moreover, as political commitments erode and divergence of views within the coalition becomes more apparent, the likelihood of successful political reforms diminishes. A second round of "reform fatigue"—both political and economic— seems imminent as general elections on November 3 approach.

In spite of serious efforts to transform economic and political life over the past twenty years, it remains very hard to predict whether the Turkish economy is on a stable path to growth and price stability; further economic reforms are tricky and unpopular and it will take some time to reform the political structure. There have been radical structural reforms in the areas of foreign trade, the financial sector, and the foreign exchange regime, but the fiscal imbalances have deteriorated continuously, almost in parallel with improvements in other areas of the economy, keeping the rate of inflation high and economic growth volatile. Failure to correct this may undermine the structural reforms achieved so far, resulting in a greater loss to the economy and a costly recovery. One should not rely on the irreversibility of reforms achieved so far for ultimate success. As recent events have shown, political uncertainty created by the illness of Bulent Ecevit, the current prime minister, can easily lead to turmoil in financial markets, reducing the effectiveness of structural reforms since rising interest rates may significantly alter debt dynamics of the public sector. Hence, implementing structural reforms alone may not necessarily guarantee economic stability. There is more to it.

Both a more predictable environment—that is, stable and sustainable exchange rates and price stability—and a greater credibility of politicians are needed to encourage private investment and consumption, which are in turn key factors for economic growth. But it remains to be seen whether politicians will behave fiscally responsibly and implement the needed economic and political reforms. Failure to do so will inevitably be punished by global financial markets.

By going into early elections, Turkey once again chose short-term instability in politics over medium-term stability in the economy. However, given the current economic conditions, parties (or the party) in the government after the elections will have little choice but to go along with the current economic program backed by the IMF, regardless of what they have said in their election campaigns.

CHAPTER THREE

TURKEY AND THE FATE OF POLITICAL ISLAM

OMER CELIK

Terms such as Islamic movement, Islamism, political Islam, radical Islam, and fundamentalist Islam cannot adequately capture the dimensions of the social reality that they aim to convey. These categories, nevertheless, are used here to describe the Islamist politics that emerged in Turkey in the 1970s as a political alternative to Kemalism. The common point among all these terms is that they refer to the discourse and activities that give Islam a central political role and rebuild society according to what are believed to be Islamic principles and Islamic law. This chapter reviews the history of Islamism and explores its prospects in Turkey.

THE PHASES OF POLITICAL ISLAM IN TURKEY

TURKISH MODERNIZATION AND THE ISLAMIST MOVEMENT

The Islamist movement in Turkey differs from those in other Muslim countries in two major respects. First, Atatürk's republican modernization policies have had a deep impact on Turkish society. Second, the political and social culture of Turkey is different from that of other Islamic countries.

Following the proclamation of the Turkish republic in 1923, the state began to implement nationalist and secular policies. The most important of these was the abolition of the caliphate in March 1924, which had preserved the idea of ummet (a community based on religion rather than nationality) by giving the Ottoman sultan the power of Islamic as well as political leadership. Devout Muslims kept their distance from the concept of *nation;* thus, to strengthen the notion of being Turkish, Atatürk had to abolish the caliphate.

With the abolition of the caliphate and the implementation of nationalist and secular reforms, the Turkish republic cut its ties with the Islamic world and put an end to the central role of Islam in Turkish politics.[1] On the very day that the caliphate was abolished, the Turkish parliament also closed Islamic educational institutes, commonly called *mektep* and *medrese* under the law of "Tevhid-i Tedrisat" (unification of education and training), which put all educational institutions under state control.

In April 1924 religious courts were abolished. In 1925 the "Hat Law" was passed as the first step of a much wider modernization of clothes and appearance. In 1926 the Swiss civil code was mainly adopted as Turkish law. In 1928 the Latin alphabet was introduced. With the abolition of Islam as the official religion, manifestations of religion in the political sphere were erased.

The secularist reforms implemented by the Turkish republic also involved a systematic effort to move Turkish minds away from Islamic concepts and practices.[2] The leaders of the new Turkey were aware that an attempt to remove Islam completely from public life would have many uncontrollable political and social ramifications. With this concern in mind, they tried to develop a new interpretation of Islam, emphasizing the role of the state. In other words, Kemalist secularism is a reinterpretation of Islam rather than its total exclusion. The most important manifestation of Kemalist secularism was the establishment of the department of religious affairs in the Turkish state. Islamists have criticized this body and its inherent inconsistency with secularism. According to secular law, state and religious affairs should be separated; however, by founding the department of religious affairs, the Turkish state proceeded to control religion. Traditional Islamic sects found this department threatening to their influence on society.

This reinterpretion of Islam in compliance with "nationalist" objectives, however, has not succeeded in defining the Turkish people's religious values. Consequently, state and religion relations have remained a major source of political and social tension in Turkish society.

On December 23, 1930, "Menemen Olayi" (The Event of Menemen), involving a member of the Nakschibendi religious order,[3] greatly affected the Kemalist elites. An army lieutenant was killed in a small Aegean town called Menemen. According to the Turkish authorities, the assassin was the radical Islamist leader Dervish Mehmet, who had stimulated an uprising in an attempt to bring sharia to the country. Some, however, claim that the perpetrators were dressed like dervishes (according to official history dervishes are people who want the state governed by religous rules) and were highly drugged. After this murder, Kemalists decided to strengthen further the political strictures on Islam.

In 1933, the faculty of divinity of Ankara University became the Institute of Islamic Research. While there were 2,259 students enrolled in the twenty schools for imams in 1926, by 1932 there were only ten religion students in the remaining two schools. In 1935, religion courses were removed from the curriculum of primary and secondary schools. This was rescinded in 1948.[4]

In its early years, the government also tried to prevent Muslims in Turkey from having relations with Muslims in other countries. Thus, Islamists in Turkey were not much aware of contemporary foreign Islamic movements such as those in Iran, Egypt, and Pakistan. However, this isolation is not the only reason why political Islam in Turkey has had a unique course of development and a different social niche compared with other Muslim countries. State and religion relations in Turkey have had a remarkable role in determining where Islam fits in the social and political picture.

One of the greatest differences between Turkey and other Muslim countries in terms of state–religion relations is that the Turkish state, in an effort to isolate Islam from state affairs and control it at the same time, used right-wing parties to manage religious movements. (Ironically, this approach also worked to facilitate the development of religious elements in politics.) All these developments explain why Islamist movements in Turkey were not able to represent a challenge to the status quo during the formative era of the republic.

Multiparty Democracy and Islamism

With the advent of multiparty democracy in 1950, the right wing
Democrat Party (DP) took power. One of its objectives was to work
against radical secular political elements. DP's approach to religion
was similar to the early republican approach, which allowed Islam to
exist as a tradition but not as a political ideology.

Political conservatives had united their various parties against the
secular nationalists of the early republic. As a result, Islamism in Turkey
was nurtured in a conservative alliance and developed with a conservative statist discourse.[5] The 1950s witnessed the incremental institu-
tionalization of Islam as a focus of Turkish nationalist values.[6] A new
era started for Islamism and nationalism and more generally for
Islamism and conservative Turkish political parties.

The DP reforms, aiming to strengthen the Islamic element in conservative politics, included policies such as the inclusion of religion
courses in the primary school curriculum as an elective, the reintro-
duction of the call to prayer in Arabic, the reopening of schools of
imam and preaching, and the establishment of a faculty of divinity at
Ankara University. Despite this bow to traditional Islam and its manifestations, DP did not allow the politicization of Islam and in this fashion remained loyal to Kemalism.

For example, lawsuits against a prominent Islamist scholar of the
time, Said-i Nursi—also called Said-i Kurdi for his Kurdish origin—
were opened for his propagating Islamic political consciousness
among the people. Here, the overlapping of Islamist and Kurdish identities especially bothered Kemalist elites. Islamists and Kurds shared an
exclusion from mainstream Turkish governance and society, which
encouraged their collaboration. In addition serious measures were
taken against minority sects, notably the Ticanis,[7] who were members
of an Ankara-based Sufi sect. The Atatürk Law, which has been often
used to restrict the activities of such minorities, was passed on July 31,
1951.[8] This law subjected to imprisonment anyone who insulted or
encouraged others to insult Atatürk's memory by word or by vandal-
izing his statues or his grave.

The 1961 constitution, which ironically was drafted by the military
following the coup in 1960, nurtured liberal democracy and plural-
ism. As a result of this further democratization, political Islamists were
allowed to take part in public discussion. In 1969, the National Order
Party (Milli Nizam Partisi) was established, the first Islamist party in

Turkey. The supporters of this party believed that Turkey's underde-velopment was caused by secularism and Zionism and that only a return to Islamic principles and ultimately pan-Islamism could reverse this situation.

Despite the greater involvement of Islam in politics during this period, the early republican division of political Islam into two groups—secular-adaptive and reactionary-conflictive—continued. Secular-adaptive Islam encouraged the adoption of Islamic interpretations to support state policies, through bodies such as the department of reli-gious affairs. Reactionary-conflictive Islam was pro-sharia and thus anti-regime. The definition of reactionary-conflictive, however, was not limited to the pro-sharia movement but encompassed all anti-state interpretations of Islam.

The Justice Party (Adalet Partisi) came to power in 1961 and con-tinued the implementation of DP's policies. In the two decades from this time until the 1980 coup, many more schools of imam training and preaching were opened. The government attached great impor-tance to the training of Kemalist and secularist imams and to the for-mation of a more contemporary interpretation of Islam.[9] Another noteworthy characteristic of this highly chaotic period was that Islam began to be used as a weapon against communism in Turkey by the government and, many Turks believe, by the United States.

A number of nationalist groups with Islamic orientation also played an important role in the integration of religion into politics. Türk Ocaklari (Turkish Janissary Corps) was a civil organization initially founded in 1912 to interpret Islam as the religion of Turks, unlike Islamic sects, which consider Turks to be a part of ummet. Closed in April 1934, the nationalists were allowed to reopen Türk Ocaklari in 1949, with a mission to unite Islam and nationalism. The fact that Turkey was seeking membership in the North Atlantic Treaty Organization (NATO) was a key factor in supporting the anti-communist doctrine of the Türk Ocaklari. Another institution that strengthened political Islam in Turkey was Aydinlar Ocagi (Intellectuals Hearth), which was founded by the conservative nationalist elite. It was an association that sought reconciliation between official secular state policies and a civil Turkish nationalism that contained Islamic elements. It tried to create a Turkish nationalist-Islamist synthesis and supported state policies within a nationalist-religious framework, albeit without much success. It was totally civil as an institution but state-dependant ideo-logically. The effort of Aydinlar Ocagi in educating and training ideologically nationalist activists and politicians did not translate into political success until the Nationalist Action Party's later popularity.

Islamism in Turkey existed within the Turkish nationalist-conservative movement until the 1970s when a "separation" between the two took place. The new "Turkish-Islamist synthesis" emerging from this process became even more defined after the coup in 1980.[10] Post-1980 Islamism became an independent movement and adopted an anti-Kemalist character. As a result, tensions emerged between Islamism and nationalist-conservative elements. From the conservative point of view, Turkish Islam had to be defended and protected as an essential part of the state. Conservatism defended religion as approved by the power holders. Turkish Islamists using religion to critique the political system, however, could not be tolerated.[11] The bond between Islamism and political conservatism was broken.

THE AFTERMATH OF THE 1980 MILITARY RULE

The most important difference between political Islam before and after 1980 is the emergence of a political Islam with real aspirations to be an alternative to Kemalism and ultimately to win power. This process started in the 1960s when a group of university students developed an Islamic political vision of their own by reading the translations of prominent Egyptian and Pakistani Islamists. In 1969 in the Nationalist Turkish Students Association elections, these students left the nationalist right camp and won the elections.[12] But this group did not gain strength until the 1980s when they formally established their individual political Islamist identity. Necmettin Erbakan, former prime minister and the chairman of all the principal successive Islamic parties, saw these university students as a prominent resource for his National Order Party. He specifically alluded to the role of the religious youth with this famous statement: "Imam and preaching schools are our backyard."

After the 1979 Islamic revolution in Iran, Islamists began to believe that Islam could thrive politically in the modern world. Indeed, after the Iranian revolution Turkish Islamists significantly increased their appeal by focusing also on the common problems of people in Turkey;[13] thus the policy of Islamist political identity was formulated. Islamist political identity accepts Islam as the only criterion for ideological identity.

It also asserts that people should be devoted to the Islamic ummet along with devotion to the nation state.

During these years the Turkish Islamic movement also began to question its past practices. This took place in two stages; first questioning of the alliance of Islamists with right-wing nationalists and second questioning of the insensitivity of Islamists to the worsening Kurdish problem. The result was a major change in the Islamist approach to the Kurdish issue, which Islamists had effectively neglected for decades because of their alliance with right-wing nationalists.

The Islamist movement, which became stronger in the more liberal period from the 1980s to the late 1990s had numerous strands, including the partisans of ummet, nationalists, statists, anti-statists, Turkists, and Kurdists. All these components eventually dwindled under the influence of Erbakan's Welfare Party, which gained significant popularity in the second half of the 1990s and ultimately obtained power in 1996. The Welfare Party recast the "National Vision," which Erbakan had developed as the political ideology of Turkish Islamism in the late 1960s.

Since 1969, the tradition of the National Vision has continued under various Islamic parties: the National Order Party (Milli Nizam Partisi MNP, 1969–71), the National Salvation Party (Milli Selamet Partisi or MSP 1972–81), the Welfare Party (Refah Partisi, RP 1981–97), and the Virtue Party (Fazilet Partisi, FP 1997–2001). Military coups on March 12, 1971, September 12, 1980, and February 28, 1997, interrupted the National Vision movement; after each coup Erbakan's party was closed and reopened under a new name. The result invariably was that their electorate shrank and their organization had to be changed.

Erbakan's National Vision provided an explanation for Turkey's problems and solutions to them. According to Erbakan, the underdevelopment of the Muslim world is caused by Israel and other foreign elements. These elements interfere in the governmental affairs of Islamic countries and cause them to be poor and underdeveloped. Muslim countries have to return to Islamic principles in order to get out of backwardness. For their salvation, Muslim states need to be governed under Islam. If Islamic unity can be attained among Muslim countries, the West will not be able to exploit them. Even though the model developed by Erbakan is primitive, it has been influential among religious youth who could not identify with state views. The failure of the modern Turkish state to deliver political, social, and economic services has transformed the traditionalism persisting in society into a reactionary mechanism against the status quo.

Both rightist and leftist ideologies suffered badly from the 1980 military coup. This created a vacuum that was filled by Islamist politics. By the mid-1990s, people had had enough of Turkey's ineffective and corrupt politicians. People who lived in shanty towns of big cities had become even poorer. Erbakan's Welfare Party, under these circumstances, became the center of opposition to the status quo. It became the party of the poor.

The National Vision of Erbakan won its first victory in the 1994 elections under the banner of the Welfare Party. Following the elections, a coalition government composed of the Welfare Party and the True Path Party (Dogru Yol Partisi) was established in 1996, but this process ended with the effective coup on February 28, 1997. The military looked at Erbakan in the same way as the Turkish Authority looked at the rebel Dervish Mehmet of the 1930s. His becoming prime minister foreshadowed a retreat to the pre-republican era.

A SUMMARY EVALUATION OF THE DEVELOPMENT OF POLITICAL ISLAM IN TURKEY

Political Islamist movements work against the status quo and constitute an alternative to the state order in many modern countries. However, they have not been able to emerge as a strong alternative to the existing system in Turkey. Turkish political Islamists may have been in the lead at times, but they have not been able to achieve continuous popularity. Moreover, people who vote for Islamist parties do not necessarily adhere to a political Islamist ideology.

However, this is not to say that political Islamism in Turkey has not had success. After the 1980 coup, political opposition found a place in the political Islamist movement. Islamists opposed the powers that be and attracted both left-wing and right-wing opponents to their side. The movement became powerful but never reached the level where Islamism developed organic relations with the Turkish public. For instance, radical Islamists in Turkey were never able to organize and recruit supporters in mosques unlike elsewhere in the world. This was a result of both the refusal of radical Islamists' to pray in mosques protesting the authority of the department of religious affairs and their inability to communicate their beliefs to the common people.

Anti-statism or opposition to the status quo has not held a traditional place in Turkish culture. Turkey inherited characteristics from the Ottoman Empire, which did not tolerate anti-statism of any sort. A widespread revolt against the state never took place in over six hundred years of imperial rule. Moreover, the mosaic of different religions and identities in Turkey as well as the country's proximity to Europe softened the harsh character of Islam that prevails in many other Muslim countries.

With rapid urbanization and the improved standards of urban living as well as the geographical extension of the secular education system, Turkey developed an educated urban middle class. The Islamists in Turkey were unable to find support from this secular group of people. Moreover, unlike Islamist movements in other parts of the world, rural populations did not constitute a significant portion of their electorate. Rather, it was those who had moved from rural areas to the cities and failed to integrate into the urban economic and social system that mostly supported political Islamists. The base of political Islam in Turkey became the uneducated poor in the urban shanty towns.

THE IDEOLOGICAL NATURE OF POLITICAL ISLAM

In order to examine Islamist ideology in Turkey, it is necessary to analyze the Kurdish problem as a domestic concern and Israel as a foreign one. However, before exploring these issues it is important to discuss the February 28 coup, which effectively ended political Islam as an ideology in Turkey and ultimately produced the Justice and Development Party (Adalet ve Kalkinma Partisi) or AK Party.

POLITICAL ISLAM AND THE FEBRUARY 28 COUP

Alarmed by political changes that Erbakan started to impose while he was prime minister, the Turkish armed forces publicly asserted that the "reactionary" Islamist danger in Turkey was growing since the day Erbakan became prime minister. The D-8 (eight developing Muslim countries, consisting of Bangladesh, Egypt, Indonesia, Iran, Libya, Malaysia, Nigeria, and Turkey) project of Erbakan's was an effort to bring Muslim countries together in some sort of alliance but was perceived as an attempt to shift Turkey's traditional foreign policy line. On the domestic front, Erbakan claimed that if a party had a sufficient number of members there was no need for democratic elections. He said that political parties could appeal to the relevant electoral authorities to verify the number of members in order to prove who had the majority of votes. After this verification process the party would be entitled to take over the government. This crude, simplistic proposal was interpreted as antidemocratic. But an even more politically adverse statement came from Erbakan: "There will be a change in Turkey. The question is whether it will be bloody or not." Such words created fear among secularists. Erbakan's dinner for Islamic sect leaders to break the fast during Ramadan was also widely and angrily noted by the secular elites. In view of the fact that, in the first years of the republic, Islamic sects were all prohibited, Erbakan's dinner at the official residence of the prime minister seemed to challenge the secular order.

The military, supported by a number of nongovernmental organizations (NGOs) such as trade unions and women's organizations, became involved in the Erbakan issue, believing that the secular lifestyle of Turkey was under threat. The commander of the Naval Forces, Güven Erkaya, described NGO's as "Unarmed Forces" and the military asked these unarmed forces for their support resulting in a public campaign against Erbakan's government. Deniz Baykal, the chairman of the Republican People's Party (Cumhuriyet Halk Partisi or CHP), characterized the military intervention in politics at the time as "Our army acts like an NGO."

The unarmed forces also consisted of the judiciary power and the mass media, which played an important role in the anti-Erbakan propaganda war. The National Security Council memorandum of February 28, 1997, made the public case that Erbakan's government was in conflict with the Turkish state. February 28 had an enormous impact on Turkish Islamists. Political Islamists in the government began to skirmish with the military, which further polarized Erbakan's supporters and the armed forces. The battle was uneven; there was little doubt that Erbakan and political Islam would lose. This soft coup marked the beginning of the decline of political Islam in Turkey.

The removal of Erbakan as prime minister was an ideological earthquake in Turkish Islamist politics. Military statements against

Islamism or any other threat to national unity made it clear that the implications of February 28 would last for a long time. The chief of the Turkish General Staff, Hüseyin Kıvrıkoğlu, publicly declared that "February 28 will go on for one thousand years if necessary." Religion-oriented parties no longer had an important role to play in Turkish politics.

As a result of the February 28 process, the Welfare Party was closed and the Virtue Party, established to replace it, soon shared the same fate. The closure of the Virtue Party indicated the severity of the February 28 process. The Virtue Party actually moderated its Islamist policies and identified itself with center-right politics; by closing it, the state made clear that it would not tolerate political Islam in any form, even if it employed democratic discourse. After the closure of the Virtue Party, the Islamist movement in Turkey still remained under Erbakan's control and returned to the policies of the old National Order Party. The current incarnation, the Felicity Party (Saadet Partisi or SP), was founded with the intent of reviving Erbakan's early ideas in order to attract the radical Islamist electorate, albeit under close scrutiny by and constant threat from the military.

THE AK PARTY AND POLITICAL ISLAM

A reformist element separated from the Virtue Party and established the AK Party in 2001 under the leadership of Recep Tayyip Erdoğan, a former mayor of İstanbul. It was established with the clear purpose of espousing center-right policies and moving away from the tenets of political Islam. By abandoning Erbakan-style politics, Erdoğan repeatedly states that religion is not central to the party's political identity. Today, the radical heritage of Erbakan's Islamism is represented by SP. The AK Party emphasizes conservative democrat politics and for that reason is against political Islam.

Some of the founders of the AK Party may have turned to the right, but they built their political careers within the tradition of political Islam. Others among the founders never adhered to political Islam. Some deputies from the center-right True Path Party and the Nationalist Movement Party (Milliyetçi Hareket Partisi or MHP) have switched to the AK Party.

By breaking with Erbakan, the AK Party had to find a political and ideological identity. Its founders had actually begun to criticize Erbakan

while they were still in his party and positioned themselves at a distance from political Islam. Contrary to the tradition of obedience in
political Islam, Abdullah Gül, a founding member of the AK Party, was
nominated as a rival candidate for party leadership in 2000 against the
then leader of the Virtue Party, Recai Kutan. The directors of the AK
Party specifically did not define themselves as the successors of earlier
political Islamists. Erdoğan indeed, defines his party as "conservative,"
something akin to Christian democratic parties in Europe.

SP, the successor to the Virtue Party, often talks about changing
the political powers in Turkey; the AK Party, on the other hand, avoids
conflict with the Turkish political powers and carries on politics along
conservative lines. SP's Islamic rhetoric continuously sends signals to
its radical supporters emphasizing the National Vision to be the official
policy of the state. The founders of AK Party know from past experiences that any conflict with the system will prevent them from becoming a mass party. They often assert that the Islamist policies followed in
the past were wrong. They also insist that using Islam as a political
tool harms the religion itself and is politically incorrect.

While SP usually refers to Islamist world policies, the AK Party
uses more Turkey-based rhetoric. Erbakan and his National Vision are
the most radical alternatives to Kemalism and maintain a rigid political
attitude. For instance, SP's leader Recai Kutan has said that they do
not aim to change themselves, unlike the AK Party; rather, they have
come to change Turkey under the National Vision. SP is now the only
significant group in Turkey representing political Islam in its more radical form.

The AK Party can hardly deny that it has been significantly
affected by Islamist ideology. In their youth, the directors of the party
were influenced by the National Turkish Students Association and
the doctrine of Akıncılar, which was close to the ideology of Erbakan.
Akıncılar was named after Ottoman warriors who fought on the front
lines during the wars. This pan-Islamist organization tried to break the
influence on youth of both secular rightist and leftist organizations.
They represented the young, radical side of National Vision from the
end of the 1960s until the 1980s. Even though they were involved in
occasional violent activities, they avoided direct confrontation with
the communists. Today, under the AK Party, they have adopted a
new, more moderate approach certainly as compared to SP, although
they do get involved in street demonstrations on issues such as the

banning of the headscarf, which means that they sometimes confront the police.

Erdoğan constantly states that the AK Party does not follow religion-based politics but that it is a conservative-democratic entity. Polls show that the vast majority of people believe Erdoğan's words, but some still have doubts. The identity of SP, on the other hand, is commonly perceived as radical.

The idea of forming a coalition government composed of the AK Party and the center-left CHP has also been discussed from time to time. If such a coalition government were established, the base of the AK Party would not necessarily be discontented. In fact, such a coalition would provide the AK Party with the legitimacy that it so desperately needs since CHP is the founder of the secular republican regime in Turkey.

The majority of AK Party voters are not ideologically Islamist. The party gets its support largely from the poor and middle-class conservatives. Such conservatives do not want the AK Party in conflict with the system. Keeping these people's support will depend highly on whether the AK Party abides by the law and conforms to the Turkish democratic system.

Despite the secular opposition, the AK Party has been the number one party in political polls. Mehmet Ali Bayar, a former diplomat in Washington, D.C., and his Democrat Turkey Party (Demokratik Türkiye Partisi) wanted to be an alternative to the AK Party, but they have not been successful in bringing the center-right together. Other traditional center-right parties have declined in popularity. This void in the right wing has allowed the AK Party to become even more powerful. The New Turkey Party (Yeni Türkiye Partisi), under former social democrat foreign minister Ismail Cem's leadership, has not been able to create enthusiasm among people. The New Turkey Party wanted to attract potential votes from the AK Party but has failed to do so. The chances of the AK Party coming first in the November elections remain high.

However, the AK Party's promise has been shadowed by Erdoğan's possible political ban, which is invariably brought up by current Turkish elite wanting to weaken the AK Party. Erdoğan faces a ban because of his earlier militant and antiregime statements as well as numerous corruption-related lawsuits. It remains to be seen whether the authorities are going to dismiss these charges on the basis that the statutes of limitations have run out. Moreover, the chief prosecutor of the State Security Court has taken the case for banning the AK Party to the Constitutional Court, which has the ultimate authority to make a decision. Some parties are apparently making their plans based on Erdoğan's political ban. There is no political party, with perhaps the exception of CHP, that seems to be able to attract the potential votes of the AK Party. Should the authorities decide to ban Erdoğan from politics, there is a real possibility for the AK Party to gain even further public support.[14]

In fact, every corruption case that Erdoğan wins increases the votes for the AK Party. Many Turks find a closeness to Erdoğan, while other leaders seem to have lost their ties with ordinary people. People in the street believe that Erdoğan speaks for them. His record as mayor of İstanbul has given him a positive professional reputation. Benefiting from Erdoğan's charismatic personality, the AK Party constitutes a genuine threat to the secular political elite in Turkey.

What will happen if the AK Party is closed? The AK Party's closure would not mean that the base of the party will necessarily move toward political Islam, but it might create a vacuum allowing political Islamists to regain at least some of their strength. SP would probably get only a negligible increase in their votes, as many religious people feel that their democratic rights are threatened by Islamist political policies. For instance, before the advent of Islamist parties, issues such as the headscarf did not attract much attention, and conservative women could wear headscarves without implying any political connotation or having to deal with any social or psychological pressure. However, as Islamists started using the headscarf as a political statement, the secularist reaction against it grew and became repressive in some cases. If the AK Party is closed, a new party with similar characteristics is likely to obtain more votes that the AK Party would have received.

POLITICAL ISLAMISTS AND THE KURDISH PROBLEM

The Kurdish problem has been a difficult one for Islamists. Turkey has always had a Kurdish problem, but it reappeared again as a major issue in the 1980s. By the 1990s Islamists could no longer ignore the reality of the Kurdish issue. A complicating factor propelling the Islamists to adopt a position was that the PKK (Kurdistan Labor Party) used Islamic symbols in order to legitimize itself. For example, the title of the book written by PKK leader Abdullah Öcalan, under the name Ali Fırat, was *A Revolutionary Approach to the Religious Problem.*

The priority for Kurdish Islamists was the resolution of the Kurdish issue. According to Islamists in general, the secular Kemalist administration tried to keep Kurds away from Islam but failed. The PKK made progress among Kurds because of the lack of concern among Islamists for the problems of the Kurdish people. In order to attract Kurds to Islamist ideology it was necessary to put the Kurdish issue on the agenda.

It is hard to say that Islamist intellectuals have a well-considered approach to the Kurdish problem. There is in fact a big division between Turkish and Kurdish Islamists. Kurdish Islamists think that Kurdish identity in Turkey and the universal principles of Islam are not in conflict. Islamists of Turkish origin, on the other hand, believe that attaching great importance to Kurdish identity will damage the conscience of ummet. Another focus of the Kurdish discussion has been on the Kurdish right to self-determination. The granting of democratic rights to Kurds under Turkish authority is the basic position for both Turkish and, since the fall of the PKK, for Kurdish Islamists.[15]

There are differences between SP and the AK Party on this issue. SP gives greater importance to the concept of Islamic brotherhood in order to solve the Kurdish problem. This brotherhood exists in all economic, social, and cultural fields. Islamic brotherhood urges Kurds to be wary of provocations and conscious of the need to protect national integrity and unity.

The AK Party program, however, indicates "The problem that some of us call the Southeastern problem, Kurdish problem, or terror problem is unfortunately a reality." This statement shows that the AK Party wants to follow a more moderate policy on this issue. What the Turkish state calls the "terror problem" nationalists prefer to call the "southeastern problem" and Kurds call the "Kurdish problem." In discussing this subject, the AK Party uses a general statement including all these approaches. The AK Party prefers to refer to the issue broadly as one of democratic rights for the Kurds instead of emphasizing Islamic brotherhood like SP did.

Until the limitation of capital punishment in August 2002, among the most important topics of discussion in Turkey among Islamists and other Turks was the execution of the PKK leader Abdullah Öcalan. SP believed MHP's support for capital punishment to be a political tactic.

To avoid losing votes, SP followed a strategy of neither approving nor rejecting capital punishment. The AK Party, on the other hand, supported the abolition of capital punishment in order for Turkey to meet the EU requirements for membership.

The most pressing concern for both the AK Party and SP, however, is the Kurdish political party, the Party of People's Democracy (Halkın Demokrasi Partisi or HADEP). Both parties seem to have no objection to HADEP's political role, and they both oppose the state's oppressive treatment of HADEP. Both AK Party and SP members have had the experience of political parties being closed, and they seek some sort of collaboration with HADEP to counter the subtle military threat that, if they make a "wrong" move, they face a political ban. Given the difficult legal conditions and to avoid the risk of losing any Kurdish votes, both parties refrain from opposition to HADEP.

The above discussion of the AK Party and SP is based on their public images. Their real approaches and intentions, especially with regard to the Turkish state, remain veiled. Islamist or conservative parties are in favor of the integrity of the state and national unity, but they certainly are against state power being used against them, that is to say, Islamist political parties, despite their reservations about the state, will support the latter if a party such as HADEP gains popularity: The ethnic orientation of HADEP does not fit with nationalist or ummet-based politics. For example, Ahmet Taşgetiren, a writer for the *Yeni Şafak* newspaper, read by mainly traditional Islamic sects and affiliated with SP, seriously criticizes the state because of its opposition to the headscarf. However, he supported state intervention against Christian missionaries, who came to the city of Adapazarı after the earthquake in 1999, and when the electoral support for HADEP significantly increased. Nevertheless, he argues that the state should give more freedom to Islamist movements.

Today Turkey is at a point where Islamists as well as conservative politicians have their doubts about the Kurdish issue. On the one hand, they want Kurds to exercise their democratic rights; on the other, they fear that such rights may provide the grounds for a Kurdish state. The Islamists cannot oppose the granting of democratic rights to Kurds since they want to appeal to the Kurdish electorate and make use of such rights themselves. Conservatives and political Islamists remain highly skeptical of politicians who get involved in Kurdish identity politics.

ISRAEL AS THE FOREIGN ENEMY OF ISLAMISM

Israel and Zionism occupy a substantial place in the discourse of political Islam. Instead of explicitly opposing Israel, Islamists prefer to reject Israel's existence through criticizing Zionism and using Israel and Zionism interchangeably. Since Erbakan's first move on the political stage, targeting Zionism directly and bluntly has become an important part of his public rhetoric. Zionism, according to Erbakan, is "a belief aiming to enslave all of humanity." The Welfare Party used such rhetoric in its 1991 election campaign.

Erbakan's approach to Israel is Middle Eastern-oriented. He could be placed within the same political group as many Arab leaders. Like them, he criticizes Israel's invasion and dominance of Palestine and tries to blame his own political failures on Israel's existence. Erbakan has frequently referred to Israeli espionage as responsible for his failures in elections over many years. After each failure Erbakan asserted that, despite his party's success in the elections, they were not rewarded because of "Zionist games."

In *Milli Gazette,* Erbakan's movement's publication, "Israel," "Zionism," and "Jews" are equated. This has a certain political objective. It would be a major political problem for Erbakan to oppose Israel's right to exist. Instead, by using "Israel" and "Zionism" as synonymous, he rejects Israel's existence through the rejection of Zionism. By considering all Jews to be Zionists, Erbakan's movement has developed a close relationship with anti-Semites. However, other Islamists in Turkey have refrained from employing his anti-Semitic language.

According to Islamists, the West consists of Christianity and Judaism, Israel is the garrison of the West in the Islamic world. Within this logic, Westerners have sometimes been the pawns of Jews, and Jews have sometimes been utilized by Christian Westerners, who have persecuted them for the most part throughout history. However, they have all been opposed to Islam. And those who are opposed to Islam have worked to prevent Erbakan's movement from strengthening its appeal and ascending to power. In this way Erbakan's movement in Turkey has put all the blame on Israel for its own failures. His movement claims that it will put an end to Israel's dominance, which gives the movement a raison d'être and a certain audience.

Erbakan's explicitly anti-Semitic stance has not won him ground among the Turkish electorate. It would be misleading to claim even that Erbakan's electoral support has anti-Semitic beliefs. Those who share Erbakan's anti-Semitic views constitute about 5 percent of his declining voter support. However, today Erbakan's close comrades still maintain his anti-Semitic discourse. For instance, Şevket Kazan, who has been in politics alongside Erbakan for many years and minister of justice in the Welfare and True Path Party coalition government, claimed that Zionists were behind the coup of February 28. Thus, Kazan not only gave an anti-Semitic message to his electorate but also claimed that there existed in Turkey a Zionist force dominant enough to manipulate the Turkish army. Meanwhile, Erbakan and his comrades sidestepped political critics by blaming the Zionists for their political failures. For them the secret force coercing Erbakan to withdraw from the government was Israel.

This kind of anti-Semitic language also is used against inter-party rivals. When Abdullah Gül, proclaimed his candidacy against Erbakan's candidate Kutan, during the congress of the Virtue Party, he was portrayed as pro-Israel in the pamphlets of the Virtue Party organizations. They implied that Gül resisted Erbakan under Israeli manipulation. In the same vein, throughout the foundation process of the AK Party the rumor that Erdoğan was manipulated by Israel was spread as gospel in Anatolian provinces. The aim was to reduce Erdoğan's and Gül's influence on the participants at the AK Party convention.

Erbakan's anti-Semitic discourse is evident in SP, which also has linked Turkey's problems to foreign forces such as the United States and Israel. The claim that September 11 was a conspiracy of Israel's intelligence agency, Mossad, was expressed in *Milli Gazette*. Although there are many fewer Islamists who share Erbakan's thoughts today, Israel is still considered to be an illegal state by SP and its supporters. Israeli prime minister Sharon's violent policies toward Palestinians especially played an important role in increasing reaction against Israel in Turkey, as well as in other parts of the world. Nevertheless, the thought of getting rid of Israel completely is not as powerful as it once used to be. Instead, the reality and the necessity of Israel's existence are accepted by most Islamist groups, which find political expression in the AK Party.

The AK Party administrators have adopted a discourse similar to that used by the Turkish foreign policy establishment. Erdoğan has asserted that Israel's right to exist should be recognized and that anti-Semitism is a crime against humanity. This is another prominent indicator that the AK Party is not an Islamist party. In response to the Israeli occupation of Ramallah in April 2002, Erdoğan spoke against the Sharon administration but not against Israel. He identified Nazi crimes against Jews with Sharon's acts against Palestinians. Moreover, Erdoğan has declared himself in favor of strategic agreements with Israel when Turkey's interests necessitate. In short, Erdoğan and the AK Party are using a language closer to the center-right parties in Turkey on the Israel issue, far from the discourse of political Islam.

POLITICAL ISLAM AND ARMY RELATIONS

Today, the relationship between political Islam and the military is per-haps tenser than ever. The military is hostile both to SP and the AK Party, while both parties try to avoid confrontation with Turkey's armed forces. The military's attitude is bound to continue until the regime is secured. SP sometimes directly confronts the army, for instance when it criticizes state efforts to prohibit students wearing headscarves from entering universities. The AK Party has proposed that issues such as that of the headscarf should be resolved under a "social consensus."

The February 28 process ended (in the sense that the military now refrains from intervention in civil politics but not in terms of the principle of fighting antisecularism) without any dialogue between political Islam and the military. It demonstrated that for political Islam to survive, it had to pursue a more moderate policy. In an attempt to overcome the handicap of military pressure, Islamists or political Islam–oriented parties have supported Turkey's effort to fulfill the Copenhagen criteria for accession to the European Union. The military sees this support as an opposition to itself since the further democra-tization that EU membership would bring means a reduced political role for the military. The AK Party administrators have claimed that they are acting merely in defense of democracy.

In April 2002, a speech Erdoğan gave ten years ago, criticizing the authorities for not being sufficiently sensitive to the security of Turkish soldiers fighting terrorism in southeastern Turkey, was shown on tele-vision. The military considered this criticism as directed toward itself. At a reception held at the president's residence, Chief of Staff Hüseyin Kıvrıkoğlu publicly and harshly criticized Erdoğan. Erdoğan later deliv-ered a speech responding to Kıvrıkoğlu. This constituted the AK Party's first direct confrontation with the military since its establishment. The open tension has since diminished but it is bound to recur, given the problems surrounding Erdoğan's candidacy. The AK Party will probably abstain from any overt conflict with the military. Erdoğan's rivals in the AK Party, on the other hand, have tried to use Erdoğan's travails to earn support in the party, claiming that the military would not allow Erdoğan to hold the offices of parliamentary deputy and prime minister, if the party wins the election. Currently, the power relations within the party are still far from defined.

Should the AK Party emerge from the elections as the number one party, a military reaction is a major uncertainty. The military does not consider the AK Party as a legal party like other right-wing parties. However, the AK Party has avoided making the same mistakes that Erbakan made. In polls, the majority of people think that the AK Party is a center-right party. If the AK Party is the first runner-up in the coming elections, the formation of a government is not likely to be granted to the party immediately. A coalition government could be formed by the other parties that pass the electoral threshold. If this option does not work and the AK Party forms the government, the tension in the Turkish political system could well intensify. Some expect that the military in such a case will not interfere in the system immediately, unlike on February 28. Instead, they will observe events closely, fearing that direct interference will further weaken the already weak political system. The most important factor determining what happens is how the AK Party acts after the elections, either in government or in opposition.

Since the directors of the AK Party went through February 28 with Erbakan and experienced the reaction of the secular system first-hand, it is highly unlikely that they will make Erbakan's same mistakes in office. The AK Party leaders can be expected to form a low-profile government that will not stray from the boundaries of the state's traditional foreign policy. For instance, they will not object more than the existing government to a possible U.S. attack on Iraq.

Even so, the military does not see the AK Party's and Tayyip Erdoğan's cases as legal ones. If the AK Party directors continue with their policy of reconciliation of differences when in government, the military restraint would likely last longer. It will not hesitate, however, to interfere on this score if it believes it necessary. Even if everything goes right for the AK Party, it will take some time before the military considers it to be legitimate.

THE SP AND THE AK PARTY AND SEPTEMBER 11

The political and ideological decline of political Islam in Turkey since February 28, 1997, has been further intensified since September 11, 2001, which had a shocking impact on those targeted and threatened by Islamists. Islamists were subsequently confined to a much narrower political sphere.

Radical Islamists see September 11 as a Western conspiracy against Muslims. Nevertheless, they have reacted against these attacks strongly and have avoided openly countering the West. However, the National Vision sect of SP expressed a strong reaction against the U.S. military operation in Afghanistan and accused the United States and Israel of designing September 11 as a conspiracy against the Islamic world. They have urged Islamists around the world to refrain from forcefully opposing the United States, Israel, and their allies for fear of being targeted in the war against terrorism.

Nonetheless, religious groupings have started reviewing their positions post–September 11. Criticism directed toward Taliban-like regimes has greatly increased. The supporters of the AK Party have developed a new approach on the issue of the Islam–terror relationship by identifying Muslim terrorists and arguing that Islam would never approve of terror. The followers of National Vision, on the other hand, have never publicly accepted Muslim groups such as Hamas and their acts to be terrorism. Depending on what happens on the Palestinian Israeli issue, the new AK Party approach may gain more supporters from this stance.

After September 11, Erdoğan sent a message to the American embassy in Ankara emphasizing the need to establish common grounds to fight against terrorism. He did not support the operation in Afghanistan. The U.S. handling of the Palestine question also has led to a significant increase in criticism of the United States by AK Party members. Erdoğan has often asserted that the Palestine issue should be resolved before the United States initiates any operation against Iraq. Another aspect of the debate among Islamists worthy of noting is Erdoğan's statement that dictatorial regimes in the Islamic world should be replaced with democratic ones. This statement most clearly emphasizes Erdoğan's distance from political Islam. Erbakan, on the contrary, has never criticized these dictatorships but has always criticized the West in his pursuit of a pan-Islamist policy. By criticizing Islamist dictatorships, Erdoğan has taken steps to try to prove that he is moving away from political Islam and that he understands the new world order after September 11. Although Erdoğan will not give active support to a U.S. operation on Iraq, he will not likely contradict the general policies of the Turkish state either. SP, on the other hand, will try to prevent Turkey from taking an active role in a U.S. attack on Iraq.

SP sympathizers believe that, in order to generate an international conspiracy against Muslims, United States and Israel planned September 11 or condoned its happening. They also believe that the Central Intelligence Agency (CIA) and Israel's Mossad worked together to frame the Islamic world. SP voters do not believe Osama bin Laden or the Taliban were behind September 11. This feeling is so strong that in a youth event attended by Recai Kutan, the chairman of SP, the audience applauded and cheered for Osama bin Laden when his image appeared on the screen. According to SP affiliates, the United States perpetrated September 11 so that it could occupy the oil and energy regions of the Muslims. The war in Afghanistan, for them, is the first step in this grand U.S. operation to take over Muslim energy supplies.

THE EUROPEAN UNION

It is important to discuss the relationship between Islamist parties and the EU. Today, both Islamist SP and the conservative AK Party support Turkey's EU accession policy. However, their support is different in nature. SP has a history that is entirely anti-EU. SP members believe that Erbakan is their "natural leader," and they will all try to do their best to bring Erbakan back to politics. This has serious implications for SP's EU policies since Erbakan has always defined the EU as a "Christian Club." The current SP leadership supports Turkey's accession to the EU for practical reasons; they believe that if Turkey enters the EU the military pressure on Islamism would be reduced. Therefore, Turkey's entry to EU, in a way, would facilitate SP's fundamental legitimization.

The AK Party is more active regarding Turkey's EU accession. Erdoğan has admitted that he was wrong in opposing the EU in the past. He said on television on July 24, 2002, that until he became mayor of İstanbul in 1994 he was anti-EU, but after his exposure to European countries during the time he served as mayor he changed his mind and started supporting the EU. Members of the AK Party in general think, as do most other political parties, that EU membership will lessen Turkey's internal political problems. Moreover, the AK Party claims that EU membership is a "civilization project" for Turkey. Getting most of their votes from moderate conservatives and liberals, the party is in the act of developing policies consistent with what is believed to be its voters' interests.

There is also a belief that if Turkey enters the EU, Islamists can make use of the freedoms accompanying membership and in time take over the system. However, even though political Islamists in Turkey would gain further democratic rights and thus a louder political voice upon EU accession, the economic prosperity and social security that EU membership would bring to Turkey would ultimately diminish their most crucial base in recruiting supporters: poverty. In other words, pro-EU policies will in fact lead to the end of political Islam. If Turkey becomes an EU member, political Islam would have no chance of survival and political Islamist anti-statist claims based on human rights violations, economic corruption, and political crises would hardly hold. On the other hand, if Turkey does not become an EU member and the economic crises persist in the country, political Islam has a potential for growth.

CONCLUSION: POLITICAL ISLAM, POVERTY, AND THE FUTURE OF THE AK PARTY

Islamists make up approximately 7 percent of the electorate in Turkey. However, the size of the Sunni-conservative electorate varies between 45 and 55 percent. In Turkey, those who want to change the regime are not able to recruit large numbers of supporters. Political Islam as such has not appealed to the masses.

Increasing poverty (approximately 45 percent of the population is now below the poverty line) and inequalities of income together with unemployment during crisis periods vastly augment the number of dissatisfied voters. People cannot find politicians to satisfy their human and Islamic needs. This has been a direct result of the state's failure in providing a model of governance capable of reconciling the clashes between Islam and politics. Center-right parties, who should meet these requirements, have been steadily melting away. Moreover, the identity of the center is changing. While the liberal share within the center in Turkey has been reduced approximately to 7 percent, center-right and center-left parties have better maintained their traditionally strong positions. Political Islam, while no longer having the possibility of reaching large groups of people ideologically, attracts more votes now because of the economic crisis in the country.

Today, political Islam in Turkey is really represented only by SP. This party continues its political life by using the discourse of democracy in pursuit of its political Islamist ideology. The AK Party argues that those who are oriented toward political Islam must adopt center-right politics. It aims to reach the center-right electorate.

As SP has a much smaller share of votes, the Turkish state no longer takes this party seriously. On the other hand, a high degree of tension prevails between the state and the AK Party. Should the AK Party be closed down by the military, political Islamists will certainly gain a trump card against the state and will try once again to seek political power. However, conservative and pious Muslims will not support political Islam in a conflict with the state. SP will survive mainly because of the economic crisis. Should Turkey experience a crisis like that in Argentina, political Islam will gain strength.

Should the AK Party come to power, it will not upset the "governance techniques" and the "foreign policy equation" normally implemented by the Turkish governments. It will avoid the changes Erbakan tried to impose when he came to power. AK Party members recognize that such an attempt would lead to another crisis. If the AK Party seeks different government approaches and creates a new discourse in foreign policy, the party is bound to encounter the same fate as the Welfare Party.

In short, the AK Party seems to be striving to become something like the center right party of pre-1980 Turkey. It will not bring piety in as a critical "alternative to Kemalism," which was prevalent in post-1980 Islamism. The party has little more reason to dispute the state than for more democratic rights for the pious such as the abolition of the ban on the headscarf. How successful the AK Party will be in its quest to become another Democrat Party of the 1950s or the Justice Party of the 1960s is yet unclear. How much the Turkish secular establishment believes in the genuineness of AK Party policies also remains to be seen.

CHAPTER FOUR

TURKEY AND THE KURDS
APPROACHING A MODUS VIVENDI?

PHILIP ROBINS

Even in a messy world, the challenge of what to do with the Kurds stands out. The Kurds are routinely identified as the largest aspirant nation not to enjoy statehood. They are often singled out as suffering from extensive and persistent human rights abuses at the hands of the states where they live. They have been at the forefront of the new transnationalism, whether suffering as refugees and from internal displacement or as asylum-seekers and economic migrants headed for the European continent. In turn, the presence and challenges perceived to emanate from Kurdish communities have had an illiberalizing effect on their host states, which have frequently acted in harsher and more authoritarian ways than might otherwise be the case. If Iran, Iraq, and Turkey can generally be identified as troubled states, the problem of how and indeed whether to incorporate their Kurdish populations has done much to contribute to this status.

At the forefront of this difficult and often negative experience has been the Turkish republic.[1] Some thirty thousand people died in a struggle over the Kurdish issue between 1984 and 1999 in Turkey, a period that was also punctuated by missed political opportunities.[2] At

Note: Research on which this paper is based was made possible by a generous grant from the Leverhulme Foundation.

its lowest point, the Turkish state has even tried to deny the existence of a Kurdish population and to ban its languages from the public space. The traditional Kurdish areas of the East and Southeast have invariably been the least developed and most impoverished in Turkey. In a state where center–periphery relations have been so important to understanding political dynamics,[3] the Kurdish areas have often seemed to be the periphery of the periphery.

The era of the harsh, bloody clash between the Turkish state and the forces of Kurdish ethno-nationalism is over, and the issue of Turkey and the Kurdish question is worth revisiting in the wake of 1999. The capture of Kurdistan Workers' Party (PKK) leader Abdullah Öcalan in February 1999, the declaration of the PKK ceasefire in August 1999,[4] and the European Union (EU) summit at Helsinki in December 1999—which gave Turkey candidate status and hence marked the beginning of a heightened political scrutiny—are all developments that have impacted upon the Kurdish issue. Turkey's February 2001 financial crisis, September 11, and the subsequent "war against terror" are other major developments that have not and will not leave the issue unaffected. Parliament's adoption of a package of liberal measures, including the legalization of Kurdish broadcasting and education, on August 3, 2002, has gone some way toward addressing the mainstream Kurdish agenda.

This chapter will first and foremost address the question of how much has changed on the Kurdish issue between 1999 and 2002. It revisits the issue of how much closer Turkey is to meeting the challenge of integrating its Kurdish population. It also discusses the strategies pursued by important Kurdish groupings, notably the People's Democracy Party (HADEP) and the PKK. Finally, and perhaps most importantly, it looks at the Kurdish issue in the context of Turkey's wider relations with the EU. But first, we must remind ourselves exactly who the Kurds are and why they are important in Turkey.

THE KURDISH PROBLEM

Simply put, the Kurdish problem in Turkey is the inability of the Turkish state to be sufficiently broadly based or flexible to incorporate all of those Kurds who define themselves ethno-nationally as such. This does not mean to say that the Turkish state has been a general failure; considerable successes in the state- and nation-building project from the unpromising beginnings of the 1920s is not the stuff of abject failure. Neither does it mean that the Turkish state has not succeeded in incorporating some of the country's Kurds; the routine presence of more than one hundred MPs of Kurdish origin in the Turkish parliament would suggest otherwise.[5] Neither, yet again, does it mean that the Kurdish problem in Turkey has been immutable and unchanging; both Kurdish identity and nationalist political ambitions have evolved, sometimes quite rapidly, over the seven decades of the modern Turkish state. What, however, is beyond doubt is that the Kurdish problem in its many manifestations has damaged Turkey at various times between the 1920s and the present. Moreover, there is no good reason for thinking that it will not continue to do so for the foreseeable future, short of a historic compromise based on a more inclusive approach.

The Kurdish problem has two components to it, a Kurdish one and a Turkish one. The Kurdish one is an agglomeration of identity, grievance, and geopolitics. Regardless of the limited assimilationist successes of the Turkish state, there has always been a significant section of the population that has continued to define itself in self-consciously Kurdish terms. The precise size of this element of the population is unknowable. A best guess might put it at around 8 to 10 percent of the population of Turkey, or equivalent to about 5.6 million to 7 million people.[6]

The notion of grievance has been central to the Kurdish experience since the creation of the modern state system in the Middle East, if not before. The best evidence for the presence of grievance is the number of rebellions that have taken place in the Kurdish areas of Turkey, Iraq, and Iran since the early 1920s. At different times that sense of grievance has changed. In Turkey it has taken the form of the resistance of the predominantly tribal political periphery to the centralizing tendencies of the modern state. It also has taken the form of religious self-assertion in the face of the secular reformism of the ideological center. More recently, it has taken the form of a minority's demand for political and cultural self-expression.

The geopolitics of the Kurdish problem springs from the traditional location of the Kurdish people and the periodic support they have received from neighboring states that have had their own disputes with Turkey. In this way, it has been much the same as the geopolitics of the Kurdish problem in Iraq, only with a different cast of country characters involved. While cross-border support for Kurdish opposition activity has often been important, especially in terms of the sustainability of guerrilla insurgency, it has not been its only or even its most important cause. In short, though Turkey's Kurdish problem may have been exacerbated by problematic neighbors, it has not been manufactured by them.

Over the past two decades or so, the Kurdish problem has acquired a new geopolitical dimension. Rather than being limited to the overlapping geopolitics of neighbors, this issue has been a more contemporary phenomenon: a transnational geopolitics of diasporas, with significant Kurdish populations moving along an authoritarian–liberal spatial continuum from and through southeast Turkey to Western Europe. This pathway was forged in the early 1980s as a military government in Ankara drove many political activists, many of whom were Kurds, to find sanctuary abroad as asylum-seekers. Rather than tailing off with the installation of a civilian government in Turkey, as was the case with many leftists, the numbers held up and even increased as the Turkish state often used brutal and authoritarian tactics in its fight against the emerging Kurdish insurgency in the southeast of the country. As the numbers of Kurdish political émigrés in the EU has risen steadily, so the Kurdish problem has ceased to be a predominantly domestic one for Turkey. It is now a shared domestic problem for the EU member states and Turkey, a reality that gives an additional edge to its presence in relations between them.

The Turkish aspect of the Kurdish problem starts from the state itself, its ideology, and its modus operandi. In the 1920s, Atatürk forged a new ideology for the Turkish state, which has become known as Kemalism, based on the twin components of secularism and Turkish nationalism. At the time, the latter was a relatively enlightened notion, based not on blood and race but on self-definition. All one had to do was to subordinate one's parochial identities to an overarching notion of subjective Turkish nationalism. From that point of view it was a relatively inclusive code. And in general it succeeded, incorporating many of the disparate peoples of Anatolia,[7] a significant number of whom, as disoriented and impoverished refugees, were recent arrivals. Where it was less successful was in dealing with that minority of people who, over the years, have insisted on retaining the primacy of alternative national identities, most notably as ethno-nationalist Kurds. The Kemalist response to such an expression has invariably been a hostile one: to conceive of it as essentially competitive, to vilify it, and to seek to suppress it.

It was this tendency to define Kurdish nationalism in an adversarial way and to seek authoritarian solutions to it that helped to transform the PKK. In the short period between 1984 and 1989, the PKK grew from a small leftist splinter group, beginning to use violence against the symbols of the Turkish state, into a sizable guerrilla army capable of pinning down more than 160,000 members of the Turkish armed forces and generating considerable sympathy across the traditional Kurdish areas. While there is no doubt that the PKK began the insurgency in 1984 and used great brutality against civilians as well as military targets, the Turkish state had itself spasmodically resorted to violence in the Kurdish areas of the country as well; its mobilization of state violence in the early days of the insurgency, affecting civilians as well as guerrillas, helps to explain the rapid growth of the PKK.

WATERSHED 1999? THE DOMESTIC ARENA

ÖCALAN AND THE PKK

Prior to 1999, the relationship between Turkey and its ethno-nationalist Kurds was characterized by confrontation and conflict. This adversarial relationship was epitomized by the often bloody struggle between the state and the PKK for physical and normative control of the southeast of the country. Though the two sides were unrelenting in their confrontation, both developed a converging interest in ensuring that a vigorous and independent political middle ground did not emerge whereby moderate ethno-nationalist Kurds would engage interlocutors from among majority opinion. A combination of threats, intimidation, violence, and a hardening unwillingness to compromise on both sides helped to fuel the bloodshed.

The situation on the ground began to change in the mid-1990s with the containment of the PKK-led insurgency by the Turkish military. This resulted from four sets of changes on the Turkish side, three at the domestic level. First, organizational changes meant that the forces that were deployed in the southeast became better trained and more highly motivated. Second, the military procurement of the

Turkish state meant that its forces became more mobile and packed greater firepower. Third, the Turkish state adopted a more uncompromising posture in its use of hard power, with the period between 1991 and 1994 witnessing the highpoint of human rights abuses in the Kurdish areas. Finally, the fourth factor that was pivotal in containing the PKK was Turkey's evolving policy toward the Kurdish territories in northeastern Iraq. Ankara created a de facto security zone in northern Iraq that, together with its deployment of increased firepower across the border, meant that PKK activities were significantly disrupted before they could infiltrate the common border.

With the PKK on the defensive, a second major breakthrough occurred with the expulsion of the PKK leader, Abdullah Öcalan, from Syria in October 1998 under pressure from the Turkish military. The flight of Öcalan robbed the organization of a settled base and relative ease of communications. Four months of uncertainty and fluctuating fortunes were followed by Öcalan's seizure in February 1999 and his trial, conviction, and imprisonment. For the PKK this was a crushingly demoralizing event, the momentary anger at his arrest soon giving way to a profound sense of directionlessness. By contrast, majority opinion in Turkey was ecstatic at the outcome, and the state nationalist Democratic Left Party (DSP) and the ultranationalist National Action Party (MHP) were returned as the leading parties in an election held shortly after Öcalan's repatriation. For many in Turkey the containment of the PKK and the arrest of Öcalan signaled the end of the Kurdish problem.

With its centralized organization and authoritarian tendencies, the loss of Öcalan literally decapitated the PKK. A leadership council was established to assume responsibilities as the new formal head of the organization.[8] Its activities have been hindered by the dispersal of its members, ever fearful of imminent Turkish military attack. It has in any case proved to be reluctant to take a bold lead, let alone to contradict Öcalan's views.

To maintain the cohesion of the organization and rejuvenate its mission, the PKK refocused its energies on a new strategic objective: the survival of its erstwhile leader. The policies of the organization have become predominantly a function of what has been deemed necessary to keep Öcalan alive. For the first ten months after his capture, Öcalan, possibly in the mistaken belief that he was involved in a "virtual peace process," earnestly encouraged such a trend. In August 1999 he announced an indefinite ceasefire, one that has more or less held and that remains in place today. PKK fighters were redeployed outside Turkish territory. The so-called Kurdish parliament-in-exile, which had been a diplomatic irritant for Ankara, was dissolved. In October of that year, two groups of PKK activists returned to Turkey and allowed themselves to be arrested to signify that the war was at an end.[9] In December 1999, PKK-affiliated organizations campaigned in favor of the EU granting candidate status for Turkey. Whatever he thought he might receive as a political quid pro quo from the Turkish state in return for such gestures and concessions, however, Öcalan was to be disappointed.

In spite of these early and not unimportant political gestures, the PKK has struggled to keep up with a political game over which it has shown little ability to exert influence. The time to have seized the initiative was after Öcalan's departure from Damascus and his flight to Rome, where he stayed for some three months between October 1998 and January 1999. Öcalan stated that with the relocation of the center of gravity of his movement from Syria to Italy, it was time to adopt a modus operandi more in keeping with European than Middle Eastern political culture. The opportunity was certainly there, as busy European governments, hitherto largely uninterested in and ignorant of the Kurdish issue, momentarily focused on the subject. But, either lacking vision or sincerity or both, Öcalan was not as good as his word. He failed to seize the chance to impress his new audience with bold and sweeping gestures, let alone reinventing his movement according to European normative standards. With European governments looking at Öcalan and the PKK and quickly deciding that they really did not like what they saw, a key moment for the Kurdish national movement was lost.

As his fortunes and those of his movement declined after he left Rome, so Öcalan at last began to display a greater willingness to embrace reform. But this has been done grudgingly and incrementally, and not in a way that has kindled interest in Europe, let alone in Turkey. Take, for example, the PKK's extraordinary Seventh Party Congress of January 2 to 23, 2000, which was billed as "a congress of a new beginning and a new establishment."[10] The congress formally announced the end of the organization's fifteen-year guerrilla campaign and adopted the "democratic political struggle" as the way forward. These statements enabled political commentators within the Kurdish movement to conclude that "the complete strategy change" confirmed by the congress was now irreversible. Yet the significance of such a move was almost completely lost on a wider audience. Hence the congress, if it is remembered at all, is best recalled for the decision to change the names of the PKK's political and military organizations, the Kurdistan National Liberation Front (ERNK) and the Kurdistan Popular Liberation Army (ARGK) respectively, with the removal of the word "Kurdistan" (though not from its parent body) as its most notable feature.

Its successor, the eighth congress,[11] held even greater potential in terms of the rebranding of the PKK because it was decided that the formal name of the organization would be changed on this occasion. The choice of the new name, the Kurdistan Freedom and Democracy Congress (KADEK), was deemed to be particularly significant, especially due to the incorporation of the word *democracy,* which has been used to bolster the organization's formal commitment to peace. Again, however, a major opportunity was lost at the time of the congress, with the changes barely registering with outsiders. For many of those who followed the congress, the name change was easily dismissed as cosmetic.[12] Those who insisted that KADEK should not automatically be deemed as a successor to the PKK and hence a terror organization, notably Iran, were suspected of other motives. The marginal impact of the eighth congress can be gauged by the fact that just five weeks after it was convened the EU added the PKK to its list of terror organizations. An opportunity to draw a line symbolically under the past by winding up a discredited organization and so begin the movement anew had been lost. It is noteworthy that the acronym "PKK" tends still to be used in conversation when discussing the organization, even among those close to it.

The reason for the skepticism of outsiders toward the PKK is not difficult to grasp. The rhetorical nature of the movement, for all its talk of democracy, freedom, and peace, remains stubbornly lodged in the lexicon of the radical left. This also can be seen in the continued beatification of Öcalan as the leader of the movement whose relationship with his followers appears to be analogous with that of an *agha,* or traditional feudal headman. When a Westerner looks at Öcalan he is reminded of a shrinking number of contemporary pariah leaders, of whom Saddam Hussein is perhaps the personification. The best example of the centrality of this Orwellian juxtaposition of hero worship and leftist radicalism is the official resolution of the eighth congress, which ends with political slogans of a distinctly 1970s vintage: "For a democratic Middle East and a free Kurdistan! No to all kinds of internal

and external reaction! Long live our freedom and the democratic struggle under the clear-sighted guidance of President APO! Long live the
vanguard of our people KADEK! Biji Serok Apo (Long live our
President APO)."[13]

Since January 2000, Öcalan has been kept semi-incommunicado in
jail on the instructions of the Turkish government.[14] Though he still
communicates his views and even issues instructions via the fortnightly
visits by his lawyers, this has greatly affected his ability to give leadership to his organization.[15] Still, Öcalan remains the symbolic leader of
the movement, and his portrait is ubiquitous at rallies and demonstrations in Europe by the PKK and its affiliates. Among many of the
Kurdish communities within southeast Turkey he continues to be ven-
erated as the man who put the Kurdish issue on the political map.[16] His
many political mistakes and miscalculations, together with the often
brutal and dictatorial nature of his leadership, are forgotten or ignored.
In Turkey, then, he has become "Mr. Kurdistan" in the same way that
Yasser Arafat, whatever one might think of him, is "Mr. Palestine."
Though the persistence of this personal devotion to Öcalan is understandable in the context of the relative lack of institutionalized Kurdish
politics, one questions if it is helpful, either in engaging majority
Turkish nationalist opinion in dialogue or in moving on from the radical politics of the 1980s and 1990s.

Shortcomings in leadership and organizational reform have drawn
attention away from what has been over the past few years a radical
paring down of the political goals of the PKK. The publicly avowed
goals of the organization and its supporters are now essentially five-
fold, half of which (that is, numbers 2, 3, and partly 4 below) were
formally met by the August 2002 liberalization package passed by the
Turkish parliament:[17]

1.   the right of free political expression, free from persecution or the
     risk of arrest;

2.   the right to educate and broadcast in Kurdish;

3.   the abolition of the death penalty;

4.   wholesale changes to the Turkish legal canon and the constitution
     to reflect such reforms; and

5.   a general amnesty for Öcalan and all Kurdish activists, including
     former guerrillas.

Gone are the demands for full independence. Gone too are the demands for collective political rights and a new political order of power-sharing with the center. In a matter of six years or so the leading force of Kurdish ethno-nationalism in Turkey has lowered its sights from full independence to a modest platform of cultural, human, and political rights. These articulated changes have been repeatedly dismissed as dissembling by the Turkish government.[18] Others wonder how sincere such a lowering of political aims actually is, and they are clearly not shared by all leading Kurdish nationalist activists.[19] As with the Iraqi Kurds, the suspicion persists that such political goals are elastic, stretching and contracting depending on the changing nature of the overall context. Nevertheless, such a diminution of objectives does provide new opportunities for the Turkish state to interact with the Kurdish national movement on a political terrain much more to its liking than before, even though the possibility of Ankara viewing the PKK or Öcalan as an interlocutor in the near future must be considered very low.

HADEP

The sidelining of the PKK as a broader political force has, however, been helpful in allowing the emergence of HADEP as a political party capable of articulating the needs and aspirations of Kurdish nationalist opinion inside Turkey.[20] HADEP is the fourth contemporary incarnation of a predominantly Kurdish nationalist party. Its recent forerunners—HEP, ÖZDEP, and DEP—were successively closed down in the mid-1990s. The future of HADEP is far from certain,[21] and it could still go the way of its predecessor parties. Even in its current form it faces periods of intense political pressure.[22] That it has survived longer than HEP and DEP is the result of a less charged political context and greater external pressures on Ankara for a more liberal political regime.

Early signs that mainstream Turkish opinion might regard HADEP as a more acceptable face of Kurdish nationalism have waned since 1999. The party began this crucial period well, gaining a renewed electoral mandate in the local elections of spring 1999. For example, HADEP polled 62.57 percent of the vote during the election campaign in Diyarbakır. Its more high-profile leadership—such as Feridun Çelik, the mayor of Diyarbakır—has tried hard to engage moderate, mainstream opinion in western Turkey. The highpoint of this engagement came on August 7, 1999, when a group of HADEP mayors were welcomed at the presidential palace at Çankaya by the head of state, Süleyman Demirel.[23]

There appeared to be the first stirrings within mainstream Turkish society in favor of an equitable settlement to the Kurdish issue. A handful of politicians, including ones as senior as then foreign minister İsmail Cem,[24] let off trial balloons that were accommodationist in essence. Influential figures associated with the political establishment, notably a retired under secretary of the Ministry of Foreign Affairs, Şükrü Elekdağ, focused on the issue, and visits were undertaken to the southeast. Cultural luminaries like Orhan Pamuk, Zülfü Livaneli, and Yaşar Kemal joined other prominent artists in signing an international declaration aimed at reconciliation.[25]

Hopes that such activity would create real momentum for action proved to be unfounded. The meeting between the HADEP mayors and the president is now seen as an aberration rather than the beginning of a high-level dialogue between the two sides. A year or so later the atmosphere had changed. Even senior locally elected representatives from HADEP were not immune to physical abuse at the hands of the authorities.[26] The apparent abduction of two senior HADEP members in the Silopi district of Şırnak province on January 25, 2001,[27] raised concerns anew that the "deep state" is alive and continues to be willing to use extrajudicial killings as a way to intimidate mainstream Kurdish opinion.[28] In the continuing absence of any news on the fate of the two officials, this issue conditioned the uneasy atmosphere between the two sides over the next eighteen months.

HADEP's is a twilight experience. It is perpetually threatened with closure; repression and violence are never far away, while its municipalities are routinely starved of funds by the political center. In the absence of any change to the national electoral barrage of 10 percent, HADEP cannot hope to win formal representation on its own. Forging an electoral alliance other than with small, marginal parties proved unfeasible in the November 2002 general election. Consequently, in spite of polling some 6.2 percent of the national vote with its allies, Kurdish nationalism will not be represented in the new parliament. In spite of these travails, however, HADEP remains both popular in its core areas and vigorous. At present, mere existence is an achievement.

POLICY REFORM

The Turkish state and government alike have not been quick to take advantage of the new realities presented by the year 1999 to address the Kurdish issue. One reason for relative inaction on the part of Ankara has simply been that the ending of the insurgency has reduced the pressing nature of the issue. The move to legalize broadcasting and education in Kurdish, passed as part of a package of measures in August 2002, only took place as a result of an external agenda: to meet the political conditions for accession talks with the EU. As a strictly domestic political issue, the subject of Kurdish inclusion has been allowed to slide down the list of priorities.

A second reason for the absence of movement on the issue is the political consequences of the capture of Öcalan in February 1999. The outcome of the general election that followed in April was a three-party coalition government that included the Turkish ultranationalist MHP as the second party in parliament, led by Devlet Bahçeli.[29] Though Bahçeli's participation in the coalition was generally low-key, the MHP has been perennially suspicious of any reforms that might be perceived as encouraging of Kurdish ethno-nationalism. An example of the Bahçeli stance was his agreement to endorse an end to capital punishment in Turkey, with the exception of cases of war, the immediate threat of war, or terrorism. While such a compromise position kept Öcalan on death row, Bahçeli did not, however, push for his swift execution.

Though the MHP view on Öcalan, the PKK, and the Kurds is ultimately driven by ideology, this alone does not explain the basic policy inflexibility. The MHP knows well the popularity among mainstream Turkish public opinion of a tough line toward Öcalan and Kurdish nationalism.[30] The populist opportunism in 1999 of the leader of the True Path Party (DYP), Tansu Çiller, in demanding that the death sentence be carried out on Öcalan is testimony to that. There is also a significant anti-Öcalan/PKK lobby within Turkish civil society, notably through such organizations as the "families of the martyrs," a well-organized and high-profile movement that carries a moral authority that politicians ignore at their peril.

The third reason for caution has been the Turkish state's view of the residual PKK insurgency threat from across the border. In spite of the absence of widespread political violence, northern Iraq is still perceived to be a platform from which the PKK could resume military activities at some point in the future. There are an estimated six thousand armed militants located in military camps spread out adjacent to the Turkish border. The continued presence of these camps suggests that the armed struggle remains an alternative, albeit dormant, option for the PKK.

Clearly, though, the most unsettling issue for the Turkish state as far as a possible future threat from the Kurds is the general uncertainty over the future of Iraq. The U.S. administration has made it repeatedly clear that it would welcome regime change in Baghdad. Furthermore, the U.S. government has been considering a number of practical ways of effecting such an outcome, including the sponsorship of local opposition groups, with Iraqi Kurdish organizations presenting the most credible and direct chance for military intervention. An upsurge in armed conflict, especially involving the world's remaining superpower, would bring new uncertainties to Iraq. These are viewed with concern in Ankara because of the renewed opportunity for state-building that they might bring to the Iraqi Kurds, especially if endorsed by a United States indebted for their contribution to the ousting of the Iraqi president. State-building efforts in Iraqi Kurdistan could act as a model and an incentive for Turkey's Kurds and could well rekindle yearnings for group political rights of a centrifugal nature. Alternative scenarios for the future of Iraq foresee a period of prolonged internal conflict and even collapse, the sort of development that could provide renewed opportunities for rejuvenated PKK guerrillas. For the Turks the fear is that, having won the war against the PKK, the wider cause of Kurdish nationalism might pluck victory from the jaws of defeat through renewed conflict in Iraq.

Against such an incongruous backdrop of distraction and wary caution, Ankara has indeed not made any substantive concessions in the direction of group political rights for the Kurds. But Ankara also has failed to act in other areas where previously it had indicated movement could take place. Notably, it has failed to deliver on a package of measures to bring about the economic regeneration of the traditional Kurdish areas, a move that it had suggested it would be happy to see once the insurgency had subsided. Of course, it was an unfortunate coincidence that the end of the security threats in the southeast occurred more or less at the same time as two devastating earthquakes in western Turkey and the onset of a broad economic crisis. Even so, there was little evidence that the government was really serious in pressing ahead with economic development, even before the emergence of the crisis.

However, the area of policy where debate has focused has been over the presence of the Kurdish identity in the public space, with most intense debate on that cluster of issues related to the use of the Kurdish languages. Prior to August 2002, the prospects for the legalization of the use of Kurdish in broadcasting and education had appeared to be slim. This issue certainly dominated the Kurdish agenda during 2000 and 2001, in the midst of a lively campaign among Kurdish nationalists in favor. After a period of apparent indecision in state circles, the line was a largely uncompromising one. The language campaign was vilified as being organized by the PKK. It was conceived of as a thin end of a more substantive wedge. This view sees the consequences of such incremental change as the binary separation of Turks and Kurds throughout society, affecting everything from businessmen's groups to professional associations. Ultimately, such an ethnocultural internal division would lead to political division.

Key state institutions added their weight to the uncompromising nature of this response. The interior ministry issued instructions to the police and gendarmerie to counteract such a campaign.[31] The Higher Education Board (YÖK) instructed university rectors to suspend and even expel students participating in the language campaign.[32] Hundreds of students were reported as having been detained across the country as a result of their involvement in the campaign.[33] Any further prospects of open debate on the matter were ended at the January 2002 meeting of the National Security Council (NSC), the ultimate de facto authority in Turkey. The NSC statement referred to "damaging activities," including "separatist activities directed by the terrorist organization on the subject of education in a language other than the official language."[34]

Against this backdrop, it was a surprise when the Turkish parliament suddenly legalized the use of Kurdish in broadcasting and education as part of a package of liberal measures adopted on August 3, 2002. The inauspicious domestic prospects for reform simply drew attention to the fact that the main impetus for the measures had come from outside and were unrelated to their substance. Though such measures are certainly welcome, the manner in which they were adopted has given rise to a cautious outlook about whether they, like many other liberal measures adopted in the past, will actually be implemented. The fact that parliament passed the package having already voted for early elections has further raised concerns about the extent to which a democratic mandate actually existed for such reforms, especially given the swift and unexpected adoption of the measures.[35]

In the absence of any movement on the issue of education in Kurdish prior to August 2002, the best that had been seen in Turkey by way of symbolic gestures toward the country's Kurdish population had been in relation to actual conditions on the ground, though even here experiences have been mixed. This has covered a cluster of measures, including the shrinking of the area in the southeast still subject to emergency laws and the promise of the rescinding of the emergency-rule area in November 2002.[36] Though positive, the tortuous pace of such change also has highlighted the fact that highly restrictive measures remain in place nearly three years after the declaration of the PKK's ceasefire. Turkish authorities do not seem to have adopted a uniformly softer approach to the policing of mass demonstrations since the virtual disappearance of political violence in the southeast of the country; for example, at least two members of HADEP were killed during marches to commemorate World Peace Day on September 1, 2001,[37] and two more during Nevruz/Newroz celebrations in March 2002.[38]

WATERSHED 2001? THE EXTERNAL ARENA

EU POLITICAL CONDITIONALITY

With little practical movement on the Kurdish issue within Turkey immediately following the Demirel meeting with the HADEP mayors, the focus of Kurdish issues switched more to the external realm. Here attention was at its greatest in terms of the EU–Turkey dynamic, especially in the wake of the Helsinki summit of the European Council in December 1999.[39] It was precisely this dynamic that resulted in the adoption of the package of measures in August 2002 that would go some way toward meeting Kurdish nationalist demands.

The Helsinki meeting recognized Turkey as a candidate state "destined to join the Union on the basis of the same criteria as applied to other candidate States."[40] No direct mention was made of the Kurdish issue, as that would have precipitated a diplomatic crisis with Turkey.

However, the EU did state that accession negotiations could not begin until Turkey had fulfilled the political criteria for membership. In accordance with the EU's Agenda 2000, adopted in 1997, the EU's accession partnership for Turkey was founded on the principle that substantive political problems should be resolved prior to accession. In spite of Ankara's premature urgings that Turkey be given a date on which accession negotiations will commence, Brussels fended off such calls on the grounds that the EU is in the business of exporting stability, not importing instability. The EU was especially conscious of this in the Turkish case. Viewed from Ankara, the political criteria were to include "particular reference to the issue of human rights." Though none would claim that human rights abuses and the Kurdish issue were precisely the same, the former had nevertheless become somewhat of a euphemism for the latter.

The Helsinki meeting also restated the mantra that the political criteria it referred to (together with the economic criteria)[41] were those "laid down at the Copenhagen European Council" in June 1993. Yet, in spite of the portentous way in which the Copenhagen criteria are routinely invoked, they actually remain only a brief and very general statement. The Copenhagen European Council stated that "Membership requires that the candidate country has achieved stability of institutions guaranteeing democracy, the rule of law, human rights and respect for minorities." It goes without saying that the criteria have nothing specific to say about the Kurds in Turkey, but neither are their platitudes especially indicative as far as Kurdish-related policy issues are concerned. Their generalities can be interpreted in different ways, depending on vantage point and context. So, for example, does stability of institutions mean any more than people of Kurdish origin in the Turkish parliament, or could it be used to insist upon a Turkish and Kurdish federation? Do human rights include political as well as individual rights? Does respect for minorities mean merely the absence of persecution or the provision of a wide range of cultural rights?

Moreover, the statement contains the seeds of a fundamental normative and juridical misunderstanding between Brussels and Ankara. While most Europeans would assume that the Copenhagen reference to "minorities" refers most obviously to the Kurds,[42] the Turkish political establishment would reject such an interpretation, claiming that the 1923 Treaty of Lausanne is quite specific in only defining minorities in Turkey as religious minorities.[43]

Copenhagen also stipulates that an aspirant member must also implement the *acquis communautaire,* the accumulation of regulations adopted by the EU over the years, including a range of liberal provisions.

The principal formal instruments that have emerged from Helsinki have been threefold. First, an accession partnership was created for Turkey's candidacy, prepared by Brussels and formally adopted at a European Council meeting on March 8, 2001. This is a first, comprehensive attempt to take the blandishments of the Copenhagen criteria and give them a tangible policy reality. Second, a "national plan" was written for the implementation of the *acquis,* published by Turkey on March 19, 2001.[44] Third, an annual report from Brussels was issued in autumn 2001 on Turkey's performance as part of a new monitoring mechanism for Turkey.

In reality, neither of the two documents had much to say concretely as far as the Kurdish issue was concerned. The Europeans divided their expectations of Turkey into short-term (that is, one year) and medium-term (that is, more than one year) time horizons. In both categories, a strong emphasis on the equality of *individual* rights dominated. Short-term demands relevant (but not exclusively) to the Kurdish issue included greater freedom of expression and association, an end to torture, human rights training, and a moratorium on capital punishment. Medium-term requirements included the abolition of the death penalty, cultural diversity in education, and the lifting of the emergency-rule regime in the southeast. The EU was noticeably more circumspect as far as the issue of any sort of *group* minority rights was concerned, an issue of direct relevance to the Kurds. It was with some relief that those working on policy toward Turkey in leading EU member states greeted the avoidance of such "time bombs." The wording of the association partnership was judged by diplomats to be "judicious," but that the substance was there. This was entirely deliberate and the product of a practical approach that sought to reconcile basic principles with a need to show sensitivity to Turkish nationalist preoccupations. Wary of a return to the difficult bilateral relationship that typified interactions for two years after the 1997 Luxembourg summit,[45] it was in many ways a very political position adopted by the EU.

With European states so cautious in their dealings with Turkey, it was no surprise that the Kurds were the more frustrated party.

"Cowardliness and hypocrisy" were the charges leveled against the EU for the accession partnership by one leading Kurdish nationalist for its omission of any recognition of either the Kurdish people or the Kurdish question.[46] In general, the absence of any mention of the word *Kurd* was seen as a disappointment.

Faced with a cautious EU document,[47] the Turkish "national plan" did just enough to satisfy the European side. In its totality, the plan was long on qualified general statements of principle but short on specific promises. For example, in its preamble, the plan stated that "Turkey intends to fulfill the Copenhagen criteria and complete the accession process, *on the basis of the fundamental principles of the Republic as articulated in the Turkish Constitution"* [emphasis added]. In other words, any changes would reflect Ankara's conception of the Copenhagen generalities. In the main body of the text, many key areas of concern, though clearly laid out, contained nothing more than a willingness to "review" existing provisions. The section on "Freedom of Thought and Expression," for example, contained undertakings in the short term to review five areas of constitutional and legal provision dealing with the subject, including the notorious Article 312 of the Turkish Criminal Code relating to crimes committed against the unity of the state. Even the official gloss could do little more than to promise that "the abolition of the death penalty" and "cultural life and the use of languages" would "be considered." In expanding on the latter, the official commentary was notable for not raising false hopes: "The official language and the formal language of education in the Republic of Turkey is Turkish but the free usage of different languages, dialects, and tongues by Turkish citizens in their daily lives will not be prohibited, though this freedom cannot be abused for the purposes of separatism or division."

In general, the national plan received a mixed reception both inside Turkey and abroad. Those more optimistic on the matter pointed to the "opening . . . up for substantive discussion" of previously taboo subjects. While the Europeans could hardly fault the aspiration, there was little way of telling whether such changes were likely to be forthcoming, and, if they were, whether they would actually be implemented. There was general resignation that the plan was "the best achievable blueprint in the current political climate."[48] Ironically, Ankara was helped in its response from the EU by the onset of the financial crisis in February 2001; member states, notably Germany,[49] were almost desperate to be supportive for fear of the potentially radicalizing political side effects of the crisis.

With both sides having set out their stalls on the range of bilateral issues, the focus has shifted to Turkey's record on legal and constitutional reform to reflect its new obligations. Turkey's two main actions in addressing the requirements of the association partnership have been the passing of a law in October 2001 amending thirty-four articles, or about one-fifth of the constitution,[50] and the adoption of the August 2002 package. From the perspective of the Kurdish issue, action with regard to the former included the lifting of the ban on statements and publications in Kurdish; an end to the ban on amnesties for politically motivated offences committed after the adoption of the amendments; and a clutch of what Amnesty International has called "welcome steps" in the direction of the improvement of human rights,[51] including constitutional provision for the right to a fair trial.

In spite of this, Ankara's track record has fallen short of what was required in the accession partnership. Arguably of greatest concern were those areas where the amendments offered new opportunities for the restriction of basic freedoms. Article 26 (3) on freedom of expression and Article 28 (2) on the freedom of the press, both of which had been used extensively to penalize those using Kurdish up to 1991, were replaced with general formulations potentially restricting freedom of expression on the grounds of national security and the protection of the indivisibility of the state.[52]

The August 2002 package was of great substantive importance as far as the Kurdish issue is concerned. In addition to legalizing broadcasting and education in Kurdish, the package also abolished the death penalty, thereby effectively commuting Öcalan's sentence to one of life imprisonment. The ultranationalists of the MHP strenuously opposed the measures and, together with some opposition Islamists, voted against the package. The fact that it was passed by 256 votes to 162 was testimony to a combination of the behind-the-scenes influence of the military and the aspirations of many Turks who see EU membership as a panacea for their many problems, most notably those relating to the economy.

While the adoption of the package was a bold and unexpected move, it was greeted with caution in Kurdish nationalist circles. In the absence of a general amnesty for PKK operatives, including former guerrillas, the package is likely to prove to be insufficient to end the stand-off between the Turkish state and the former insurgents. The fact that the liberal reforms were driven by EU conditionality rather than a historic decision to embrace the country's ethno-nationalist Kurds within a new, more inclusive partnership makes one doubtful about its likely efficacy, certainly in the shorter term. There are also concerns about how and indeed whether the legalization of broadcasts and education in Kurdish will be permitted, especially if other matters, notably Cyprus, stymie hopes that a date for accession negotiations will be announced at the EU summit in Copenhagen in December 2002. As ever, in the case of Turkey, it will be the implementation of such formal provisions that will decide whether these changes are substantive or merely window-dressing.[53]

SEPTEMBER 11

It was against the general backdrop of a cautious and wary interaction between the EU and Turkey that the events of September 11 and their aftermath have unfolded. The immediate effect of the crisis was to place international terrorism at the top of the U.S. foreign policy agenda. For countries like Turkey, the new terrorism agenda generated the potential to bring Ankara and Washington closer together. Revelations that indicated a strong Middle Eastern dimension to September 11 and rising speculation that Iraq would be the second target of the "war against terrorism" led to a further appreciation in Washington of the strategic value of Turkey to the United States. Ankara's willingness to do whatever was required, notably sending a contingent of troops to Afghanistan, underlined the practical usefulness of Turkey as an ally for the United States. The fact that Turkey emerged as part of the North Atlantic Treaty Organization (NATO) consensus that September 11 represented an attack on the United States, for example, made it possible for Washington to invoke Article 5 of the treaty and rally its allies.

The new Atlantic preoccupation with terrorism prompted a sense of vindication on the part of many Turks. Much was said and published of a defiant nature suggesting that the world, and especially the Europeans, had been soft on terrorism prior to September 11 and hence that the Turks had been ill-served by their supposed friends. A charitable interpretation would see this outpouring as a collective catharsis, potentially capable of clearing away the bitterness associated with the prolonged period of the PKK insurgency. A less indulgent view would be to see such sentiments as evocative of a proud and harsh unwill-ingness to compromise at all with a rival variant of ethno-nationalism. Wisely, European governments have avoided being drawn into public exchanges on the issue.

That is not to suggest that Europeans have been unmoved, either by September 11 or by the forceful emergence of terrorism as a top international agenda item, or that this bundle of issues has not had some impact on their Turkey policy. In the European case, the issue has been an important one but one that has been played out in a more complex way than across the Atlantic. Europeans have found them-selves torn in two directions. On the one hand they have been keen to support the United States, and for reasons of self-interest to ensure that terror networks on the continent are closed down. On the other, Europeans cannot simply ignore groups that have large followings inside member states, whether they be émigré or indigenous support-ers or both. In the case of the PKK, leading EU member states have rarely if ever shown much enthusiasm for Öcalan or his organization, whatever the perceptions from Turkey.[54] But member states individu-ally also have found themselves uneasy at the prospects of the pur-suit of a hard line against the PKK given its nearly three-year ceasefire, especially if they want to encourage good future behavior. At some point, policy toward a terror organization that is apparently no longer utilizing terror is likely to be revisited.

This collective European dilemma appeared to be resolved, at least in the medium term, on May 3, 2002, when the EU, under pres-sure from both the United States and Turkey, finally decided collec-tively to place the PKK on its list of terror organizations. This provoked a bitter response from PKK supporters in Europe, who, with a sur-prising degree of historical hyperbole, accused the Europeans of engi-neering "a second Lausanne."[55] Once again, the PKK's response was indicative of the failure of the organization to deliver on its promise to reinvent itself as a European-style political movement. In one florid piece of rhetoric issued shortly before the decision—a crude attempt, one assumes, at deterrence—Europeans were warned that such a step would amount to "a declaration of war" on the PKK,[56] the implica-tion being that the organization might resort to violence in response. The fact that the speech was made by an executive committee mem-ber of the newly created KADEK, and one who also happened to be the brother of Abdullah Öcalan, was equally revealing. The ferocity of the invective against the Europeans prompted some European officials to conclude privately that such responses confirmed that the decision had indeed been a sound one.

In his fiery speech, Osman Öcalan also warned that if the EU took this decision, "we will advise the Kurds to cease all official relations with EU countries."[57] In the event, nothing as sweeping by way of retaliation has taken place. Nevertheless, the PKK and its supporters did state that they would cease all interaction with the governments of Britain, Denmark, Spain, and Sweden,[58] which were perceived to be in the vanguard of support for the move. This, though, was unlikely to do any damage other than to the PKK itself, especially considering the role that northern European states such as Denmark and Sweden have played as keepers of the collective conscience of the EU.

A response that will be more problematic for the EU to deal with is the accusation that the terror list decision has effectively "criminalized" all Kurds from Turkey. Such a charge resonates with an existing campaign being run on behalf of Kurdish arrivals in Europe, which has been aimed at antiterrorism and immigration legislation. It is considerably harder for embattled governments to fend off[59] because of its attempt to tap into the highly emotive race issue in continental Europe.

CONCLUSION: THE WAY AHEAD

The struggle between Turkey and the Kurds has punctuated the history of the modern Turkish state. It has taken many forms and has often involved violent resistance. There is no reason to believe that, short of a mutually respectful political accommodation, the Turkish–Kurdish cleavage will not continue to be a blight domestically and externally for Turkey over the years to come. Although the August 2002 package was an important step in a positive direction, it would be premature to suggest that such an accommodation has yet been clinched.

In many ways, this has been a propitious time for action to address the Turkish–Kurdish cleavage. For the foreseeable future, the PKK-led insurgency is over. As an organization, the PKK has been decapitated and contained. The extent of the PKK's political objectives seemed until recently to have been to save their erstwhile leader from execution, thereby giving Ankara crucial policy leverage over the organization. An end to the violent conflict and to the polarization of the dispute has given new opportunities to the middle ground. HADEP has emerged as a political party representative of mainstream Kurdish nationalist aspirations and willing to work within the existing political system in Turkey. For many, it enjoys democratic legitimacy. The demands of the Kurdish camp have been greatly moderated since the early 1990s, and, post–August 2002, equate mainly with the desire to function normally within the party political arena in Turkey.

With the Kurds perennially cast as the *demandeurs,* it is the Turkish response to this agenda that has been and will continue to be crucial. When the Kurdish insurgency was a reality, there was a widespread consensus against making concessions as this would be tantamount to rewarding violence and therefore encouraging confrontation. With the capture of Öcalan and the end of the insurgency, there was little incentive on the part of Turkey's political class and state establishment alike to give priority to the issue; that is, at least, until the emergence of some clear EU conditionality for reform, which resulted in the adoption of liberal change in the direction of cultural rights and the abolition of the death penalty. Those changes have brought Turkey and its Kurds closer to a historic reconciliation than has been the case for a long time, perhaps even since the very creation of the modern Turkish state.

In spite of this moment of hope, the future is likely to remain uncertain for some time to come. The clarification of government policy toward broadcasting and education in Kurdish will have to await the November general election and the policy uncertainties of its outcome. By that stage, the whole domestic liberalization process may have been derailed if the EU fails to give Turkey a date for the start of accession negotiations at the Copenhagen meeting in December 2002. Furthermore, a basket of issues to do with the PKK, not the least its ability to retain a proximate military option, will in great degree be dependent on the future course of events in Iraq. In the meantime, preliminary reports from HADEP about the obstacles being placed in its way at the commencement of the parliamentary election campaign are not encouraging as far as the creation of a level party political playing field in Turkey is concerned. Turkey and the Kurds have indeed been moving in the direction of a modus vivendi, but they are not there yet.

CHAPTER FIVE

AN INSIDER'S VIEW OF TURKEY'S FOREIGN POLICY AND ITS AMERICAN CONNECTION

YALİM ERALP

For many years now, almost every Turkish political leader proclaims after a visit to Washington that a "new chapter has opened" in relations between the two countries. Prime Minister Bülent Ecevit's visit to the oval office on January 16, 2002, was true to form, yet another "new chapter." Turkey's leaders like to show the Turkish public that they have the U.S. president's endorsement. As in most countries, the trips of leaders abroad are invariably portrayed as successful to the public. Visits to Washington also show the importance of the United States, not only in Turkey's foreign affairs but in the country's domestic politics as well.

But the fact that the statement of a new chapter in the relationship came from Ecevit, who opposed many U.S. policies in the past, shows how much the relationship with the United States has improved. A much winding road was traveled to come to the present excellent state of relations.

A Look at Recent U.S.–Turkish Relations

The decade following World War II was marked by developments that completely changed Turkish foreign policy. The Truman Doctrine of 1947 ushered in the new era. This was followed in 1950 by the Turkish government's decision to send troops to Korea to fight alongside Americans. When Turkey attained North Atlantic Treaty Organization (NATO) membership in 1952, it felt secure in the face of Soviet threats. A sizable American military presence in the country punctuated that security.

In the early 1960s Turkey's confidence in the U.S. tie declined and a sense of insecurity intruded. The new generation of military officers that led the Turkish Republic's first coup in 1960 felt that Turkey had been too deferential to the United States in opening up the country to a sizable American defense presence and should better control U.S. military activities in Turkey. The new, highly agitated political left agreed with the military, leaving little room for the right-wing Justice Party government to maneuver. Moreover, many in the government were unaware of secret military arrangements with the United States, further limiting its freedom to act. The aftermath of the Cuban missile crisis heightened public suspicions, as Turks assumed that a deal had been struck with the Soviets over their heads on the withdrawal of Jupiter missiles in Turkey.[1]

The sense of insecurity reached its peak with the famous, or in Turkey more accurately infamous, Johnson letter. In an attempt to prevent Turkish military intervention in Cyprus, President Lyndon Johnson wrote Prime Minister Ismet İnönü on June 5, 1964, that U.S. military materials provided to Turkey could not be used by Turkish forces in Cyprus. The letter further stated that Turkey was not covered by the NATO collective defense agreement should the Soviet Union attack in retaliation for a Turkish intervention in Cyprus.[2] Although the letter was kept secret until 1966, according to retired Ambassador Osman Olcay, it enraged İnönü. He responded immediately, expressing disappointment, indeed anger, in diplomatic language. However, İnönü accepted an invitation to visit Washington on June 19, 1964, and the differences on Cyprus were narrowed or papered over in the ensuing communiqué. The İnönü government fell not much later; İnönü's son-in-law, Metin Toker, claimed that the United States had engineered his fall, and that was widely believed in Turkey.[3]

Not only was the Turkish government dismayed with the turn of events, but a widespread anti-American feeling also emerged, and serious public doubts arose over the depth of U.S. interest in a stable Turkey. A prime target of the rising and vociferous Turkish left at the time was the Peace Corps, who were popularly suspected of being spies. Eventually the Turkish government asked for their departure. Years later, a high-ranking general in a conversation with me equated American nongovernmental organization (NGO) activities in southeastern Turkey with those of the Peace Corps.

In 1969, Turkey negotiated greater control over U.S. bases in the country. The new agreement satisfied Turkish requests to a large degree, including concerns over the jurisdiction of U.S. service personnel. The bases were now labeled "joint bases" in contrast to the prevailing public perception of "U.S. bases."

If the 1960s were a period of rising strains in bilateral relations both over U.S. military activities in Turkey and the U.S. approach to Greek–Turkish relations, the 1970s were worse. The decade started with a disagreement over poppies. Turkey was deeply angered at American insistence that the cultivation of poppies be stopped. The poppy quickly became a high-profile issue in both countries. While Prime Minister Süleyman Demirel managed to resist American pressure to ban cultivation, Nihat Erim, who became prime minister after the military staved off a leftist coup, gave in to American pressure despite the advice of the Turkish bureaucracy. The poppy ban of 1972 resulted in sizable losses of revenue for one hundred thousand Turkish farmers with little recompense from the United States. After Ecevit took over the government in 1974, he lifted the ban but imposed strict controls over cultivation.[4] In hindsight, despite the strain in relations, the episode was a classic example of finding a middle ground satisfactory to both sides. The poppy has long ceased to be an issue in U.S.–Turkish relations, although drug trafficking through Turkey remains a matter of concern to both countries.

When the Greek junta tried to overthrow Archbishop Makarios of Cyprus in July 1974 and annex the island to Greece, Ecevit sought a joint intervention with Britain, convinced that the union of the island with Greece was unacceptable to the Turkish public. When Britain washed its hands of the matter and refused Ankara's importuning, Turkey intervened alone. The U.S. government worked hard to avert a Turkish–Greek war but this time sent no "Johnson letter." American diplomatic efforts this time failed to stop a Turkish military operation in Cyprus. As a result, Congress imposed an arms embargo on Turkey, which shocked not only the Turkish government but the country as a whole. Turks felt that their country was the victim of a Greek-dominated Congress. It took four years of negotiations to end the single biggest blow to U.S.–Turkish relations. The embargo led to the start of an indigenous arms industry and the diversification of military procurement, since Turkey felt it could no longer rely on the United States as its sole supplier.

Ecevit became prime minister again in 1978, at a time when his social democratic party was using the era's Third World slogans. There was even much discussion of joining the nonaligned movement. Ecevit and his party's sensitivity to Soviet concerns collided with the American desire to fly U-2 spy planes over Turkey in order to monitor the implementation of the SALT Treaty. Deputy Secretary of State Warren Christopher flew to Ankara in 1979 in an attempt to persuade Prime Minister Ecevit to allow U.S. planes in Turkish airspace. Ecevit, fearing Soviet reaction, told Christopher to ask for the Soviets' consent for this operation; an idea unacceptable to the U.S. administration. A month later, when the Turkish government wanted $50 million in economic assistance from the United States, Christopher said: "I don't want to say anything that I will regret later, but the United States has no money to waste." (This was a reference to chronic government subsidies to Turkey's state economic enterprises.)

THE CHANGE BEGINS

Although Prime Minister Demirel and the deputy prime minister responsible for the economy, Turgut Özal, initiated a radical liberalization of the economy in the beginning of 1980, the political situation deteriorated badly. Virtual anarchy including left–right war was rife. The military took over on September 12, 1980, to restore order. The Turkish public believed that the U.S. administration approved or even stimulated the military coup because of American fears of a destabilized Turkey.

After the Shah's regime in Iran was replaced by the Mullahs and the Soviet Union invaded Afghanistan in 1979, Turkey once again became a strategic focal point for the United States. Americans now wanted to build several new airfields in eastern Turkey. The United

States gave the impression that it was preparing for possible military intervention because of the fluid situation in the region. The Iran–Iraq war also had begun. Although Turks feared being dragged once again into Middle Eastern affairs as they had with the Baghdad Pact of 1955,[5] the Turkish government did agree after much deliberation to the building of airfields in the southeastern cities of Mus and Batman. Indeed, many Turks thought that the Carter administration had started a policy of responding to the "red" (Communism) with the "green" (Islam)— that is, that the United States intended to contain Communism by supporting Islam. Turks also believed that the United States felt that Islamic regimes cooperating with the United States would better withstand the challenge of Communism because of the contradictions between Communism and Islam. It is still widely believed in Turkey that the junta's policies were in line with that strategy.[6] Turkey improved its relations with antisecular Arab regimes, while relations with Israel were downplayed. The state of relations between Israel and the Arab regimes at that time did not permit Turkey to have good relations with both sides; at least, that was the impression in Turkey. After September 11, 2001, many Turkish intellectuals claimed that the United States was the victim of its own creation: bin Laden. Using Islam had backfired, as secular Turks saw it.

As the elections of 1983 to restore civilian rule approached, the ruling Military Council screened the parties and the candidates and determined which would be allowed to take part in the elections. It excluded many. One probable candidate for exclusion was Turgut Özal, whose loyalty to secularism the military questioned. However, an article subsequently appeared in the *Wall Street Journal* that in effect said that if Özal were not permitted to run, the U.S. administration would be angry with the military. At the State Department I was told that the article was inspired by the U.S. administration. In the end, Özal was allowed to run and his party won an absolute majority.

Özal was a pragmatic man. He stood for change; he wanted to open up Turkey much wider to the outside world, hated bureaucracy, and loved new ideas. He wanted to move closer to the United States, seeing American support as vital for Turkey's growth and its security. Americans liked Özal, a devout Muslim who stood for liberal ideas and was very voluble. Indeed, Deputy Secretary of Defense Paul Wolfowitz, in his Turgut Özal Memorial Speech at the Washington Institute for Near East Policy on March 13, 2002, made similar observations. Özal was perhaps the first Turkish prime minister not to complain to a U.S.

president, Ronald Reagan at that time, about a "U.S. tilt to Greece," about the level of assistance, and so forth. He always proclaimed he wanted trade, not aid. He wanted Turkey to be a genuine partner of the United States.

Özal also wanted good relations with Turkey's neighbors. During his first visit to Washington, D.C., as prime minister, in 1985, he met with leaders of Jewish organizations. (This became a routine in all his visits to the United States.) He also met with Iakovos, the Archbishop of America, who was banned in Turkey. Although closer relations with Israel had to wait for better times, Özal was on the same page with the United States regarding Israel, Greece, Armenia, aid and trade, and ethnic and religious rights. Even during the time when the Kurdish People's Party (PKK) was carrying on its war in Turkey, Özal wanted to defuse tension by opening the Kurdish issue for public discussion.

Özal's policies and personal approach significantly improved U.S.–Turkish relations. Nevertheless, there were difficulties with the United States in this period, particularly over trade restrictions and quotas. The military and foreign affairs bureaucracy also wanted to renegotiate the Defense and Economic Cooperation Agreement (DECA). They believed that the bases were particularly valuable to the United States and that the congressional annual limits on aid to Turkey under the agreement had to be eliminated. Özal, however, was against a renegotiation of the DECA, and Turkey's campaign to eliminate the annual congressional limitation on military assistance failed. Another contentious issue was the continuing effort by the Armenian lobby to get Congress and the White House to issue resolutions on statements characterizing the events in 1915 in Anatolia as genocide. One day, Özal called me to ask whether the New York Times would make the approval in Congress of the resolution on "genocide" a headline. I explained to him that this was not the issue. Other Armenian demands—financial and territorial compensation—would follow, and that *these* would be unacceptable to the Turkish public. These examples show how Özal wanted to deal with American ethnic lobbies.

Iraq's invasion of Kuwait in 1990 had a sudden, decisive impact on U.S.-Turkish relations. Özal had privately told me that he always considered Iraq a bigger threat to Turkey than Iran. Not surprisingly, Özal quickly sided with the United States after the invasion despite domestic opposition, including from his own prime minister, Yıldırım Akbulut. He closed the oil pipeline without waiting for the United Nations (UN) Security Council resolution. He also wanted to send a military unit to Iraq to join the allied forces there, but met with stiff opposition from the military. The commander of Turkish forces, General Necip Torumtay, resigned, mainly because of his unhappiness with Özal's policy on Iraq, a truly remarkable occurrence in Turkey. The principal opposition leader, Süleyman Demirel, also opposed Özal's policies allowing the Americans to use Turkish bases for the air war; at one point Demirel denounced Özal for turning Turkey into "an American aircraft carrier." Many Turks also feared that the war could result in the break-up of Iraq and an internationalization of the Kurdish question. But once in power, Demirel continued—albeit less vociferously—Özal's policies of supporting the United States and its allies on Iraq.

Özal also wanted Turkey to be on "the winning side for once" and hoped for significant economic and financial benefits by supporting the United States in Iraq. However, despite some U.S. and Arab financial assistance and a rise in textile quotas, Turkey suffered serious financial losses because of the continued embargo on Iraq. The embargo and economic losses continue today and have influenced Turkish attitudes with regard to another war against Iraq.

A Kurdish issue emerging from the Gulf War also became an exacerbating factor in U.S.–Turkish relations. When Saddam Hussein destroyed the Kurdish uprising in northern Iraq, shortly after the end of the Gulf War, almost half a million Kurds arrived at Turkey's borders. U.S.-led Western assistance saved the Kurds, and Western military power permitted them to return home. Through the allied Operation Provide Comfort and the prohibition on Iraq to fly fix-winged aircraft north of the thirty-sixth parallel, a political catastrophe for Turkey as well as a humanitarian one for the Kurds were avoided. But this episode has been a painful one for Turkey. The continuing allied flights through Turkish airspace and occasional bombing make Turkey uneasy. The uneasiness reached its peak during the 1991 parliamentary election campaign, when opposition leader Demirel promised that Provide Comfort would be terminated. Following his taking over as prime minister in 1991, the general staff wrote a memo to the foreign ministry supporting the termination of Provide Comfort. When they understood that Demirel was not serious, however, they simply wrote another memo, this time recommending the extension of Provide Comfort. When asked why he had changed his attitude on Provide Comfort, Demirel responded: "What was I to do; damage relations with the United States?"[7]

Later, when Tansu Çiller became prime minister, she would face the same parliamentary problem over the extension of Provide Comfort. Even some high Turkish officials in the 1990s claimed that U.S. helicopters in southeastern Turkey were aiding the PKK. Additional arguments were put forth for Provide Comfort's extension: another exodus by the Kurds to Turkey or the "cover" Provide Comfort gave to Turkish forces, which often raided Iraqi territory in search of PKK camps. Over time, governments "learned to live" with Provide Comfort. The situation is no different today—eleven years later—under Prime Minister Ecevit. The differences among various Turkish leaders on this neuralgic public issue have turned out to be ones of nuance and style—more the management of domestic public opinion—and not serious clashes with the United States.

The Kurdish issue has also caused friction from U.S. concerns for the rights of Kurds in Turkey. The United States feared that the fight against the PKK was tearing the social fabric of Turkish society. American demarches for the recognition of greater rights for Turkish Kurds were met with stiff resistance. Turkish governments have always shown an abiding fear for Turkey's dismemberment if Kurdish ethnicity became an issue. The existence of a de facto Kurdish entity next door in northern Iraq has heightened these fears. Many Turks still genuinely believe that the U.S. administration is intent on creating a new Kurdish state in northern Iraq and that Turkey will soon be faced with a fait accompli. Despite U.S. assurances to the contrary, the fear of an independent Kurdish state resulting from another American war against Saddam Hussein is much on the minds of Turkish leaders and the Turkish public.

Çiller became prime minister in June 1993 and was invited to the White House the same year. The first item on her agenda was the lifting of the embargo against Iraq. She believed that her image of modernity and political change and the fact that she stood for secularism would help persuade the administration. At this meeting, and in frequent conversations thereafter, Çiller pointed out that there are essentially two models in the Islamic world: Turkey and Iran. If Turkey was not supported better financially, the Islamic vote in Turkey would increase. In response to her requests, Vice President Al Gore proposed that the two sides should find a formula to help Turkey financially, but little in fact was done. Her principal success with the United States was on the energy question. She stressed the importance of the Caspian basin and the need to build pipelines carrying energy from the Caspian and from Azerbaijan through Turkey to the West. The much-discussed Bakü–Ceyhan pipeline is to finally start construction in 2002, with American and other external support. Another issue of importance for Turkey was achieving a customs union with the European Union (EU). On this issue as well, the U.S. administration helped Turkey greatly by putting pressure on the Europeans, who agreed to the union in 1995. On the other hand, Turkey's attempts during the 1990s to amend the DECA were met each time with American resistance. Turkey also basically failed to reduce U.S. trade restrictions.

One issue on which Turkey and the United States have seen eye to eye for five decades has been the importance of NATO. Indeed, Turkey has constantly feared that the end of the Soviet Union would lead to lesser interest in the alliance and ultimately to the erosion of the organization's core functions. Turkey also has had a continuing concern that Russia might deviate from a policy of cooperation with the West. NATO—the only major Western organization in which Turkey is a full-fledged member—remains Turkey's principal attachment to the West and a vehicle to participate in Western policymaking. NATO has also served as a useful political cover for some difficult decisions with regard to Greece. In recent years, Turkey has come to see NATO as protection against unfriendly neighbors such as Iran and Iraq, although it has always been fearful that the alliance would not come to its defense in any conflict with these "out of area" countries. In security matters, the Turkish establishment looks to the United States as its principal defense partner. It considers the role of the United States irreplaceable, despite the budding Common Foreign and Security Policy of the EU. Turkey also looks to the United States for help, if necessary, to prevent crises between Turkey and Greece or at least to keep them from worsening. This was the case during the Aegean crisis in 1987 over the exploration of the seabed and in 1996 over the disputed ownership of Kardak/Imia, a small rock island off the shores of Turkey.

For many Turks, the principal event of the past few years was the capture of Abdullah Öcalan, leader of the PKK. Although never acknowledged officially, Turks believe that the United States played a vital role in his capture, which has obviously helped to cement ties with the United States. Moreover, the United States, unlike the Europeans, backed Turkey when Turkish forces massively intervened militarily in northern Iraq in 1995 to chase after the PKK. The United

States also supported Turkey when it issued an ultimatum to Syria to expel Öcalan from its territory. It helped persuade Russia, Italy, and Greece not to give asylum to Öcalan. To Turks, only the United States recognized the dangerous nature of the fight against the PKK and its threat to the stability in Turkey.

Turkish governments have usually preferred Republican administrations, largely because they believe that Republicans are less influenced by American ethnic lobbies. Every year the Turks were deeply irritated by the actions of the U.S. Congress in restricting, delaying, or reducing military assistance. The Turks declared the Greek and Armenian lobbies to be "alien influences" in the U.S.–Turkey relationship, bent on diminishing U.S. support for Turkey and creating major problems for Turkey on issues such as Cyprus or, in the case of the Armenian-Americans, the "Armenian genocide." There is only a small Turkish lobby in the United States, whose numbers and political and financial clout can in no way be compared with those of the Greek and Armenian lobbies. Recently, however, the government of Turkey has worked hard to join forces with the Jewish lobby in promoting Turkish interests in the United States.

THE SITUATION TODAY: A GROWING UNDERSTANDING

For all the U.S. support, the Turks still have lingering doubts or uncertainties about the United States. While there is a genuine belief that the United States is indeed concerned about Turkey's instability, many Turks feel less certain how the United States sees Turkey in a world without Russian competition. No administration has explained much, if anything, to its Turkish counterparts about what "big emerging markets," and Turkey's description as one, means. Nor has the United States or Turkey defined the frequently used term "strategic partnership." Instead of laying out some sort of large vision of Turkey's role in U.S. policy, Turks see American leaders and officials trying to change a bit of policy here and there or suddenly asking to use the bases for war in Iraq. There has been no serious blueprint from either side as to what domestically, economically, and diplomatically Turkey should do to play a prominent regional role. Turkish leaders have frequently left the oval office wondering what White House intentions really are.

Nevertheless, as Turkey grew economically and opened up to the outside world, greater understanding between the United States and

Turkey gradually replaced the disagreements and distrust of the 1960s and 1970s. The relationship matured as both countries adjusted to the end of the cold war and a new international situation. Whatever disagreements continue to exist, both countries have seen to it that these do not fundamentally damage the relations. Indeed, Turkey has turned to the United States on many issues and U.S. support has not been lacking. Help from the International Monetary Fund (IMF), the achievement of the customs union with the EU, and the Bakü–Ceyhan oil pipeline are good examples of the closeness of the relationship and of continuing U.S. support. And this list is far from exhaustive.

THE DECISIONMAKING PROCESS IN TURKEY

The foreign policy decisionmaking process in Turkey is not very transparent. The government and the National Security Council (NSC), which became a constitutional institution after the 1960 coup, dominate foreign policy decisionmaking. Other actors, such as the foreign ministry, play a less significant role. The parliament does not play much of a role at all.

Whether it is the civilian government or the NSC (that is, essentially the military) that has the final say in foreign policy is often discussed in Turkey. Despite the fact that, according to the latest constitutional change, the NSC merely "advises" the government, the NSC most frequently has the final say. Although the composition of the NSC is in fact dominated by civilians (the president, the prime minister, deputy prime ministers, the minister of foreign affairs, the minister of the interior, the minister of national defense, and the minister of justice), the military (the chief of staff, heads of four services, and the secretary general of the National Security Council) dominate the NSC. Indeed, the NSC is the main vehicle for the military establishment to express its official views in the decisionmaking process. During the periods of military rule, the military naturally would have the final say on policy. Indeed, the Rogers Agreement that provided the return of Greece to the military committee of NATO was made without the knowledge of then Foreign Minister İlter Türkmen. But the tilt toward the military in security and foreign policymaking persists today and even increased after the military's "postmodern coup" of September 28, 1997, ending the Islamic-led government coalition.

Before each NSC meeting the military coordinates its views and agrees on a common position. The secretary general of the National Security Council—a four-star officer—is aided by a sizable bureaucracy of military personnel, civilians, and academics not only on foreign policy and security matters but also on social, economic, and legal issues. The civilian government, on the other hand, does not usually coordinate its position prior to the meeting. Even when it does, its members can usually only agree on the lowest common denominator. At the end of the day, the military's views often prevail. The military's clout, of course, goes beyond the organizational advantages.

Since the establishment of the republic in 1923, two state institutions have been widely respected—the general staff (army) and the foreign ministry. In recent years, the ministry has lost much of its luster and power relative to the military. The army, always influential in some aspects of foreign policy, has grown even more so, as its political involvement has risen. But there are other reasons for the decline of the foreign ministry. As the demise of the Soviet Union resulted in many more neighboring and Turkic countries, the foreign ministry's workload increased enormously without an increase in personnel or financial resources. Because also of the increased number of international meetings, more senior people are desperately needed to help with the workload of the foreign minister. New actors such as NGOs, business circles, fledgling think tanks, academics, and syndicates have started increasingly to influence foreign policy, each in their own way.

Within the ministry itself, coordination between departments is often lacking, creative thinking is not encouraged, officers tend to know only their "own" dossier, area specialists do not exist, and, other than French and English, knowledge of foreign languages is rare. The advisory role of ambassadors is minimal, if their views are sought at all. Sometimes the ambassador is the last person to be informed about a decision relating to his country. The appointment of ambassadors is often random and expertise is frequently not taken into consideration. With regard to Central Asia, the Caucasus, and the Balkans, new but unaccountable "nationalist" actors such as advisers to the Office of the Prime Minister or advisers in other ministries entered the foreign policy arena, claiming that they represented the Turkish government. All these forces have combined to complicate the work of the ministry and lessen its weight. Planning has become extremely difficult if not impossible. In contrast, the general staff, usually supported by the

National Security Council secretary general and his vastly expanding staff, lacks neither personnel nor financial resources.

The pervasive military involvement in policy is defended on the basis that "national security" in Turkey is viewed in a much wider sense than elsewhere. Questions such as the domestic fight against terror, against antisecular activities in the country, and against Kurdish separatism are all considered matters pertaining to national security. All these areas are heavily controlled by the military. Every decision by the government on these issues must have their approval and the military is often aggressive in seeking decisions.

The military deeply distrusts politicians; its members have seen many politicians fail and lead Turkey into difficult economic and political situations. They also believe that the approach of politicians to secularism in Turkey is mainly guided by their desire to get votes by exploiting popular religious sentiments, in turn undermining secularism. In an interview, former president Demirel responded positively to the question of whether the politicians feared the military. He went on to say: "If the Parliament is closed, the Prime Minister is hanged, and the military-made constitution is praised, you cannot ask me whether the military's views are predominant."[8]

The political establishment in Turkey has been both unable and unwilling to limit the military's influence. It is unable because democratic institutions are not fully consolidated, because of the fragmented political situation, and because governments are usually fragile coalitions. It is unwilling because politicians like to hide behind the military when unpopular decisions have to be made, because the military has a much better standing with the public (although this has recently been somewhat tarnished by their ambiguous attitude toward the EU), and because the military is still widely regarded as the final bastion against an Islamic government.

The government's weakness shows itself in a variety of ways. For example, when the ban on the use of Kurdish was lifted, a journalist asked President Özal about its belated timing. Özal reportedly responded: "I have been defending the lift for a long time; now I have surmounted the National Security Council."[9] It is commonplace for the political elite to wait until the military expresses its opinion on important issues, and then they usually salute. For example, before expressing their own opinion, they waited for the military to state that execution or nonexecution of the PKK leader Öcalan—a matter in fact of deep interest to the military and to millions of Turks—did not concern them and that this was a decision for the parliament.

When I, as ambassador to the Organisation for Security and Co-operation in Europe (OSCE), explained to President Demirel in July 1999 how the issue of school instruction in the mother tongue and broadcasting in Kurdish should be treated (by allowing Kurdish language courses and private TV channels), Demirel asked me to explain this to General Hüseyin Kıvrıkoğlu, commander of the Turkish Armed Forces. When the legislation to enlarge the scope of freedom of thought was under parliamentary consideration in order to meet the Copenhagen criteria for EU membership, some ministers complained privately to the press of military intervention in the process. Newspaper headlines such as "The army has given green light to TV broadcasts in Kurdish" are common. Indeed, military statements on such issues are not lacking. However, when the parliament suddenly enacted legislation in August 2002 to meet the EU criteria, including freeing instruction and broadcasts in Kurdish and abolishing capital punishment, the politicians apparently and surprisingly did not bother to ask the military's views.

Not only does the civilian government often bow to the military on security issues, but there are civilian leaders who ask for military views even where the military does not expect or want them to. When President Ahmet Necdet Sezer decided not to go to Iran in 2000 for the summit of the Economic Cooperation Organization (ECO) because of tensions in relations between the two countries, Foreign Minister İsmail Cem suggested to Prime Minister Ecevit that Ecevit should travel to Tehran. Ecevit responded by saying that the issue should be discussed in the military-dominated NSC. Before it enacted the new law on religious foundations in 2002, the government also consulted the military. When Çiller became prime minister in 1994, General Gures, then the armed forces commander, suggested to her that a military adviser should be appointed to the Office of the Prime Minister. The position has since been turned into a permanent one.

Foreigners also believe that military views dominate decision-making and unwittingly help perpetuate the situation. Statements emanating from the NSC are closely followed in other countries. Even statements by military leaders outside of the framework of the National Security Council are considered important abroad as well as in Turkey. For instance, when General Atilla Ateş, then chief of ground forces, warned Syria on September 16, 1998, against further harboring PKK leader Öcalan, it was taken very seriously by Syria as well as by foreign emissaries. During Vice President Dick Cheney's visit to Turkey on March 19, 2002, the American side insisted on meeting separately with General Kıvrıkoğlu, the Turkish commander. (The Turkish military as well as the civilian leadership prefer to maintain military-to-military meetings only.) The Turkish government was embarrassed and included General Kıvrıkoğlu in the meeting with Prime Minister Ecevit. When the American side insisted on a separate meeting with Kıvrıkoğlu, ostensibly to discuss Iraq, the government bowed to this request and the general was flanked by the foreign minister in order to save face.

The foreign ministry's role is also complicated by the way political leaders handle foreign policy issues. Özal, for instance, often wanted to change Turkey's approach to specific foreign policy issues. He distrusted the foreign ministry, disliked its conventional bureaucratic attitudes, and often kept the foreign minister in the dark. He worked with only a handful of advisers from the ministry as well as with some journalists and businessmen; business was indeed a part of foreign affairs for Özal. When he wanted to lift visas unilaterally for Greeks, Özal went ahead despite the ministry's opposition. The foreign ministry equally disliked Özal; there was a continuous turf battle between the two. Not surprisingly, Özal's views usually carried the day.

Cyprus, however, is an important example of the contrary. Here, Özal could *not* override the concerns of both the military and the bureaucracy. His approach sometimes collided with the military. Another important example was Iran. The military considered Özal soft on Iran. One day, as the spokesman for the foreign ministry, I received instructions from President General Kenan Evren to lash out at Iran. Özal had instructed me five minutes earlier not to say anything about Iran. Such clashes were not uncommon during the Özal years, particularly during the Gulf War and the ensuing exodus of Kurds from Iraq and their subsequent return.

Demirel was a different man in that he was conventional and he trusted the foreign ministry, dutifully following the ministry's script. Çiller was a combination of both men when it came to relations with the foreign ministry. She often wanted change in the approaches to policy issues and worked with a handful of advisers from the ministry, but she did not completely sideline the ministry as Özal so often did. She also took care not get out of step with the military. Mesut Yılmaz worked with the ministry and his advisers but had his own personal input, which distinguished him from Çiller. Özal's approach to policy was shaped from top to bottom; in the other governments policy was usually made from the bottom up.

Prime Minister Ecevit today is different from the Ecevit of the 1970s. His foreign policy ideas and approaches to social democratic issues have changed radically. Today, Ecevit follows the script of the foreign ministry; naturally his views on the EU and Cyprus vary but the aging prime minister is a "hardliner" on these issues, particularly Cyprus. Coalition governments are often divided on neuralgic foreign policy issues. The present ambiguity in Turkey's EU policy has been to some extent the result of differences in the current coalition. The National Action Party of Devlet Bahçeli and the Motherland Party of Yılmaz have put forth totally different views on Turkey's future; the Motherland Party is liberal and pro-EU. The National Action Party is conservative and staunchly nationalistic.

The media's role in foreign policy decisionmaking in Turkey should not be underestimated. Turkey's leaders, both civilian *and* military, are extremely sensitive to media criticism, Özal being perhaps an exception. Özal spent much time with the press to explain his views and to spin his approach to numerous issues. Often, as in many countries, Turkish politicians try to manipulate the media by strategically leaking documents and providing specific information to favored journalists or columnists. Despite the demonstrated lack of credibility of the media in various public opinion polls, political leaders pay plenty of attention to them even as they want to avoid them; indeed many despise and fear them.

The Turkish media have evolved tremendously over the past decade. They have become much better informed and less staunchly nationalistic. Today, the media question even long-standing policies on Cyprus, Greece, Armenia, and the Kurdish issue. They recently broke new ground by criticizing the military establishment both in domestic and external affairs. Even military procurement, a long-time taboo, has become subject to criticism. As a result, the military establishment and the foreign ministry take much more time to inform the media and try to control it. Background briefings have become common. But while the elite has its favorite commentators, it has generally found it more difficult to convince the media. It is not uncommon for the government to continue to add more nuances to its statements to stave off criticism. For instance, the government tilt toward the Palestinians in

April and May of 2002, after the Israelis' entry into Jenin, was due in considerable measure to media pressures and domestic public outcry. In sum, the establishment has had to take into account the views of the media, including the media's strong support for EU membership.

Turkey's parliament is politically important, but its role in foreign policy remains minimal. The government rarely shares information with the whole parliament, let alone the opposition. Foreign policy debates take place in the media but infrequently on the floor of parliament. Indeed, when a foreign policy issue is tabled by the opposition, the discussion often turns into a debate as to who is more nationalist and who defends one's kin better. The substance of the issue is rarely discussed. However, where the Balkans, the Caucasus, and Central Asia are concerned, advocates of various lobbies (Georgian or Abhkaz, for example) play a significant role. The foreign ministry is indeed sensitive to possible accusations of inaction from such groups. International agreements brought before the parliament for ratification are rarely screened in any depth except in cases involving domestic ethnic considerations.

The evolution of the Cyprus issue is an interesting case for analyzing the complexities of policymaking in Turkey today. Prime Minister Ecevit made the decision to intervene in Cyprus in 1974. At that time, he stated that the best solution, also from a strategic point of view, would be a federal state and that a division of the island would be detrimental for Turkey. Interestingly, and possibly influenced by the military's thinking, he recently seems to have changed his view. He stated on May 28, 2001, that "two states on the island should be possible." As an example, he quoted the velvet divorce of Czechoslovakia, whose two resulting countries are now both EU candidate members. Even within the present coalition government, in addition to the widely differing views of the Motherland Party and National Action Party, there is disagreement between the leader of the coalition, the Democratic Left Party (DSP) minister Şükrü Sina Gürel, a "hardliner" responsible for Cyprus; and the more compromising former foreign minister Cem. Cem has recently left the government to establish his own party and was replaced by Gürel.

Indeed, for the past year Turkey has had an acrimonious debate on the EU and Cyprus issues—which have become intractably linked—between conservatives and liberals and with the serious involvement of the military. Recently, there have been disagreements within the military on EU issues. An unofficial statement by a high-ranking general in March 2002 was quickly contradicted in an official statement by the Office of Chief of General Staff, not a common occurrence in Turkey.[10] Very much like the civilian side, the military sometimes seems confused on these issues, although on most issues it maintains unity.

The foreign ministry fully understands the consequences for Turkey if no solution for Cyprus is found, but it cannot force the decision. A Turkish compromise on Cyprus in return for the possibility of EU membership is denounced in nationalist circles. Interestingly, those who oppose a compromise on Cyprus are also lukewarm about membership in the EU and often resist liberal ideas. Moreover, many in all camps are skeptical of European intentions and of whether Turkey will ever get into the EU. The now infamous e-mail messages of the EU representative in Ankara denigrating Turkish discussion of the issue, which were deliberately leaked to the press early in 2002 in order to discredit the EU, were a sign of the discord within Turkey. This has increased suspicions in the public about EU intentions, while pro-EU Turks have seen to what extent anti-EU groups can go.

Pro-EU NGOs—led by the Turkish Industrialists and Businessmen Association (TUSIAD)—on the other hand are united in wanting a solution in Cyprus so that one of the main obstacles on the way to Turkey's membership will be cleared away. They have started lobbying for EU membership through newspaper ads, declarations, panel discussions, and meetings with the Turkish military.[11] Many businessmen believe that Rauf Denktash, the president of Turkish Cyprus, is neither interested in a solution nor in EU membership, although they generally fear to denounce him publicly.

As for Denktash himself, he has long been deeply involved in Turkish politics and knows how to exploit it. As soon as criticism about him appears, he immediately flies to Turkey to give one or two lectures and stir up nationalist feelings or to get guarantees from political leaders.

Many policymakers are unaware of the intricacies and formulations of peace proposals for Cyprus and their possible ramifications. For instance, it is not difficult to convince some political leaders that Denktash has broken important ground in negotiations since most are not well versed in reading between the lines. Fine print in such negotiations is important. Many have forgotten, for example, that after the

1997 EU Luxembourg summit, where Turkey's candidacy was refused and that of Cyprus was accepted, Turkey stopped supporting a federal solution in favor of a confederal one.

This case study shows the complicated, messy, and less than democratic nature of foreign policy decisionmaking in Turkey. For it to improve, politics in Turkey would need as dramatic an overhaul as the economy is going through under IMF pressure. This is not likely, at least in the short term.

THE NEW MILLENNIUM: NEW FOREIGN POLICY CHALLENGES

The terrorist attacks of September 11 on the United States shocked Turkey. Turkey immediately distanced itself from agitated Muslim countries, in part fearing it would be thrown in with the rest of the "Islamic world." Despite pronouncements of condemnation by their governments, most people in the Arab world demonstrated in favor of Osama bin Laden. Such demonstrations did not take place in the Turkic world—that is, Turkey, Azerbaijan, and Central Asian republics. That difference can in great part be explained, I believe, by the influence of secularism in Turkey and a different Turkic interpretation of Islam.

Turkey has taken its usual and expected place beside the United States in the war against terrorism. Many in Turkey saw in this attack a vindication of Turkey's secularist and antiterror stand in the long war against the PKK. Some writers in Turkey even dubbed the new policies of greater sensitivity to terrorism and secularism in the West as "28 February" on a global scale, a reference to the beginning of the Turkish military's destruction of the coalition government headed by the Islamist Necmettin Erbakan.

TURKEY'S POSITION IN THE WORLD

From a Turkish perspective, the September 11 attacks were a reaffirmation of Turkey's increased political significance as a secular and democratic Muslim country and its strategic importance as a reliable ally in unstable regions of great importance such as the Middle East, the

Caucasus, and Central Asia. The months following the attacks contrasted with the days of the demise of the Soviet Union, when Turkey desperately tried to find a credible role for itself. At that time, there were genuine fears in Turkey that it had lost its strategic importance for the West and would gradually lose its support from the United States and its allies.

It is always difficult for the successor country to an empire to accept a minimal role and to be considered insignificant. Turkish leaders invariably seem to feel the necessity to issue periodic official statements asserting Turkey's continuing relevance as an important Western-oriented outpost or, more frequently, as a "bridge between East and West." This rhetoric seems to fit the American concept of Turkey as well, which American leaders also often repeat. Yet, as Ian Lesser points out, an arm's-length relationship between Turkey and its Middle Eastern neighbors could have limited success, and a growing political role of Islam would risk estrangement of Turkey from the West.[12] Indeed, Turkey's opening to the Arab world has had limited success; however, Islam's political role in the country has increased. Turkey's "bridge" role has not brought any tangible results or much global acknowledgment beyond some laudatory statements from abroad, usually made to please the Turks, who very much want to hear them.

Following the September 11 attacks, Prime Minister Ecevit started to reemphasize publicly and frequently Turkey's role as a model for other Islamic countries including Afghanistan. He stressed the Turkish model in his statement at the EU-Islamic Conference. Indeed, in February 2002, Turkey—wanting to show to the EU its international reach—organized a meeting in Istanbul between the EU and members of the conference to encourage greater understanding between the Christian and Islamic worlds. After the meeting, the then foreign minister Cem stated that the "bridge" role did not adequately describe Turkey's importance. Rather, Turkey was, he said, a "meeting place, a crossroads of civilizations."

Turkey's interest and willingness to play a larger role on the international scene manifests itself in other ways as well. As UN peacekeeping missions in the 1990s mushroomed, Turkey—taking pride in its disciplined armed forces—participated alongside its allies in such disparate places as Somalia, Bosnia, and Kosovo. Turkey was also one of the first countries to send troops to Afghanistan. Despite uncertainties and difficulties, Turkey decided after much American importuning and funding to assume the command of the International Security Assistance Force in Afghanistan in April 2002.

TURKEY'S POSITION IN THE MIDDLE EAST

Turkey's relations with its Middle Eastern neighbors have always been uneasy and hardly warm. Its imperial legacy left a long shadow. Turkey has long been careful not to be dragged into inter-Arab conflicts and rivalries but rather to develop good bilateral relations with all countries. With moderate Arab countries relations have been satisfactory. With countries such as Saudi Arabia and Iran, however, Turkey remained at arm's length. Turks are convinced that these countries have tried to erode secularism in Turkey, that they have spread much largesse around for that purpose, and, in the case of Iran, that it has carried out terrorist acts on Turkish soil. Relations with Iraq have been complicated by the loss of trade from the embargo, the Iraqi Kurdish question, and the general support to U.S. forces in the area by Turkey. Relations with Syria have significantly improved since the expulsion of Öcalan and his capture, as well as the death of Hafez Assad. Turkey understands that these regimes are neither modern nor predictable. Indeed, many of these regimes see a democratic and secular Turkey as a threat to themselves. It is an uneasy relationship for both sides. Trade with the area is important for Turkey, especially given its continuing economic crisis.

Over the past decade, Israel has become an important partner for Turkey—politically, strategically, and economically—without endangering Turkey's relations with Arab states. Israel, for its part, finds in Turkey a strategic partner in a region where it has no friends. Turkey recognized Israel quickly in 1949, but until the 1990s formal relations were complicated by the Palestinian issue. Turkey has always supported the Palestinian right to statehood and what was happening in the area affected Turkish policies. Relations between Turkey and Israel were unstable, and there was no exchange of ambassadors for a long time.

In the 1990s Turkey decided to solidify relations with Israel for a number of reasons: to balance its alleged pro-Arab policies, to bolster its intelligence, to expand trade and investment, to secure help against

Syria if necessary, and to increase support from the United States. Özal even proposed a "peace water pipeline"—from Turkey, through Syria, to Israel and Jordan—that did not materialize, among other reasons, because of little enthusiasm from Arab countries not wanting to share water with Israel. Turkey has signed agreements with Israel on trade, tourism, scientific exchange, and defense, despite protests from Arab countries. The intelligence relationship is close and Israel has been a source of military technology, particularly for defense items that Turkey has trouble procuring from the United States. Israel modernized Turkish F-4 and F-5 aircraft and recently M-60 tanks, despite the vastly increased tension between Israel and Palestine and the domestic political uproar in Turkey. Indeed, the agreement for the modernization of tanks was signed on March 12, 2002, the day that Israeli tanks moved into Ramallah. The media strongly protested the agreement but nothing changed.

Finally, Turkey has been deeply interested in obtaining the support of the Jewish lobby in the United States. Turks felt that American Jews could act as a powerful counterweight in the U.S. Congress to the Greek and Armenian lobbies and help build broad political support for Turkey in the United States. Turkey enlisted the help of the government of Israel and the Jews in America to win approval of the customs union in the European Parliament.

Events in the Middle East in 2002 often have been a difficult balancing act for Turkey and frequently put the government at odds with the press and public opinion. Prime Minister Ecevit called Israeli actions in the West Bank "genocide" in March 2002, but in the face of an uproar from American Jews and criticism in Turkey, he made amends and quickly dropped the use of that term. Except for the religious political parties, the public did not take much issue with the substance of Turkish–Israeli relations until the events of March 2002 in the West Bank. By and large, Turkey has been unbiased in the Israeli–Palestinian issue. Through diplomatic channels Turkey criticizes both Israel and Palestine depending on the case, and both find in Turkey an *interlocuteur valable*. Even though Turkey is fully aware of the vital role the United States plays in this issue, Turkey, as a successor state to the Ottoman Empire that once ruled Palestine, believes that it can act as a facilitator because of its good relations with both parties. That is one reason why Turkey proposed Istanbul as the venue for an international conference on Palestine.

Israeli prime minister Ariel Sharon and his policies, however, have not been well received in Turkey. The very negative public opinion of Sharon will undoubtedly have an impact on how further Turkish–Israeli relations will evolve. One has to remember that, though a secular state, Turkey's population is overwhelmingly Muslim.

TURKEY AND THE FORMER SOVIET UNION

The end of the Soviet Union left Turkey with no common border with Russia and a host of new neighbors in the Caucasus and Central Asia. With most Turkic countries the Turks feel a kinship. Moreover, the Caspian basin has become a huge new energy source, opening major commercial opportunities. Turkey recognized the three Caucasian countries simultaneously. Relations with both Azerbaijan and Georgia developed rapidly in many areas. Turkey's growing relationships made possible a concrete, enormous project: the Bakü–Tbilisi–Ceyhan energy pipeline. Significantly, it was Turkey that proposed that the Bakü–Ceyhan pipeline should go through Supsa in Georgia. Turkey has tried to provide both countries assistance in all fields, as it considers their security and independence vital to its own interests. It lobbied to remove American restrictions on aid to Azerbaijan, which were finally ended after September 11. Turkey helps Georgia even militarily, apparently with some coordination with the United States. Turkey believes that the present chaotic situation in this region serves Russia's purpose, as weak regimes perpetuate the latter's relative preponderance. Turkey's aim has been to work to stabilize these countries, in great part by pursuing greater U.S. involvement in the area, as with the Bakü–Ceyhan pipeline.

In comparison to relations with Georgia and Azerbaijan, those with Armenia have lagged far behind. The contentious issue of the Armenian genocide bedevils any effort to improve relations. But the principal issue has been the Nagorno-Karabakh dispute. Turkey closed its borders with Armenia under Azeri pressure because of Armenia's occupation of Nagorno-Karabakh. Turkish–Armenian relations are not likely to improve unless Azeri–Armenian relations improve. Despite bilateral meetings at the highest levels, the U.S.-sponsored reconciliation committee, and meetings among businessmen, relations between the two countries remain frozen. Even though Turkish products find their way into Armenia via Iran and Georgia (at much higher prices), many Turks are eager to see the border opened. Opening the borders, the Turkish government believes, may give Turkey some leverage over Armenia as well, in turn perhaps facilitating a solution to Azeri–Armenian problems. Moreover, trade relations, it is hoped, can gradually lead to some sort of broader reconciliation between Turks and Armenians and lessen Armenia's considerable dependence on Russia. In any event, it is generally recognized in Ankara that the present situation between Armenia and Turkey cannot last. Ultimately, Turkey wants a peaceful and independent Caucasus so that it can benefit from the energy resources of the Caspian basin without Russia's interference. Turkey also sees its active role in both the Caucasus and Central Asia as an element increasing its "value" in the eyes of the EU.

The newly independent Central Asian republics initially attracted great attention from the Turkish political and economic elite. Some right-wing politicians in Turkey professed to see in Central Asia an alternative to the EU and favored much closer cooperation among Turkic republics. There was, however, little support for such a construct in any of these countries including Turkey. In several countries in Central Asia, Turkey did assist in institution-building by sending advisers in numerous fields. Conscious that these newly independent countries relied heavily on Russia, Turkey wanted to lessen their dependence. Turkey also felt a similar need to counterbalance the activities of antisecular Iran and Saudi Arabia.

Turkish businessmen moved in quickly and started to invest, winning many bids in the fields of infrastructure and industry. However, the sometimes patronizing attitude of Turkey was not well received by the leaders in those countries, and Turkish businessmen added significantly to the already vast corruption in the area. In addition, Central Asian countries felt that they were exploited by Turkish politicians seeking domestic electoral gains. Activities by some Turkish religious circles also caused irritation in those countries.

Both in terms of economics and politics, the Turkish government soon realized that Turkey could not shoulder the vast needs of these countries alone. Moreover, besides Russia, Turkey was also competing for influence with two rich, often disruptive, players: Iran and Saudi Arabia. Turkey again turned to the United States for help in trying to maintain reasonably stable, independent states in Central Asia, particularly after September 11. Turkey sees itself as and in effect has become something of a spokesman for these countries in international fora. It played an important role in securing their membership in the Partnership for Peace in NATO and in the OSCE. Turkey maintains close political, economic, and commercial relations with most of Central Asia, although relations with Tajikistan lag behind, as this country is not Turkic.

Turkey's initial push in the Caucasus and Central Asia obviously did not leave its relations with Russia untouched. Frequent statements by senior Turkish leaders telling the world of "Turkish influence from the Adriatic to the Great Wall of China" caused great irritation in Russia. Not surprisingly, Russia started to see Turkey as a competitor for influence, trying to fill the vacuum left behind by the collapsing Soviet Union and turning the new states against Russia. All this created tensions in relations between Turkey and Russia, despite official assurances from the Turkish side that it had no intention of replacing Russia. As Stephen J. Blank has correctly pointed out, the present Turkish policy is to combine two strategies: to build cooperative ties with Russia and at the same time to build a controlled policy to spread Turkish influence and keep Russia away from Turkey's borders.[13]

Economic relations with Russia have significantly expanded, first with the famous and very large "suitcase" trade, later with Turkish investment and construction in Russia, and more recently with the decision to lay a natural gas pipeline under the Black Sea to Turkey. The most important specific disagreement remains Russia's concern over Turkey's aid to Chechen terrorists. Turkey has repeated often that it does not help the Chechens and that it supports Russia's territorial integrity. But under Turkish law, people who have carried out armed actions for the Chechen cause are not considered terrorists. Ironically, Russia accuses Turkey of using double standards on terrorism, an accusation Turkey often holds against Europe with regard to the PKK. Turkey has been more careful on this issue since September 11. The influx of thousands of Russian tourists that come to Turkey each year may slow if the negative perception of Turkey's attitude toward Chechnya continues.

Both countries have long considered themselves as rivals. Notwithstanding democratic changes in Russia over the past decade, Turkey has continued to look at Russia with suspicion. Only recently has that begun to change. The economic relationship in particular has become very important to Turkey. Moreover, Russia has now become a partner of NATO and the United States, a relationship with the West that will have implications for Turkey. Turkey will have to adjust its policy to changed times and seek greater cooperation with Russia, particularly in Central Asia and the Caucasus.

TURKEY AND THE EU

In the 1990s, Turkey started criticizing the EU for being a "closed Christian club" and openly accused the EU of discriminating against Turkey on religious grounds. Turkey reacted harshly when the EU rejected Turkey's bid for candidacy in 1997 at its Luxembourg summit, virtually breaking off all dialogue. It was evident that the EU was not keen on Turkish membership. But at Helsinki in December 1999, the EU ostensibly changed its mind on potential Turkish membership and formally declared Turkey a candidate.

This sudden shift of policy surprised many observers, as not much had changed in Turkey. Turks have put forward several theories explaining this change. One is that the EU is not really serious about Turkish membership but uses it as a lever to solve the Cyprus question. They expect that, at the end of the day, even if the Cyprus issue is resolved, Turkey will be kept out. Another theory is that the EU became convinced that leaving Turkey in the lurch in the long run would cause instability and encourage radicalism in the country.

But if Turkey wants to meet EU criteria to begin accession talks, let alone gain full membership, some further crucial steps have to be taken, even though it has taken important legal steps already. The main remaining hurdles, as seen by the Turks, were abolishing the death penalty in particular, and respect for human rights in general, allowing instruction in Kurdish and Kurdish TV broadcasts, finding a solution in Cyprus, and limiting the political power of the military. In a very surprising development in May 2000, the parliament, after deciding for early elections, sat in marathon session to pass legislation to help meet the Copenhagen criteria in the field of human rights. Parliamentary actions stunned the Europeans as well as most Turks. Turkey will also have to clean up its serious economic problems.

Europeans generally understand the unique role the Turkish army has played in Turkey's history, but they believe that the military's involvement in political life should lessen. The European concern regarding Turkey's National Security Council and the role of the military goes well beyond the number of participating civilians in the NSC. Nor is the concern limited to whether the NSC merely "advises" the government, as stipulated in the changed version of the constitution. Some have suggested that the secretary general of the National Security Council should be a civilian. Ultimately, the EU wants the military, as in all the other EU countries, to play no political role at all and disapproves of any military overriding of civilian decisions, tacit or explicit. Hence, the EU has preconditioned accession on institutional changes to help ensure civilian control over the military and better consolidating a liberal democracy in Turkey.

Even though the military establishment finds it difficult to deal with the pressures of EU membership, I believe it is not seeking alternatives to the EU. The military prefers EU membership, but with as little change in Turkey as possible on neuralgic issues such as Kurds and including keeping their own prerogatives in the decisionmaking process. In short, they want the EU to take into consideration Turkey's "peculiarities." As guardians of secularism and territorial integrity of the fatherland, they fear that "EU liberalism" may erode secularist policies, promote Islamic parties, and ultimately lead to Kurdish efforts at secession. But without limiting the political role of the military, Turkey will not likely accede to the EU. Still, the military also understands the economic benefits to Turkey of EU membership. Given the immense technological developments in weaponry, how the Turkish military establishment will continue to finance its modernization given the fiscal difficulties of the country is a question that has not yet fully been taken into account by the military.

Notwithstanding all the uncertainties, the changes in the EU's approach to Turkey and the preconditions, EU membership is strongly supported by the Turkish public. They believe it will lead Turkey to rapid and sustained economic progress; various polls show support as high as 70 percent. Many feel that this year may be the last chance for EU membership and recall with deep regret the grave mistake of not having taken the opportunity to apply for membership in the 1970s along with Greece. Indeed, EU membership has become Turkey's highest foreign policy priority since the EU declared it a candidate at the 1999 Helsinki summit. Turkey would like to fix a date to start membership negotiations in 2003, without which it fears that it will lag ever further behind other candidates and that its membership could be postponed indefinitely. Some economists fear that, without fixing the start of membership negotiations by the end of 2002, Turkey may face difficulties rolling over its internal debts.

But political reforms have been embroiled in politics, primarily by the opposition of the nationalist National Action Party as well as the True Path Party of Çiller, both of which compete for the same nationalistic electorate. In addition, many Turks do not realize how much the world has changed and that with that change have come new meanings for concepts such as sovereignty, ethnic rights, and so forth.

The Turkish way of reasoning and its approach to these neuralgic issues is a problem indeed. Misconceptions about Kemalism play a role. Many Turks do not realize that Atatürk's reforms were dynamic, not static. For instance, a retired general once remarked that the EU was against the nation-state concept and as such did not accord with Atatürk's views. Such statements have led many Europeans to conclude that Kemalism itself stands in the way of Turkey becoming an EU member.

In addition, Turks usually express themselves as being "not against" something; they rarely say that they are "for" something. Turks tend to think in concepts such as "giving in" or "giving away something." "Win-win" scenarios are uncommon in Turkish thinking: one side wins, the other side loses. Turks usually believe that they have lost in negotiations, regardless of the topic. Indeed, certain segments of the ruling elite, including some military officers, see EU norms as being forced on Turkey, whereas these norms are of course common to all candidate states. In a sense, Turkey wants to get into the EU on its own terms.

My own view is that the Cyprus problem is as important as the human rights issue, and that policy is probably more difficult to change in the former area. I am not sure that this fact is fully understood by the Turkish elite. Despite the EU timetable for Cyprus, in Turkey the question has never been publicly put as a choice between the future of the sixty-five million people in Turkey and the fewer than two hundred thousand Turks in northern Cyprus. Moreover, the military is convinced that the civilians and the bureaucracy are not negotiating with the EU as aggressively as they should. In addition, many Turkish politicians, as well as General Kıvrıkoğlu, have criticized the EU for supporting terrorist organizations in Turkey; hence the intermittent anti-EU statements by the military. Recently, the EU—after enormous Turkish pressure—put the PKK on its list of terrorist organizations, an action welcomed by the military establishment, which considered it a litmus test for the EU.

If and when a negotiation date for EU accession is set, many of the doubts about EU intentions will likely dissipate; Turkey will probably take further steps both internally and externally to meet EU membership requirements and its economy will pick up. But the present doubts about EU intentions prevent Turkey from taking the steps that are required. The Sèvres syndrome (referring to the post–World War I 1919 treaty of the allies, which split Turkey up into different countries, was soundly rejected by Atatürk and ultimately was replaced by the Lausanne Treaty of 1923) is indeed still a factor in elite thinking. Indeed, many Turks, including members of the elite, fear that Turkey may break up as a result of liberal policies. It seems essential that Turkey get rid of its fear that once the Cyprus problem is solved, the EU will turn its back on it. In this regard, I would have thought that Turkish proposals on Cyprus would have been tailored more so as to facilitate future Turkish membership in the EU. For example, one may envisage the application of the three freedoms (free circulation, free settlement, and the right to buy property) as dependent on continuing Cyprus negotiations and the full withdrawal of Turkish forces synchronized with Turkish entry into the EU.

At the end of the day, the power to get out of the present deadlock on Cyprus lies in Ankara, provided that it can put forth some creative measures. But the outside world will also need to lean heavily on the Greek-Cypriot side; the Greek Cypriots have little incentive to negotiate a compromise given the assurance that Greek Cyprus will become an EU member even in the absence of a solution. Many people on both sides, not surprisingly, look to greater U.S. involvement to get out of the conundrum.

THE FUTURE OF U.S.–TURKISH RELATIONS

In the past decade, the U.S.–Turkish relationship has moved from the military partnership of the Soviet period into a much more multifaceted one. Frequent political consultations, expanding trade relations, and close bilateral cooperation during the Gulf War, in Afghanistan, and elsewhere have become common; there is greater understanding, greater appreciation, and greater interest in an even more ramified relationship. This would be more likely if the highest levels of the U.S. administration were to come forth with a more detailed perspective on the American approach to Turkey and how relations can be seriously deepened, not just rhetorically. For Turkey, one way of deepening relations is for the United States to treat Turkey on an equal footing with the countries of the EU (as Turkey has a customs union with the EU) and, for example, to see textile quotas significantly expanded. Turks would welcome more efforts to encourage private investment, which has been very limited. The U.S.–Turkey Joint Economic Council in February 2002 decided to create qualified industrial zones to help Turkish exports, and other ways to increase Turkish exports to the United States are being discussed. Most importantly, continuing U.S. support in IMF and World Bank lending is essential and expected.

The immediate problem facing U.S.–Turkish relations, however, is a possible American attack on Iraq. Even serious talk of an operation sends the fledgling Turkish stock market down. Turkey feels that the American obsession with Saddam Hussein is unjustified; Turks question both the threat Iraq poses as well as the benefits of a relatively more open regime in that country versus the enormous potential costs of achieving it. Turks fear two things in this regard: (1) the inevitable negative effect of war on the Turkish economy, particularly on its most important tourist sector, which is in crisis already, and (2) their expectation of the creation of some sort of Kurdish entity in northern Iraq in the war's aftermath. Only through close consultation at the highest levels and some assurances on what follows Saddam Hussein might the United States quell those fears.

If the United States is bent on removing Saddam Hussein through military means, Turkey will probably have to provide bases for the operation whether it wants to or not. But it will not likely provide military units, as fighting an Arab nation, unless in self-defense, is still anathema both to the Turkish government and to the public. In addition, Turkey will have to have prolonged and detailed consultations with the United States on whether and how the Kurds in Iraq are to be armed and trained and what sort of system and government will follow after Saddam. Turks are wary of the Kurdish leaders in northern Iraq and will want to monitor the situation closely to prevent the establishment of an independent Kurdish state. Turkey would not be happy with a federal Kurdish state as a part of Iraq either. The Turkoman population in Iraq is expected to be useful in controlling possible negative developments in northern Iraq. Nor should it be overlooked that the Turkish military is already a major factor in northern Iraq.

Concrete U.S. plans and intentions on Iraq are still unknown. Although Turks are confident in U.S. technology and its war machine, they are not sure that the United States is well-enough equipped to control and shape Iraqi politics after Saddam Hussein. As Turks feel that even a superpower can make mistakes and that Turkey will feel the impact of those mistakes more than any other country, Turkey proceeds with extreme caution on Iraq and urges the United States to do the same.

THE EU: THE BIG ONE

Perhaps the biggest long-term uncertainty that will affect U.S.–Turkish relations is whether or not Turkey will be allowed to enter serious negotiations for EU membership and ultimately win acceptance.

SCENARIO ONE: NO ACCESSION

If attempts to become an EU member fail, Turkey faces a potentially explosive situation. Some segments of the establishment, which are anathema to the EU, would consider special relations with the United States as an alternative. Turkey has for many decades looked to the United States for support on many issues, including most recently major financial rescues through IMF loans. In a way the United States has bankrolled Turkey. Without EU accession, Turkey would depend to an even greater extent on the United States in economic matters. Remarkably, some circles in Turkey believe that some members of the Bush administration would like to keep Turkey out of the EU in order "to make better use of a lonely Turkey." I believe that this is nonsense. In such a case, the United States would have to bankroll Turkey for years to come.

A country with a stagnant economy can hardly be a strategic partner of the United States. If in the short term Turkey cannot get a date from Brussels to start serious membership negotiations and does not become an EU member in the medium term, U.S.–Turkish relations would remain within a regional and truncated context. Financially dependent on the United States, Turkey would effectively be limited to implementing whatever "tasks" are given to it by the United States and end up as a difficult and sulky partner, as successive economic crises have gone a long way to remove the last vestiges of Turkish self-confidence.

Turkey would have to rely more on the United States for investment, financial rescue as necessary, and probably its export trade. Turkey would have to turn to countries other than the United States as well as a sort of substitute to the EU. Relations with Israel could become important, in part to help strengthen relations with the United States given Israel's clout in the United States and in international financial circles. Turkey also would focus on relations with Russia and neighboring countries for greater trade and investment opportunities. Cooperation with Russia in particular would likely grow in many fields. There also would be attempts by nationalist circles to try to significantly expand ties with the Caucasus and Central Asia. As to the Balkans, Greece is an EU member already, and Bulgaria, Romania, and most republics of the former Yugoslavia expect to become members. If Turkey remains outside the EU, Turkey's role in the Balkans would be further reduced, despite its historic ties with the region.

It is difficult to forecast the internal ramifications of a possible failure to gain accession. Many Turks think they would be dire. My own view is pessimistic, that a sense of withdrawal would prevail, that self-confidence would be difficult to reestablish, that nationalist feelings and slogans such as "Turks have no friends but Turks" would be on the rise, and that ethnic strife in southeastern Turkey could resurface. Turkey's European vocation, by and large, despite official statements to the contrary, would come to an end. The search for identity would intensify. In the eyes of many countries in the region as well as in Central Asia and the Caucasus, Turkey would be considered as a Middle Eastern country. Turkey's status and prestige would diminish.

A failure to gain real access to eventual membership would have disastrous economic repercussions as well. The Turkish Industrialists and Businessmen Association has indicated that without the serious likelihood of EU membership, Turkey would not be able to attract the necessary foreign investment and the economy would grow slowly if at all. I fear that the ruling elite in Turkey fails to appreciate fully the wider implications of a failed accession effort.

From a European perspective, Turkey would be regarded as a failure, despite official European attempts to cushion the blow. For fear of a radicalized Turkey at its doorstep—the so-called nuisance value—Europe would try to keep tight, albeit at arm's length, relations with Turkey through "special" relations, as advocated by some circles in the EU. There would be attempts on the part of some in Turkey to end the customs union with the EU and replace it with a free trade area with the United States. For Turkey, to put it succinctly, the failure to march toward membership would result in every sense in a much greater dependence on the United States and NATO. Having enacted important legislation to meet the Copenhagen criteria in extraordinary sessions of the parliament in August 2002, Turks now expect the EU to respond by setting a date for membership talks to begin. That remains uncertain, and there may be much last-minute bargaining on Cyprus on the eve of the Copenhagen EU summit.

SCENARIO TWO: ACCESSION

If Turkey begins a serious process of integration into the EU, U.S. expectations of Turkey in many areas (growing democracy, improved economy, and so forth) would be fulfilled. The U.S. efforts during the 1990s to deepen democracy and liberalize the political scene and economic life in Turkey coincide with the EU agenda on Turkish membership. As a member of the EU, Turkey's "shopping list" in Washington would be much shorter. For many matters, in particular the economy, Brussels would obviously become more important than Washington. The Turkish government would perforce focus much of its energies on adjusting to Brussels.

This does not mean that the United States would lose its relevance for Turkey. Even though Turkey would have to follow EU norms and policies, it would still need U.S. investment, science and technology, and education. Rescue operations by the United States, through the IMF, on the other hand, would be less likely. Turkey's geographic location at the most eastern edge of the EU would still continue to be extremely important for the United States in security matters, despite the evolving European Common Foreign and Security Policy. Turkey would still be a partner of the United States in the fight against terrorism, in helping to find solutions in the Middle East, and by contributing to the support of U.S. policies in the Caucasus and Central Asia, regions where the United States is more involved than the EU. Turkey could become, even more than now, a useful and confident partner.

Just like Britain on the western edge, Turkey would be a partner on the eastern edge. And just like Britain, it would want to maintain special defense ties to the United States.

In the final analysis, despite the necessary adaptation to the policies of the EU, Turkey would try to make its relations with the United States as complementary as possible with its position in the EU. Despite recent disagreements, the United States and the EU still share a general understanding of global issues and ultimately common values. Where U.S. policies may differ with the EU on some regional issues, Turkey can, just like Britain, follow a policy that is sensitive to U.S. concerns. Moreover, many of the U.S. requirements in regions where Turkey may play a role are issues beyond the direct purview of the EU.

CONCLUSION

It is difficult to make a broad assessment of the effectiveness of Turkish foreign policy in just a few pages. Foreign policy is the mirror image of a country's internal situation. During the past half-century, Turkey's internal political and economic situation has been fluid and unstable, and so was its foreign policy. Despite this serious and continuous drawback, Turkey made only one grave mistake in terms of foreign policy—turning its back on the EU in the 1970s when offered the opportunity for membership, while Greece went in. By and large, Turkey has exploited its geostrategic location well, as shown by the numerous financial rescues of the international community, largely prodded by the United States.

Turkey has had some other foreign policy successes. Despite limited financial resources, Turkey has played an important role in Central Asia, the Caucasus, and the Balkans. Through membership in NATO it is considered an important and reliable country to be reckoned with. NATO membership, the 1960 Cyprus agreement, and the EU's formal declaration of Turkey as a candidate were notable successes. Turkey succeeded in differentiating itself from the Middle Eastern countries and stressed its European vocation.

But significant problems have persisted. Necessary internal reforms and adaptations to changing conditions have been late and unenthusiastic; even the present internal reforms, so useful to Turkey on their own, are being made under foreign pressure, which diminishes

Turkey's ability to be proactive. Turks have not fully understood that present-day diplomacy is not solely the domain of the foreign ministry and the military; only slowly are they realizing that the parliament, the business community, the academic world, labor unions, the media, and NGOs can contribute to the shaping and execution of a country's foreign policy. Unfortunately, for a long time Turks have been inward looking, convincing themselves that they are always right and the outside world is wrong. Local rather than global politics have carried the day when Turkey must seek the maximum benefit from globalization. The question, "what damages 'Turkish pride' more"—fulfilling EU norms or the fact that half the population of Turkey would like to leave the country—must be answered, and now. Indeed, the parliament responded in a significant way by enacting important legislation to meet the EU criteria.

Some see the EU as the last and only chance for modernity, reform, and change in all fields. Throughout history, except during the Atatürk era, Turkey has only changed through outside persuasion. Therefore, if Turkey does not reform now as required for EU membership, it is unlikely to do so at all in the near future. Indeed, Deputy Prime Minister Yılmaz has said publicly that without Turkish integration in the EU, Turkey will be like one of the inward-looking Baathist regimes in the Middle East.

Turkey is now at one of the most important crossroads since the establishment of the republic in 1923.

CHAPTER SIX

THE POST–SEPTEMBER 11 UNITED STATES THROUGH TURKISH LENSES

CENGIZ ÇANDAR

It is almost a universally accepted truth that "the world will never be the same" after September 11, 2001, the day the territorial immunity of the world's sole superpower was brutally violated. American grief was turned into American anger. The United States compellingly reasserted its global might.

This new chapter in world history started at a moment when the relationship between Turkey and the United States was as close as it had ever been. Such positive relations have not always been the case, however; indeed, the bilateral relationship has never been conflict-free. There have been twists and turns, and sometimes the relationship seemed near break-up. The 1980s, however, with Turgut Özal at the helm of Turkish decisionmaking, began a new era of Turkish–American relations, crowned by close cooperation in the Gulf War and changing Turkish perceptions of the United States. The change in relations also coincided with the collapse of the cold war's international order, the new unique position of the United States, and technology-driven globalization. Turkey's free-market reforms and vast International Monetary Fund (IMF) infusions of funds further cemented Turkish–American ties.

After September 11 new dynamics came into play. How Turkish–American relations will evolve in this new, emerging world remains to be seen.

The making of foreign policy in Turkey, probably more so than in most other countries, is the province of the elite. An examination of elite perceptions of the United States, and particularly the impact of September 11 on them, sheds light on the culture and thinking of Turkey's political class. This chapter takes a close look at the perspectives of the military and the changes in their perceptions of the United States after September 11. All this facilitates understanding of the complex relationship between Turkey and the United States.

An analysis of only the civilian and military elite is insufficient, however. New research on Turkish public opinion provides an essential addition to the analysis of Turkish foreign policy attitudes. Indeed, elite perceptions increasingly are no longer shared by the public. Popular perceptions—public opinion—for example on such issues as the Arab–Israeli conflict, have come to play an increasingly important role in influencing elite perceptions and hence Turkish foreign policymaking. In short, democracy is having an impact on Turkish policy. Finally, the chapter discusses the impact on Turkish perceptions of U.S. policy toward Iraq and Turkey's possible accession to the European Union (EU). I close with some observations on how changes in Turkish society and political culture may affect U.S.–Turkish relations.

PERCEIVING SEPTEMBER 11

I saw the World Trade Center in New York collapse on television while I was writing my daily column for a Turkish paper. I wrote: "A new page has opened in the world's history. Nothing will be the same. The events that unfolded yesterday in New York and Washington will prove to be more important than the fall of the Berlin Wall and the termination of the Cold War."[1] This prophecy was hardly unique. Timothy Garton Ash wrote "It may seem wild to suggest that how the United States responds to a terrorist attack, however large and horrific that attack, will shape the whole international system. It may yet be true. If the fall of the Berlin Wall was the true end of the short 20th century, there is a good case for arguing that the demolition of the

World Trade Center was the true beginning of the 21st. Welcome to another brave new world."[2]

Since the turn of the century the already strong relationship between the United States and Turkey has grown closer, largely because of Turkey's increasing dependence on the United States as the republic's worst-ever financial crisis unfolded. American support to secure the needed IMF credits was essential. To facilitate the arrangement, a Turkish vice president of the World Bank, Kemal Derviş, took over as the "economic czar" of Turkey. Most Turks believed that Derviş had the full confidence of the U.S. administration and that he would secure continued American financial support for Turkey. The financial crisis in 2001 made the United States the "indispensable nation," at least according to most Turks.

After September 11, Turkish officials were quick to express their solidarity with the United States and share its grief. Fearing that September 11 would negatively impact Turkey because the terrorists were Muslim, Turkish leaders publicly emphasized that terrorism should not be linked to any one religion, culture, or ethnicity. Turkey's foreign minister, İsmail Cem, warned:

> We are also against those who want to move this struggle to some other framework through erroneous interpretations and actions. Turkey is naturally the foremost opponent of those who want to portray this as a clash of religions; a clash between two different religions or cultures. To add any religion as a prefix to terrorism is the greatest disrespect to all religions. There can be no Islamic, Christian or Jewish terrorism, and we are openly conveying our thoughts in this regard to all friendly and concerned countries.[3]

Other prominent members of Turkey's secularist establishment shared Cem's concern. Former undersecretary of the ministry of foreign affairs Özdem Sanberk wrote in the *Financial Times* on September 18, 2002:

> The idea that people of Muslim background must be anti-Western or anti-American is a dangerous myth. In my view it has two causes. The first is a persistent failure of western public opinion to inform itself properly about Muslim countries and to rely instead on clichés and oversimplifications.

The second, which grows out of the first, is excessive readiness to accept claims by marginal extremists and radicals to be legitimate leaders and spokesmen. . . . Another result of these prejudices was a sort of "Bantustan" approach to Muslims and their world. Time and again, one hears some in the West suggest that Turkey ought to be "more Islamic" in its coloration. Atatürk's successful attempt to build a unified modern nation state in Turkey, with the twin goals of democracy and modernization, seems to be insufficiently appreciated in the western world, even though its own security rests to some extent on the existence of a strong, stable, and pro-western Turkey.

Sanberk's attitude leads to a paradoxical situation in which extremism in Islamic countries is actually fueled by the West. For Sanberk and the Turkish elite alike,

Turkey's Islamist movement, for example, is largely financed, and to some degree even organized, out of western Europe as are, incidentally, violent leftwing movements—to all of which the liberal western media turn something of a blind eye. The climate of chronic mutual mistrust is most acute in Turkish-European relations but hardly touches Turkish-U.S. relations. The Americans generally seem readier to accept Turkey on its own terms as a country constructing a modern democratic industrial society despite all its shortcomings. Twice in the past 12 months it has helped out generously in Turkey's worst-ever economic crisis. Europeans, although also supporting the IMF credit, give the Turkish public the impression that anyone who is opposed to the existing order in Turkey will be given a friendly hearing.[4]

Sanberk's article epitomizes the Turkish establishment's immediate response to September 11. The fear of a clash of civilizations led the latter to criticize Europe more than the United States. The United States was the target of the terrorist attack, and any indication of a clash of civilizations should have been expected from American policies rather than European ones. However, the Turkish establishment placed the blame, in this respect, on Europe.[5] Sanberk's assessment of the significance of September 11 was similar to that of

Turkey's military leadership. It is important to look more closely at the Turkish military's top leadership, as their views are decisive in policymaking.

General Yaşar Büyükanıt, the deputy chief of staff—considered to be the "strongman" of the military and the top candidate for the highest military post—gave the Turkish military's assessment in a speech two weeks after the attack. He declared bluntly, "On behalf of the Turkish Armed Forces, I condemn this blind terror in the strongest way and with hatred." He proceeded with a veiled but unmistakable criticism directed at Europe:

> New communication systems make distance increasingly irrelevant and help spread rapidly values such as human rights and the rule of law. However . . . they also open new avenues for wicked leaders, organizations and individuals to pursue their aims. As a result, lofty values such as human rights, freedom and democracy are being abused in developing countries as a justification for ethnic conflicts, separatism and destructive acts. This situation compels those responsible for security and defense to work on a broad spectrum, to find solutions to various issues, to produce threat scenarios, and even expand their imagination to take measures to meet these threats. . . . The attack on the United States teaches basic lessons to many countries. Turkey is at the top of the list of the countries that does not need to learn. Turkey experienced terror for many years and spent great efforts learning what terrorism is.[6]

Conveying the Turkish military's support for the American approach to the Kurdish Workers' Party (PKK) rather than that of the Europeans, he stated, "Turkey has fought terrorism for 16 years; it has lost more than thirty thousand citizens. This terror was directed from abroad and supported by many countries and I have to state with regret that it is still supported by those countries. . . . What makes us feel sorry is that those countries, which serve as a base for terrorism, are those who are also trying to teach us human rights."

The PKK, the nemesis of Turkish generals, was not included on the "list of terrorist organizations" compiled by the EU. This fueled the ongoing suspicions of Turkey's military leaders toward the EU. The

PKK was finally added to the list in spring 2002, but this did not dispel the Turkish military's unhappiness with the EU. The EU's national minorities policy, as well as the lenient attitude of member countries toward PKK-affiliated Kurdish groups and associations enjoying liberties to pursue anti-Turkish activities in their host countries, was seen by the military as European ill-will toward Turkish national unity and territorial integrity. The Turkish establishment was always wary of European attitudes on the Kurdish question and interpreted them as incentives to Kurdish-motivated terrorists.

In short, Turkish generals saw in September 11 the justification of their long war against the PKK and of their traditionally security-oriented policies in the face of European skepticism. The EU's criticism of Turkey has been focused on Turkey's failure to consolidate its democracy and on human rights violations, particularly against Kurds. Turks disliked European criticism of their military tactics against the PKK, including their large-scale incursions into Iraq. The fact that the EU has made it clear that the strong domestic political role of the military in public life impedes Turkey's prospects for EU membership obviously contributes further to military antagonism toward the EU. All these factors, plus the EU's lack of enthusiasm for Turkey's accession, have generated mistrust and a certain contempt of Europe in the Turkish military. Focusing on Europe after September 11 was a backhanded way of expressing Turkish support for the U.S. approach to terrorism.

LINGERING ANTI-AMERICANISM

For its special status in Washington, Turkey owes much to the vision and efforts of one man: Turgut Özal, Turkey's prime minister from 1983 to 1989 and president from 1989 until his death in 1993. Özal represented the pro-Western reformist-modernist tendency, which is rooted in the turn of the nineteenth century. Özal's views and policies were a unique mixture of his admiration for America's scientific and technical success and might with his strong attachment to pre-republican Ottoman-Muslim values. Özal was never under the influence of the European democratic-intellectual tradition. His references were American from the days of his early youth.

Until Özal, being pro-Western generally was synonymous with Europe for the modernizing Turkish elite. This manifested itself, for instance, in the European writers and philosophers the Turkish elite were familiar with and the administrative structures the Turkish state chose to adopt. The rise of American influence on the elite was a break with a tradition dating back to the French Revolution of 1789.

Despite Özal's U.S. orientation, the fifty-year-old U.S.–Turkish alliance, and the military and political camaraderie in conflicts ranging from Korea to Yugoslavia, certain skepticism toward America remains amid the general closeness, which provides the basis for a latent anti-Americanism. This skepticism has three causes: (1) the Johnson letter and the arms embargo, (2) the leftisms of the 1960s, and (3) the Islamic factor.

First, in the Turkish national subconscious there still lies a feeling of betrayal from both the infamous 1964 Johnson letter, which prevented a Turkish military intervention in Cyprus during the intercommunal strife that was aimed to salvage the outgunned Turkish Cypriot community, and the imposition of the arms embargo a decade later following Turkey's military intervention on the island. These two episodes had a devastating effect on Turkish feelings toward the United States. Turkish knowledge of how the U.S. system operates is poor, and the distinction between the American executive branch and Congress is not clearly made. The Turkish public also projects Turkey's own monolithic state structure on the United States. Thus, the role of Congress in imposing the arms embargo on Turkey in 1974 was overlooked. Rather, it was perceived as the betrayal or the evidence of unfriendliness of the entire American government.

Second, in the 1960s the Vietnam War became very important in shaping Turkish elite perceptions of America. Anti-Americanism erupted in Turkey, as it did almost everywhere else. Indeed, Turkey's *present* media, business, and military elite was largely shaped during that period. Although anti-Americanism is by no means prevalent anymore, it left traces in the minds of the elite that emerge from hibernation when the appropriate circumstances present themselves.

The third cause of skepticism is Islamism—that is, the Islamist political movement. As elsewhere in the Muslim world, Islamism in Turkey is one the main sources of anti-Americanism. This emanates from its ideological anti-Western tradition, as well as the mindset of the Islamist constituency and its social fabric. The Islamist constituency, coming mostly from a rural background resistant to globalist market dynamics and usually affected adversely by them, takes refuge in piety and has a negative attitude toward external influences. America, as the "world hegemon," in their view epitomizes all destructive external cultural influences. The concept of a "clash of civilizations" adds to their fears and imbues a confrontational stance against the United States.

Yet, none of this opposition has had much practical impact on Turkish policy after September 11. Islamist anti-Americanism, which was shared by some segments of secularist public opinion, did not go beyond a few protest demonstrations following the Friday prayers in urban centers and vitriolic articles in the Islamist press. There were no nationwide protests and only fractional public opposition. The Turkish government granted the United States the use of Turkish airspace and supported the American war effort in Afghanistan logistically at the outset of the crisis after only a slight hesitation. The Turkish parliament overcame the feeble resistance of the opposition parties and swiftly voted for the dispatch of Turkish special forces to Afghanistan. A Turkish general took part in the coordination of the American-led campaign at the operations' headquarters in Tampa, Florida. Turkey also offered intelligence assistance to the United States and sent troops to take part in the International Security Assistance Force (ISAF) in Afghanistan following the collapse of the Taliban regime and the establishment of an interim government. In April 2002, Turkey, encouraged by the United States, took over the command of the ISAF from the United Kingdom with little murmur of public disapproval.

Turkish support for America's fight against terrorism, however, was not unalloyed. Anti-Americanism in Turkey flared up during the American military campaign in Afghanistan. Islamists, antiglobalists, and many shades of pseudo-Marxists found in the Afghan war an opportunity to try to reactivate anti-American views. After the usual denunciation of terror, Turkish Islamists expressed outrage at the military campaign against the Taliban regime and al-Qaeda. But in the end, Turkish Islamist anti-Americanism turned out to be more bark than bite.

There was in fact no consensus among the variety of Islamists on how to interpret September 11 and how to react to the military campaign against the Taliban regime. The lack of consensus can be explained first by the fact that Turkish Islam has traditions and ideological sources different from the Islam of the Taliban and its ideological kin Saudi Wahhabism. The latter emanate from puritan versions of

Islamic interpretation and both are anathema to Turkish mainstream Islamic practices. Secondly, the attack on America on September 11 occurred during a period when Turkey's Islamism was healing its wounds and trying to reconcile Islam with modernity. Islamists were trying to recover from their traumatic political experience: the Turkish military removal of the Erbakan government in 1997 and the subsequent banning of the Islamist Welfare Party and, in 2001, of its successor, the Virtue Party. September 11 put Turkish Islamists into another embarrassing and traumatic situation. When the American military campaign got under way in Afghanistan, the Islamist reaction was widespread but lukewarm and somewhat confused.

AMERICA THE FRIEND, AMERICA THE ENEMY

The somewhat ambiguous reaction to current U.S. policy and the public's confused impression of the United States are reflected in a recent scholarly survey on Turkish public perceptions of foreign policy and international relations. The survey indicates that Islamist convictions occupy a minor place in Turkish attitudes toward friends and foes. It also warns against making generalizations on how Turks perceive international relations and react to foreign policy matters. The survey, the first of its kind, was conducted between November 1 and November 30, 2001—during the height of the American operation in Afghanistan. It produced surprising results.[7]

One question requested the respondents to rank "nations," on how "friendly" they are toward Turkey. On a scale from 1 to 10, the "least friendly" were to be given 1 and the "most friendly" a score of 10. Azeris (or Azerbaijani Turks) got the highest mark with 6.6. Surprisingly, the Japanese and Saudis followed with 5.4 and 4.8, respectively. Palestinians and Americans scored 4.6; the Kurds were next with 4.5. To complete the row: Europeans (4.3), Iranians (3.9), Israelis (3.2), Russians (3.1), Greeks (2.3), and Armenians (2.2).

One of the most striking results of the survey was on the question, "Which country is Turkey's best friend in international relations?" Of those polled, 34 percent responded "none," indicating persistent strong isolationist tendencies and Turkey's introvert nature. Nonetheless, when respondents were asked to name specific countries, the

United States surpassed all the others, with 27 percent. Interestingly, Azerbaijan and the Turkish Republic of Northern Cyprus, though considered as "Turkey's kinsmen," received only 6 percent and 2 percent, respectively. Pakistan's share was 4 percent, Europe's 7 percent, and the Muslim countries' 9 percent. The remaining 8 percent had no opinion.

The results of the question, "Which country is Turkey's number one enemy in international relations?" were equally interesting. Not very surprisingly, 34 percent of respondents picked Greece. The United States scored quite high as well, however, in second place with 21 percent. This indicates the sizable potential for anti-Americanism. Ideologically motivated prejudices and the usual causes of anti-Americanism elsewhere might explain this high score. As for Turkey's immediate neighbors—two of which President George W. Bush characterized as part of the "axis of evil"—Iraq and Iran were considered "enemies" by only 5 percent and 3 percent, respectively. Syria, which harbored Turkey's "public enemy number one," PKK leader Abdullah Öcalan, was considered "an enemy" by only 2 percent. These are all striking results. "Europe" was perceived as an enemy by 8 percent, "the other Muslim countries" by 4 percent, and "the whole world" by 4 percent. Only 3 percent of the Turks saw "no enemy whatsoever," while 8 percent of the respondents had no view.

An Ankara Social Research Center field survey on public perceptions of the conflict in the Middle East was conducted in early May 2002; that is, not long after the Israeli military incursion into the West Bank and the siege of Yasser Arafat's compound in Ramallah in March 2002.[8] This survey reveals the massive support of Turks for the Palestinians. In response to the question, "How do you feel about the Israeli occupation of the Palestinian territories?" only 3.7 percent found it "justified" and 87.4 percent "unjustified"; 8.9 percent gave no response. To the question, "Which party is on the right side, in general, concerning the Israel–Palestine conflict?" 72 percent responded Palestine, 7.6 percent Israel, and 20.5 percent gave no response. With regards to the American stance in the Israel–Palestine conflict, 7 percent of the respondents found it to be "neutral," 2.9 percent thought it to be pro-Palestine, and 76 percent considered it Israel-biased; 14 percent did not respond.

These figures may seem surprising in a country considered to be Israel's only strategic partner in the Middle East. However, the view of Israel as a partner is more an elite perception. The survey reflects clear popular sentiment in a Muslim Turkey and shows how recent good bilateral relations with Israel at the government level have not altered Turkish popular perspective toward the Israeli–Palestinian conflict. The notion entertained in some American circles and among the Turkish elite that Turks have a historical animosity toward the Arabs is fundamentally challenged, at least when it comes to Turkish attitudes toward the Arab–Israeli conflict. Turkish opinion is also influenced by the perception of the Palestinians as underdogs.

The Turkish government was not unaffected by the Turkish public's and media outrage in reaction to the escalating violence in the Middle East in April and May 2002. On April 4, Prime Minister Bülent Ecevit, bowing to the pressure, declared that Israel "committed genocide against the Palestinian people in front of the eyes of the entire world."[9] Other prominent Turks echoed similar sentiments without the "g-word." In response to international pandemonium Ecevit apologized for his remark.

All this, not surprisingly, had some backlash in Turkish–American relations, particularly in American conservative circles close to the administration. A *National Review* article, titled "The Turks, Too: Joining Anti-Israeli Left?" while trying to be self-assuring could not conceal its unease and ended with a stern warning. Referring to Ecevit's remarks, it said:

> What of Turkish-Israeli relations and, more importantly, Turkish-American relations? Naturally, Israel reacted with anger to Ecevit's baseless accusation, but many Israelis know Turkey well enough to see it in context. They know, too, that many Turks know it's a lie. In America, it's different. Our government sees Turkey as a key ally, but most Americans know little about Turks and tend, regrettably, to confuse them with Arabs, missing the huge differences between Turkish society and Arab societies; between a modern world of freedom, tolerance, and opportunity, and a bleak, savage society without them.[10]

The American conservatives' faith in the Turkish military's positive attitude toward Israel has a good foundation. For example, under strong military pressure and despite media disapproval, Turkey signed an "agreement for tank updates" with the Israeli Military Industries on March 29, a few hours after Israeli tanks surrounded Yasser Arafat's compound in Ramallah. Calls in some of the media to rescind the deal were dismissed.

The deterioration of the situation in the Middle East in April 2002 created a genuine wedge between the popular mood and party politics on the one hand and the military's position on the other. A consensus among the Turkish people is rare. Turkish popular solidarity with the Palestinians translated itself into various forms of expression. Many from all walks of life joined in publicly expressing sympathy and support for the Palestinian people. The Islamists, the Marxist left—long nonexistent on the political stage—trade unions, academic institutions, ordinary people, state officials, nongovernmental organizations (NGOs), conservatives, and liberals mounted a wave of protests against Israel. In magnitude they could hardly be compared to those in the Arab world, but the nationwide scope of the activity was unprecedented in Turkey. More recently, despite the continuing violence in the area, the level of indignation about the Arab–Israeli conflict seems to have declined, raising questions about the depth of Turkish feelings.

Does all this indicate an impending reorientation or subtle change in Turkish foreign policy? Hardly. The main decisionmaking body of Turkish foreign policy—on major issues of strategy and security—is the military, and the military is staunchly pro-Western. However, popular opinion no longer can simply be brushed aside.

The military watched the anti-Israel fervent closely and was uneasy with the criticisms over the tank deal between Israel and Turkey. The chief of staff, General Kıvrıkoğlu, baselessly accused the critics of being "inborn anti-Semites and those whose interests lie with the foreign firms spreading slanders against the military because they have lost the bid."[11]

During the ordeal of April 2002 in the Middle East, the military component of the Turkish elite was unyielding and solid as ever, running counter to Turkish public opinion. One has to conclude from this episode that, as long as Turkey's foreign policy is ultimately determined by the military and remains largely unaffected by civil society, the United States can rely on Turkish cooperation and coordination in its policies in the Middle East and elsewhere. But those days no longer seem so assured in the longer term.

THE UNITED STATES IN THE EYES OF THE TURKISH MILITARY

The military as the self-appointed protector of republican values, with its core belief in being "the backbone of the state" and its claim to be the main channel for the conduct of Turkish–American relations, deserves special attention. As the guardian of Turkey's ruling elite, it occupies a special place in understanding Turkish perspectives of the United States.

BEFORE SEPTEMBER 11

The military was the first and foremost Turkish institution to have deep and consistent relations with the United States, notably with the Department of Defense. The bond between Turkey and the United States did not originate from cultural affinity or from a large Turkish immigrant population in the United States, nor from commercial ties. Rather, it emerged from a pragmatic response to common security needs and goals. The military has been for a long period of time the preeminent Turkish institution dealing with the United States. Most American aid to Turkey has been for military purposes.

The military in Turkey has above all important ideological under-pinnings. Its "role" as the guardian of the Kemalist-nationalist legacy, the principles of the republic, and national unity intrinsically separate it from identification with any foreign power. Hence, the close military ties with the United States after Turkey's accession to the North Atlantic Treaty Organization (NATO) in 1952 were always presented or justified as a practical "business deal" and as collective security essential against the Soviet Union. Turkey needed NATO for security, but the military was always keen to demonstrate and reassert its nationalist creden-tials. It has been sensitive to being pictured as "pro-American."

The reality is more subtle. The military has not been unambigu-ously pro-American. The arms embargo against Turkey in 1974 in mil-itary eyes was totally unjustified. It was an unjust punishment by an ally, a punishment for fighting for both a national cause and a strategic interest. The arms embargo created a deep, acute, and lasting feeling of betrayal in the Turkish public, but above all in the military since it affected them directly. It crippled Turkey's strategic advantages over

Greece. The fact that even the cold war did not prevent the United States from imposing the embargo on an ally added insult to injury. After nearly four years of painful negotiations the embargo was lifted, but the damage was done. Nothing could at that point alleviate the Turkish military's distaste and lack of confidence in U.S. policymaking.

The 1980s did not have the drama of the 1960s or the 1970s. Nevertheless, during this decade U.S. military aid to Turkey was tied to military aid to Greece. The infamous seven-to-ten ratio proved to be unchangeable despite the Turkish military's conviction that its requirements demanded otherwise. The military was deeply angered by this ratio and believed that American arms sales were hostage to the powerful Greek lobby. Given the absence of an effective Turkish lobby in the United States, any change in the ratio seemed unattainable. Both the difference between the two political cultures and the lack of understanding of the complexities of the American political system helped sustain misperceptions of the United States. The Turkish military, convinced of its indispensable strategic value, simply did not understand the inability of the administration to lead Congress on issues of strategic importance to the United States. The military coup in 1980 further harmed U.S.–Turkish relations.

In November 1999 Turkey gave a very warm welcome to President Bill Clinton on his five-day visit—the longest of its kind. But warm as Turkish–American relations had once again grown in the 1990s, it was not possible to dispel totally the Turkish military mistrust for its Western partners, including the United States. A twenty-one-page booklet entitled "Main Issues," a publication of the general staff distributed to the armed forces in November 1999, did not spare the United States from bitter criticism. This document points out the ambiguities in U.S. foreign policy and how in some cases human rights and democracy were often pushed down the priority list in favor of other foreign policy objectives. Its depiction of the United States highly reflects the subconscious of the Turkish military on American policy.

> While refraining from selling Cobra helicopters to Turkey under the pretext that they might be used in operations violating human rights, the United States has not hesitated to sell them to Morocco for the same purpose (to be used against terrorists) under President Carter's special order, in October, 1977. The same U.S. government, while blaming Turkey for its human rights violations, has granted most-favored nation

status to China. President Clinton, despite intense public pressure, did not bring up the human rights issue during Chinese President Jiang's visit to Washington, in early 1997. And during his visit to China, Clinton only addressed this issue implicitly. Similarly, when Boris Yelstin killed many people—including some parliamentarians—in the shelling of the Russian parliament, Western countries accepted this as a necessary measure to restore democracy. . . . The United States, again, had found Turkey's intervention in Cyprus— where Turkey has the right of guarantee secured by international agreements—unjustified, and imposed an arms embargo for many years. But on the grounds that the lives of a few hundred students were in danger, the United States did not hesitate to invade Grenada; or under the pretext of "restoring democracy" to land troops in Haiti.[12]

An unofficial paper written in January 2002, "The Viewpoint of Turkish Civilian and Military Intelligentsia in Historical Perspective," prepared by Turkish General Staff (TGS) officers, reflects their assessment of relations with the United States and underlines important points in these relations. It is worthwhile to quote the last part of the text verbatim to grasp the Turkish military perceptions of the United States over time.

Despite all the tensions, parallel with the [technological] innovations in the post–Cold War period, American-Turkish relations have undergone a positive structural change. The intensity of bilateral relations in the military and political spheres reached its peak with the 1991 Gulf War Campaign. In 1991 with the aim of diversifying and naturalizing the relationship a new concept called "enhanced partnership" was promoted. Cooperation between the United States and Turkey is now placed under the title "the agenda with five fields of cooperation"; energy, economy and commerce, regional cooperation, Cyprus, and defense and security cooperation.

The closer relations and cooperation developed during the Gulf crisis have also influenced the outlook of Turkish intellectuals on America. The civilian intellectuals, who are more open to outside political influences are polarized

between "positive" and "negative" positions with respect to
the Gulf War. Intellectuals with military background also differ in opinion; however, their differences are not as deep and
clear as their civilian opposite numbers. Nevertheless, civilian and military-oriented intellectuals are united, to a large
extent, in their common evaluation that the outcome of the
Gulf War affected Turkey's security and economic interests
negatively. They, therefore, believe that "the activities of the
United States should be followed with skepticism" and "a
cautious attitude should be adopted toward America."

Although the Gulf War stimulated mixed reactions in various quarters of Turkish society, Turkey and the United States, as two close
allies, have consulted each other in crisis prevention and management,
regional conflict containment, deterrence of international norms and
conduct violations, fighting terrorism, and preventing the proliferation
of weapons of mass destruction. The joint activities in Bosnia and
Kosovo in the context of the NATO-led stabilization force in Bosnia
and Herzegovina (S-FOR) and the Kosovo force (KFOR), as well as in
Northern Iraq, are important examples of regional cooperation.

AFTER SEPTEMBER 11: "CAUTIOUS PRO-AMERICANISM"

Two years after Clinton's visit, September 11 seems to have further
changed Turkish military attitudes toward the United States.
September 11 compelled the Turkish military to undertake a new
strategic assessment of the international system, which, in turn, led to
a decided and different attitude from the long-lingering skepticism
toward the United States. There may still be some element of mistrust
in the subconscious of the Turkish military, but the new world order
after September 11 and the impressive demonstration of American
military might in Afghanistan influenced the Turkish General Staff to
adopt a "pro-Americanism" different in content and scope from before.
    In January 2002, a top-ranking general of the TGS, who asked to
remain anonymous, discussed at length with me the unpublicized
views of the military establishment about the United States in the
aftermath of September 11. While repeating the Turkish military's skeptical attitude toward the United States, he said that this is not unique to

the United States: "The Turkish military feels its obligation is to the country's security. It reserves the right to be always skeptical of anyone and anything that is non-Turkish." Emphasizing that he is conveying the "institutional viewpoint" of "headquarters," he added, "Among all countries, it is, nevertheless, the United States towards which the Turkish military has the most benign attitude."

He continued:

> From the perspective of the military, the best choice for Turkey is to be a fully independent country, which exercises leadership of some region of the world [with an allusion to the Turkic republics of former Soviet Union]. But the realities of the international system and the overriding principle of interdependence do not allow Turkey to do so, and the military establishment realizes this. Following September 11 the Turkish military sees a convergence of Turkish and American interests since Turkey also suffered much from terrorism. The commitment of the sole superpower to fight terrorism globally is in Turkey's interest. Moreover, the establishment of military tribunals in the United States to put terrorists on trial, while the European Union declines even to include such organizations as the PKK, the DHKP/C [Revolutionary People's Liberation Party/Front],[13] etc. on its terrorist list, is another reason why the Turkish military feels that Turkish interests are best served by cooperating with America.

Shortly after this conversation and much pressure, the EU finally included the abovementioned organizations on its terrorist list.

During our lengthy conversation, this high-ranking member of the TGS singled out Germany for some very critical remarks. My impression is that the TGS views on international relations have been largely shaped by nineteenth-century concepts of big-power rivalries and global struggle for spheres of influence. In this respect, the Turkish military sees the United States as "friendly" and as a "strategic partner," as opposed to—using the TGS characterization—the "German-influenced" European Union. Germany, for quite a long time, has been an undeclared venue for the Turkish military's mistrust. This is partly due to its being the host country for more than three million

Turkish citizens and the activities of separatist Kurdish and Islamist fundamentalist organizations. Germany, especially during the long tenure of Helmut Kohl and his Christian Democrat Party, also has been the main stumbling block to Turkey's quest for membership in the EU. Turkish military leaders tend to see the EU's national minority policies and emphasis on Turkey's poor human rights record as an indirect German-led effort to dislodge the United States from a sensitive geopolitical and energy-rich zone extending from the Balkans to the Caucasus and the Middle East, where Turkey sits as the main regional actor of stability and security.

Given this TGS view, National Security Council (NSC) secretary-general Tuncer Kılınç's well-publicized and controversial speech in June 2002 proposing a rapprochement with Russia and Iran "without neglecting the cooperation of the United States"[14] is, by no means, coincidental. The NSC has been the most influential foreign policy organ in the Turkish state for some time. It is dominated by the TGS and, as General Kılınç remarked in a symposium at the War Academy in March 2002, reflects the prevalent views of the top military leaders. General Kılınç argued that Turkey should seek "alternative alliances" in the face of the EU's manifest insensitivity toward Turkish national concerns. General Kılınç intended to voice the displeasure of the TGS publicly regarding the policies of the EU while giving precedence to strong ties with the United States. Although this speech was largely discounted in the media, it did not prevent unsurprising speculation that it expressed the views of the top military offices.

The text quoted below, also from the 2002 paper "The Viewpoint of Turkish Civilian and Military Intelligentsia in Historical Perspective," explains the Turkish military's official assessment of U.S.–Turkish relations, specifically post–September 11:

> The terror generated by radical Islam has been carried to a global scale through the September 11 attacks. The war against terrorism started by the Bush administration increased Turkey's importance for the United States because of Turkey's geographical location and its secular Muslim identity. At a period when postulates such as "clash of civilizations" or "inter-religious conflict," instigating an Islamic versus Christian confrontation were in circulation, Muslim Turkey's support for the American military providing its airbase facilities

elevated the bilateral relations to a sort of "strategic partnership" level. . . . It is obvious that future U.S. policies will be
decisive in further shaping the opinions of Turkish intellectuals. . . . Recently, the United States has been displaying a
positive attitude towards Turkey and consideration for
Turkish national interests. The sincerity of this recent attitude
and its continuity, will determine the (positive) evolution of
Turkish opinion of the United States.

Three main points in this text should be emphasized:

1. The military sees September 11 as an opportunity to
   enhance Turkey's importance in the eyes of American
   decisionmakers.

2. Turkey complied with the needs of the day and provided
   necessary logistics and support for the United States. The
   U.S.–Turkish relations thus moved from an "enhanced
   partnership" to a higher level that might be called a "strategic partnership." Already close relations grew even closer.

3. Yet, the Turkish military's attitude towards the United
   States always contains a note of caution. They are satisfied by the recent positive American approach to Turkey
   but whether this view will persist will depend on American
   conduct. This caution presently can be explained in part
   by the Turkish fear of an attack on Iraq. The Turkish military and other foreign policy makers are opposed to any
   change in the status quo in Turkey's periphery. In their
   minds, the risk of Iraq's break-up and the uncertainties
   about the intentions of the Kurds of Northern Iraq out-
   weigh the opportunities that the removal of the Saddam
   Hussein regime in Iraq would present.

The signals coming from Washington after September 11 that Iraq
would be a likely target have caused uneasiness in Turkey. The frequent mention of Turkey as a reliable American ally in the opinion
columns of the *New York Times* and other mainstream American media
and high expectations of an active Turkish participation in over-
throwing Saddam Hussein have especially enhanced Turkish appre-
hensions.

IRAQ: THE ACID TEST

Morton Abramowitz, in the introduction to his book *Turkey's Transformation and American Policy,* observed in 2000 that "the acid test of the U.S.–Turkish relationship is likely to come in Iraq when Saddam departs the scene."[15] Because of September 11, the "acid test" may come even before Saddam's departure from the Iraqi scene.

On the one hand, Turkish authorities, above all the military, are keen to cooperate in preserving and deepening the newly attained closer U.S.–Turkish relationship. This is particularly important given the U.S.-supported and IMF-supervised economic program to overcome the grave economic crisis. On the other hand, the highest officials seem never to miss an opportunity to voice their dissent with any American military operation against Iraq. The Turkish objections are at times explicit, at times muted, but they are incessant.

Prime Minister Ecevit has been the most persistent of these voices. Toward the end of his long political career and especially on the eve of Turkish elections scheduled for November 3, 2002, that would terminate his prime ministry, he has become even more vocal in his criticism of the American policy seeking regime change in Iraq. Turkey's veteran prime minister went as far to urge the U.S. President George W. Bush to make up his mind on military action against Iraq. It is noteworthy that he directed his most explicit criticism of American Iraq policy on the day of the first ever visit to Ankara of General Tommy Franks, the commander of the Central Command. Only a few hours following Franks' departure, Ecevit told the press:

> The American administration, on the one hand, is giving the impression that it's getting prepared for a military operation [against Iraq] and on the other hand, it announces that no decision has been taken yet for a military intervention. This contradiction is affecting Turkey negatively. We remain under great strain. Furthermore, developments in Northern Iraq are taking place thanks to U.S. guidance, protection and encouragement [to the Iraqi Kurds]. It is Turkey, more than anybody else, that is suffering from this American approach.[16]

As a matter of fact, his remarks, only ten days before Turkish election day, has become the peak of his persistent and consistent campaign directed against the American Iraq policy. It moved from veiled

criticism of American policies to vitriolic accusation. He blamed the
United States for not merely encouraging but actually guiding the Iraqi
Kurds toward independence, which Turkey is determined to prevent.
In a special interview with the daily *Milliyet,* after blaming the United
States for its assistance to the Kurds in northern Iraq, he said: "We
could say that a Kurdish state has come into being in Northern Iraq.
Turkey is being dragged into a war [by the United States] against its
will. . . . We do not want to fight. Thus, we will spend all diplomatic
means to that end. We do not want to have losses of life. We do not
want to send our youth to a war."[17] The next day, in an election, he
repeated this theme and went further: "The U.S. should be stopped
[from undertaking military action against Iraq]. . . . A great number of
our young people may lose their lives." He added that "in order to
involve Turkey in the war against Iraq, it is very probable that the U.S.
is fomenting trouble in Northern Iraq."[18]

Ecevit's remarks are not too surprising, since he vehemently
opposed Turkish cooperation with the United States during the 1991
Gulf War. Before the fighting began and after the war, he met with
Saddam Hussein in Baghdad. Nonetheless, his efforts to normalize
relations and promote trade with Iraq were widely supported in
Turkey, as has been his reluctance to ally Turkey to the United States
to achieve regime change in Baghdad. Not only Ecevit but also many
other Turks have repeatedly spoken out against any military campaign
in Iraq, fearing it could destabilize the region and harm the Turkish
economy, which was suffering from its worst recession in decades.

Turkish authorities, the President Ahmet Necdet Sezer and likewise the influential National Security Council, have insisted that any
action against Iraq should have United Nations approval. The official
Turkish position has been much closer to the French and Russian position than to its close and staunch American ally.

The Turkish business community is also not enthusiastic to see a
military operation unfold next door to remove the Saddam Hussein
regime. The continuing embargo against Iraq is varyingly estimated
to have cost Turkey over $30 billion since 1992, and many Turks
believe it has contributed to the current economic crisis. In this respect,
one of the most America-friendly and most credible pressure groups,
the mouthpiece of Turkey's biggest industrialists and businessmen,
TÜSİAD, voiced its disapproval of an American attack on Iraq, as far
back in 2001. Its chairman, Tuncay Özilhan, asserted that the business
community looks at this purely in economic terms. He added, "We

can see that Turkey's exports to Iraq are increasing. These are exports from the Southeast, which are very important at a time when Turkey needs production and exports. A new intervention may cause problems in Turkey, especially economic ones"[19] When an American-led military action on Iraq loomed inevitable, another powerful spokesman of Turkey's business community, the chairman of the Union of Chambers of Commerce and Industry, Rifat Hisarcıklıoğlu, estimated that "other sectors aside, the annual loss of the tourism sector alone would amount to 10 billion dollars." In an implicit bargaining discourse, he said that "if Turkey and Britain do not support a military operation in Iraq, the success of such an operation is not guaranteed."[20]

Military displeasure with possible U.S. military action against Iraq has been constant. Chief of Staff Kıvrıkoğlu visited Diyarbakır, near the Iraqi border, at the end of 2001 to reiterate that Turkey does not want any military action against Iraq. He did so in strong terms and on more than just that occasion. Despite the fact that an American military operation to remove Saddam seems almost inevitable, he said: "our perspective is clear. If something happens it won't be limited to the closing of oil pipelines like in 1990. For Turkey, a much greater threat would be on the agenda: an independent Kurdish state."[21]

NSC the secretary-general Kılınç remarked in an interview to a Lebanese daily newspaper in December 2001 that the Turkish military's resolve on the issue remained unchanged. "Turkey," he said, "will not participate in any attack against Iraq, and any Kurdish action that may jeopardize Iraq's territorial integrity will be met by an immediate Turkish military intervention, because Turkey cannot permit the establishment of an independent Kurdish state."[22]

Three key pillars of Turkey's policymaking—the executive, the military, and the business community—are opposed to a U.S. military operation to overthrow Saddam. On the other hand, Turkey's growing dependence on Washington will likely still ensure some degree of Turkish support for U.S. military operations if the United States can satisfactorily guarantee the maintenance of Iraq's territorial integrity. The Turkish government hopes that it will not be asked for military support, which it cannot refuse without serious consequences for U.S.–Turkish relations. It is quite possible that, despite its serious reservations, the Turkish government could make an about-face and follow Washington's lead on Iraq.

Deputy Secretary of Defense Paul Wolfowitz's visit to Turkey in July 2002, while the country was gripped in political turmoil, resurfaced

Turkey's concerns about military action against Iraq and its own participation. The visit attracted much attention in the media and from the public, despite their immersion in the ongoing domestic political squabbles. Wolfowitz, accompanied by Undersecretary of State for Political Affairs (and a former ambassador to Turkey) Marc Grossman and the SACEUR (Supreme Allied Commander in Europe), General Ralston, was blunt in his dealings with Turkish officials. He told Prime Minister Ecevit that "Whether Turkey participates or supports the operation against Iraq, the United States is committed to undertake action to remove the 'Iraqi menace.'"[23]

Before his formal talks in Ankara with Turkish officials, including the chief of staff, Wolfowitz delivered a speech to Turkish elites in Istanbul emphasizing the American administration's objection to an independent Kurdish state in Northern Iraq. Wolfowitz sought to alleviate Turkish fears further by giving them an incentive to follow the American lead. He said,

> It is vital to Turkey for the people of Iraq to govern themselves democratically, with full respect for the rights of minorities, including the Turcomans, and to maintain the territorial integrity of Iraq. A separate Kurdish state in the North would be destabilizing to Turkey and would be unacceptable to the United States. Fortunately, the Kurds of Northern Iraq increasingly seem to understand this fact and understand the importance of thinking of themselves as Iraqis who will participate fully in the political life of a future democratic Iraq. A democratic Iraq will stimulate economic growth with neighbors like Turkey and will stabilize the region.[24]

The message that Wolfowitz sent from Istanbul and in his face-to-face contacts in Ankara did not dispel the discomfort of the Turks for the increasingly looming U.S. military operation against Iraq. The Turkish position was conveyed to Wolfowitz under four headings:

1. An independent Kurdish state is unacceptable.

2. Turcoman rights must be ensured. In this respect, even if a federal Iraq is established following the removal of Saddam's regime, the oil-center city of Kirkuk, which is considered as mainly inhabited by Turcomans, and the province of Mosul cannot be part of the Kurdish federated zone.

3.   The Iraqi administrative structure that would replace Saddam's Baathist rule should have the consent of all ethnic groups in Iraq.

4.   Turkey's economic losses should be compensated.[25]

Prime Minister Ecevit, the military leaders, and other Turks also stressed to Wolfowitz that the Turkish economy, already facing very difficult circumstances, would be negatively affected by a military action in Iraq, possibly leading Turkey's fragile economy into further chaos. Thus, the American side was asked to consider rescheduling or erasing Turkey's foreign military sales (FMS) debt to the United States, worth $6 billion.[26] Ways of compensating Turkey for economic losses as a consequence of military action against Iraq were also discussed between Turkey's economy czar, Kemal Derviş, and Wolfowitz.

Despite Turkish worries that Iraq may disintegrate and continuing Turkish reluctance to support a military action against Iraq, Turkish leaders seemed to realize the inevitability of an American operation and the American determination to oust Saddam's regime. Thus, an aura of bargaining surrounded Wolfowitz's visit. The Turkish government will most probably end up following Washington's lead on Iraq.

THE EU FACTOR

Lastly, another important determinant for future U.S.–Turkish relations is Turkey's prospect for EU membership, something that the United States has supported for a long time. Turkey's EU membership has been the most polarizing issue in Turkey in 2002. Whether Turkey is allowed to join the EU will largely determine Turkey's economic and political future; it will also have strategic and geopolitical implications in a crucial part of the world and affect American regional and global interests. If Turkey's EU accession bid fails, the implications for Turkey's security, foreign policy, economy, and political reform will oblige Washington and Ankara to reformulate their relationship.

On this crucial issue, the military and some conservative domestic forces are skeptical about the desirability of Turkey's accession to the EU. On the other hand, the business community and roughly 75 percent of the Turkish people favor EU accession as quickly as possible. The most significant manifestation of support for the EU was put forward by a joint declaration of 175 organizations, associations, and prominent personalities in June 2002. This ad hoc group included TÜSIAD and its Islamist equivalent MÜSİAD; a leftist confederation of trade unions, DİSK, and the confederation of employers, TİSK; human rights groups; and the chamber of agriculture, the chambers of industry and commerce in Anatolia, and, above all, their influential parent organization, TOBB (Union of Chambers of Commerce and Industry of Turkey), which represents the small and middle-sized firms. The event was hailed in the press: "Turkey's civil society say: EU!"[27]

Proponents frequently describe EU accession as "the greatest project of Republican history" or "a civilization project." Adversaries, on the other hand, emphasize the danger of compromising national sovereignty, which they say would ultimately lead to Turkey's break-up (because EU membership requires the recognition of ethnic identities and thus of Kurdish rights) and loss of its independence. Though they have never been explicit, the conventional thinking of opponents to the EU is that the void from Turkey's exclusion from the EU could be filled and balanced by a strategic connection to the United States.

The Turkish elites believe that the Clinton administration in particular exerted constant pressure on the EU on behalf of Turkey. In contrast, the Bush administration, while formally supporting Turkey's accession, has focused more on the bilateral relationship, securing above all Turkish cooperation and involvement in its looming confrontation with Iraq. The Turkish pro-EU advocates did, however, receive a very strong and outspoken boost recently from Paul Wolfowitz.

Clinton, hosted by the Turkish-American Business Association, delivered a dinner speech in Istanbul on July 9, 2002, titled "Turkey, the EU and the United States." Concluding his speech, he said: "Our relationship is strong and will continue to be strong. When you enter the EU, it will be better for the United States. I want you to do everything necessary in order to enter the EU. . . . Your success is very important for the United States." Responding to a question on "why the United States should support Turkey's entry to the EU that might emerge as a global rival to the sole superpower," he was more explicit:

> When I took the office of Presidency, many Americans were displeased with the EU's growth. But I always thought positively about the EU's growth. America cannot remain as the only superpower forever. Rome did not. The Ottoman Empire

did not last. Therefore, we should develop ourselves to become a part of the group that shares our common values. This is the reason why I support the EU. Of course, one day the EU will surpass the United States economically. But if we belong to the same group with our common values, who cares!

Clinton's desire to see Turkey firmly anchored in the Western world explains the rationale for his administration's intense lobbying of the Europeans on behalf of Turkey. But this was not exclusively Clinton's project. Paul Wolfowitz, representing an administration with serious divergences on foreign policy issues from that of Clinton, addressing a similar audience in Istanbul on July 14, 2002, also expressed a strong American commitment to supporting Turkey's EU bid. According to Turkish Economic and Social Studies Foundation (TESEV) director Özdem Sanberk, who hosted Wolfowitz, his speech has been the most important American policy declaration on Turkey since President Clinton's memorable speech delivered at the Turkish parliament in November 1999.[28] Wolfowitz said:

> The process of economic reform is closely linked to the question of Turkey's aspiration to join the European Union. When Atatürk created the Turkish Republic nearly a century ago, he envisioned a Turkey that was modern, western and secular. . . . Turkey is now at the crossroads. As profound as our friendship with Turkey alone may be, it is even more profound when added to Turkey's fundamental relationship with Europe. Turkey's full integration into European institutions is in the best interest of the people of Turkey, the people of Europe, and of the United States. . . . Turkey's aspiration to join the European Union is a development that should be welcomed by all people who share the values of freedom and democracy that grew out of European civilization and suggest the name Western values. But they are not just Western values or European values. They are Muslim and Asian values as well. Indeed, they are universal values. Europe has a strategic opportunity to help Turkey realize its aspirations to join the EU and to demonstrate to 1.2 billion Muslims in the world that there is a far better path than the one offered by the terrorists.[29]

From the vantage point of the Bush administration, the global war against terrorism requires a European Turkey to serve as a role model for the Muslim world. Turkish aspirations to join the EU might become another element of Turkey's dependency on the United States and, paradoxically, could be a new field in mutual cooperation. The recent accentuation by the Bush administration of Turkey's EU bid could be considered as one of the by-products of September 11 that further reshapes U.S.–Turkish relations.

A Foregone Conclusion?

One has to refrain from generalizing or oversimplifying when discussing the future of Turkish–American relations in the wake of September 11. The new world is still in the making. Nonetheless, for the foreseeable future it is hard to predict any fundamental changes that would affect the vastly strengthened structure of Turkey's bonds with the United States.

Turkey itself is passing through a turbulent period of transition whose duration, scope, and dimension are difficult to measure. During this period of transition, Turkey's ruling and influential elites cannot afford to jeopardize the U.S.–Turkish alliance and fail to cooperate with the United States for these basic reasons:

1. The uncertainties of Turkey's EU accession create an unspoken but prevailing fear of isolation from the West among the Turkish elites. Thus, they will be keen, in adverse circumstances, to preserve Turkey's close relationship with the leader of the international system (the United States).

2. The awareness of common interests and the convergence of strategic preferences will keep the Turkish establishment as close as possible to the United States.

There are additional safeguards protecting the U.S.–Turkish relationship against the unexpected shocks that so often come in a globalizing world. The inevitable generational change in the political class—including the business-minded and modernist Muslim politicians and intellectuals, who are much different from the stereotypical fundamentalists of the last quarter of the twentieth century—will reshape the political stage to be more harmonious with American political culture than their predecessors. In addition, in the first quarter of the twenty-first century scores of thousands of Turkish students will graduate from American educational institutions, further enhancing the tie between the two countries and facilitating better communication between the two nations on different levels.

Foreign policy is still the privileged domain of the elites in Turkey and there is still a disconnect between public and elite opinions on important issues. This disconnect, however, will not prevail as long as Turkey, on the road toward the EU, progresses in transforming itself into a truly democratic society and integrates further into the global system. Public demand will increasingly be more effective in shaping policy in an electoral democracy that will draw Turkey closer to both the United States and Europe.

This is the framework within which any differences between Turkey and the United States on important issues like Iraq and the Middle East will be managed. Even if such differences arise, it is unlikely that they will alter the main positive trend of the U.S.–Turkish relationship: mutualism.

CHAPTER SEVEN

THE CYPRUS PROBLEM
THE LAST ACT

M. JAMES WILKINSON

INTRODUCTION

The last run of "The Cyprus Problem" as we know it is under way. The drama, which has resembled a long-running Broadway play, gained international renown in 1963–64, when ethnic strife erupted on the island and United Nations (UN) peacekeepers were dispatched. The stage was reset in 1974, when a Greek coup-attempt against the government in Nicosia and a Turkish military offensive in response split the island into two "ethnically cleansed" parts.[1]

For a quarter-century the plot has remained the same: leaders of the Greek- and Turkish-Cypriot communities meet under UN aegis and pledge to find a solution; special envoys from the United States, Europe, and even Russia make cameo appearances; the talks break down with recriminations all around; and the players recess until the next cycle. The production last reopened in January 2002 with Rauf Denktash (age 77) and Glafcos Clerides (age 83), veteran heads of the Turkish-Cypriot and Greek-Cypriot delegations respectively, paired in lead roles as they have been for the past decade. They have known each other nearly half a century—they participated as young lawyers in the constitution-drafting exercise for Cyprus that led to the island's independence from Britain in 1960.

On November 12, 2002, the UN tabled an all-encompassing new proposal, and when the curtain falls on its consideration, there can be no more reruns of the same play. Absent a European Union (EU) policy flip-flop, the setting will be too radically transformed by accession of Cyprus to EU membership. If the two Cypriot communities ultimately agree, both will enter the EU under one Cyprus flag; if not, a Greek-controlled government will don the EU mantle, and Turkish Cypriots will be left out in the cold. Cyprus has been put on a road either to reunification or permanent division.

In comparison to previous formulations, the current UN plan draws on Belgium's experience for an extraordinary devolution of powers to the smaller Turkish-Cypriot community. It also, however, provides for return of more territory and property to the Greek Cypriots than earlier versions. This is a new set of apples and oranges for the two Cypriot leaders. Both likely will accept the UN proposals as a basis for negotiation, but they will not find it easy to strike a balance of benefit acceptable to their constituencies. Although Turkey's new political leadership appears intent on resolving Cyprus, there is much historical baggage on both sides and no guarantee of success for the bicommunal talks.

THE TURKEY PROBLEM

The catch is that, in an effort to force the pace of Cyprus negotiations, the EU has linked Turkey's membership prospects to resolution of the Cyprus problem. The timing of the UN proposal was keyed to the December 2002 European Council meeting, which will almost certainly issue a membership invitation to Cyprus and also consider whether or not to set a date for starting formal membership negotiations with Turkey. In effect, the UN action compounds the pressure on Ankara to act positively on Cyprus in hopes of eliciting an EU commitment that advances Turkey's EU membership bid. The political and substantive complexities posed for both sides by the UN document, however, may well necessitate many more weeks of negotiation. Whichever way the European Council comes down in December 2002, the Cyprus issue will continue to shackle Turkish–EU relations until a lasting accord on the island's future is achieved.

There is no lack of warning as to the possible consequences for the United States if the EU plan goes awry. Reaction in Turkey could accentuate political discord and strengthen anti-Western forces. The repercussions could constrain Turkey's participation in such activities as the international security force in Afghanistan, and possibly even generate pressures against the extensive cooperation now extended to the United States and the North Atlantic Treaty Organization (NATO), including U.S. operational use of Turkish bases near the Iraqi border. In Washington, pro-Greek sentiment in Congress could complicate administration efforts to fortify pro-Western leaders in Ankara if they are confounded by yet another Euroshock.

Washington should be pressing hard for agreements in principle, particularly on the form of government, to lock the two sides as securely as possible into an ongoing reconciliation process. If progress remains elusive, the United States should put forward a transition plan that will buy time and avoid precipitate actions by all parties. The EU, for its part, should begin moving from questionable pressure tactics focused solely on Ankara to a strategy that builds bridges to Turkish Cyprus and lays out clearer intentions toward Turkey.

The sections below look at the pressures building on a regional agenda transformed by the focus on Cyprus, the dangers on the horizon, the differences that have undermined the UN process until now, why international opinion has generally favored the Greek Cypriots, why the Turkish Cypriots have been out of step with the rest of the world, the Hobson's choice facing Turkey, the downside of the EU strategy driving events, and why the United States should ratchet up its engagement.

THE SOUTHEAST EUROPEAN AGENDA:
TELESCOPED AND TOPSY-TURVY

A polemical cartoonist might draw Rauf Denktash and Glafcos Clerides holding in their hands the power to decide Turkey's future course. An exaggeration to be sure, but the kernel of truth in such an image would dramatize the extent to which the EU's Cyprus deadlines have recast the region's political agenda.

After years of desultory negotiations, the need to find a solution for the island's division has acquired a sharp and concrete urgency. It is not that there is anything new on Cyprus itself: the barbed wire marking the boundary along the so-called Green Line is still ugly, but bloodshed has been rare, people on both sides long ago settled into comfortable routines of daily life, and negotiations have turned into fruitless repetitions.

The sense of impending crisis flows from EU decisions that in effect have set deadlines for bicommunal negotiations and put the onus on Turkey to budge the Turkish Cypriots. This EU policy unfolded over the past several years, expressed mainly through promulgations at European Council summits. No one seemed to pay much attention in the beginning, and the full implications have only recently become apparent to the wider public.

Lost Time

Cyprus and the EU have had partnership relations since 1973, and the official countdown to Cyprus membership dates from mid-1995, when the EU formally activated accession procedures. Although the EU made positive pronouncements before 1995 about membership for Cyprus, timing was not specified, and the EU's involvement in the Cyprus problem was correspondingly restrained. While the Cypriot sides were negotiating under UN sponsorship in the 1980s and early 1990s, Brussels was an interested bystander, not inclined to twist arms. The United States carried most of the water for the international community.

The EU's 1995 decision on Cyprus's accession escalated its engagement with the dispute on the island. A linkage between bicommunal negotiations and Turkey's relations with the EU was soon made more explicit. The December 1997 European Council meeting in Luxembourg laid down forceful (and, some Turks would say, arrogant) markers, with statements that accession negotiations for Cyprus "will contribute positively to a search for a political solution to the Cyprus problem," and "strengthening Turkey's links with the European Union also depends on that country's . . . support for [UN-sponsored] negotiations" on Cyprus.[2] At the time, these pronouncements were salt poured in the larger wound made by the council's action shunting Turkey out of the membership queue.

The EU's approach at Luxembourg proved unproductive, and the December 1999 European Council in Helsinki granted Turkey active candidate status. The EU gave with the right hand but took away with the left by also decreeing that a solution to the Cyprus problem would *not* be a prerequisite for the membership of Cyprus itself. The effect of the Helsinki language[3] is to provide for entry of the Greek-controlled government and population of the island, even if the Turkish Cypriots object and are excluded. Taken with the EU's overall posture, the message for Turkey is simple and pointed: move on the Cyprus problem or risk debarment from the club.

Most Turks were gratified to be given an official place in the waiting room, but at the same time many perceived the EU's Helsinki edict as a pro-Greek ultimatum demanding that mainland Turks abandon their ethnic brethren on Cyprus. Ankara has threatened to annex the Turkish-Cypriot sector of Cyprus if the Greek side is taken into the EU before any settlement of the island's division. This EU action–Turkish reaction set up the ominous confrontation now hovering over negotiations.

The schedule foreseen by the Helsinki summit ensures that a day of reckoning cannot be put off for long. The membership invitation will almost certainly be issued to Cyprus at the end of 2002, and EU member-state ratifications will be completed in 2004. Cyprus, a strong economic performer and smoothly functioning democracy, has progressed easily through the EU preparatory hoops. There seems no question it will be in the top ranks of the EU's preapproved candidates when the European Council meets in December 2002.

Meanwhile, two years after Helsinki, there has been no visible progress in bicommunal negotiations on Cyprus. As deadlines move closer, pressures are intensifying on Turkey's fragile relationships with the EU and Greece.

SHIFTED PRIORITIES

The Cyprus problem might earlier have been likened to one corner of a triangle, with Greek–Turkish and EU–Turkish relations in the remaining angles, such that progress or deterioration at any one node influenced the other two in the corresponding direction. All three corners came back into full play in 1999 with the reinitiation of Greek–Turkish détente in mid-year, the boost from cooperation on earthquake disasters a few months later, reaffirmation of Turkey's EU candidacy at Helsinki, and efforts by the international community to jump-start talks between the two Cypriot community leaders. By mid-2002, Cyprus had leapfrogged ahead on the timeline—it is the developments concerning Cyprus through the end of 2002 that will largely shape Turkey's approach to both the EU and Greece.

When Cyprus negotiations restarted in January 2002, there was talk of an early settlement, but hopes were quickly dashed as both sides held their old familiar ground. As the year advanced, the impending crunch over Cyprus sharpened debate in Turkey, not over what compromises would be necessary or acceptable to reach a Cyprus solution but rather over how much EU membership is really worth and what the alternative of nonmembership might entail.

The EU debate took center stage in Turkey at mid-year when the governing coalition in Ankara disintegrated, primarily due to loss of confidence in ailing Prime Minister Bulent Ecevit. Parliament voted to hold early elections on November 3, 2002, and several political leaders vowed to make the balloting a referendum on EU membership. Legislation was rushed through on two central EU demands: ending the death penalty and providing more freedoms for the Kurdish minority.

The unanticipated and rapid passage of the EU-related laws led many Turks to believe that this positive action virtually obligated Brussels to upgrade its membership negotiations with Ankara. Turkey and the EU currently have an "accession partnership," which should progress to two succeeding, more formal stages: first, the screening process, which evaluates ability to meet requirements of the EU's core body of law and regulation, known as the *acquis communautaire;* and, following that, direct accession negotiations. In its bilateral meetings with the EU in 2001, Turkey had proposed that the process be advanced to the screening stage, but Brussels declined.

European leaders applauded the new legislation, but the EU's October 2002 progress report indicated further reforms were required as well as effective implementation of those just passed. The report again declined to recommend that a date be set for upgrading membership negotiations and deferred the question to the European Council's December 2002 meeting. Given that Europeans will want to see how the Justice and Development Party (AK Party) will perform after its decisive win in the November balloting, the issue may well be fudged with some formula to set a date for setting a date. With the new UN proposal now on the table, a sudden leap forward on Cyprus is possible at any point and could elicit a more forthcoming EU stance. Additional major change in the Turkish system, however, will take considerable time. Tension seems sure to persist as the Europeans press for more Turkish actions, whether on Cyprus or domestic reform, and the Turks demand more credit for actions already taken.

THE STAKES: CYPRUS AND BEYOND

The United States and Europe face a pivotal fork in the road ahead. If the EU's linkage strategy exacts a solution for Cyprus, all well and good—capitals will be able to concentrate fully on building the bridges from Ankara to Brussels and Athens. If the Cyprus talks fail and the EU proceeds with its membership scenario, Washington and Brussels will be acutely challenged to keep Turkey's relations with the West on an even keel.

The stakes, at least in the short term, for the people of Cyprus are evident. Sometime before the end of 2004, the two communities will be preparing for a new government or bracing for permanent partition. The latter outcome from the perspective of human rights would be seen by many as a tragedy for Cyprus and a major failure of Western democracies. Still, the Greek Cypriots are virtually certain to join the comforting fold of the EU, and the Turkish Cypriots, while they face the economically less appealing possibilities of remaining in limbo or being annexed to Turkey, are not threatened with immediate catastrophe at home. In sum, the future form of the Republic of Cyprus will be determined, but day-to-day life on either side of the Green Line will not be greatly changed overnight.

The medium and longer term present a different picture for the island's residents. Adjustments to "bizonality" would be demanding, but mutually agreed reunification is sure to bring extensive change for the better on both sides as the benefits of EU membership kick in, in particular EU development assistance to boost the ailing Turkish-Cypriot economy. On the other hand, the prospect of permanent division would anger many, including a substantial number on the Turkish-Cypriot side where there are still diverse connections to Britain and considerable pro-EU sentiment. On the Greek side, a split could precipitate troublesome irredentism, even though the island long ago emerged from the poverty and ultranationalist fervor that fueled the vicious terrorist movements in the period from 1950 to 1974.

RECONCILIATION BETWEEN GREECE AND TURKEY

The touchstone of Greek–Turkish relations since 1974 has been Cyprus. Lack of any demonstrable benefit for Greek Cyprus dissipated the "Spirit of Davos," the reconciliation effort undertaken in 1988 by Prime Ministers Andreas Papandreou and Turgut Ozal at the height of their respective powers. Ozal visited Athens that summer, but soon thereafter Papandreou put on the brakes under pressure from domestic criticism over Cyprus and looming national elections (which he lost). Although later foreign ministers such as Michael Papakonstantinou of Greece and Hikmet Cetin and Emre Gonensay of Turkey took positive initiatives, government-to-government relations did not recover sustained momentum until George Papandreou and Ismail Cem launched their bilateral effort in 1999.

But the Spirit of Davos did break the ice, and an extensive network of bilateral connections evolved through the 1990s, notwithstanding persistent imbroglios between Ankara and Athens over Cyprus, the Aegean, and Kurdish issues. Greeks and Turks cautiously worked together on a wide range of programs and projects such as Black Sea Economic Cooperation; peacekeeping and peacemaking tasks in the Balkans under U.S., NATO, or UN umbrellas; limited but persistent private sector exchanges; reestablishment of the long moribund NATO Command and Control structure for the Aegean; and myriad government-to-government contacts undertaken in fits and starts with varying degrees of productivity.

The several encouraging ministerial meetings and substantial number of private sector contacts, however, never combined to reach a critical mass sufficient to stabilize bilateral relations. The Imia/Kardak crisis of 1996[4] nearly brought the sides to military conflict and accentuated Greek fears of Turkish designs on Greek islands. Revelations that the Greek government assisted Kurdish separatist leader Abdullah Ocalan before his capture in February 1999 stoked Turkish suspicions over Greece's long-term intentions.

Against this background, the progress achieved by Foreign Ministers Cem and Papandreou following their bold initiative in mid-1999 was substantial. Bilateral cooperative agreements were signed, trade mushroomed, and the two ministers reaped broad public support. These achievements went far to defuse the flashpoints and construct an auspicious foundation for further cooperation, even if Ankara and Athens have not yet seen their way clear to take up Cyprus directly between them.

On March 12, 2002, no doubt with one eye on the looming Cyprus crunch, the two foreign ministries launched discussions on the core of disputes related to the Aegean. Although quiet in recent years, disagreements over oil-drilling rights on the Aegean floor have caused armed confrontations, contested island boundaries brought the Imia/Kardak showdown mentioned above, and differences over air control regimes have produced innumerable challenges between armed planes of the two air forces. Initiating bilateral talks on the Aegean marked a new plateau for Greek–Turkish rapprochement. Athens described the dialogue as one "without agenda," but the format opened the way for exchanges on a variety of subjects. The move was thus a meaningful concession by Greece, which until then had rejected Turkey's call for a bilateral dialogue on issues across the board, insisting that only the continental shelf was negotiable.

The Greek–Turkish talks on the Aegean also have an important EU dimension. As was the case with Cyprus, the Helsinki summit imposed a deadline and linkage to Turkey's EU candidacy. The language did not mention either country by name, but Turkey was clearly the prime addressee.

[Candidate countries] must share the values and objectives of the European Union as set out in the Treaties. In this respect the European Council stresses the principle of peaceful settlement of disputes in accordance with the United Nations Charter and urges candidate States to make every effort to resolve any outstanding border disputes and other related issues. Failing this they should within a reasonable time bring the dispute to the International Court of Justice. The European Council will review the situation relating to any outstanding disputes, in particular concerning the repercussions on the accession process and in order to promote their settlement through the International Court of Justice, at the latest by the end of 2004.[5]

Greek–Turkish relations shifted into neutral when the mid-2002 political turbulence in Ankara led to Cem's resignation as foreign minister. Subsequently, the new strongman of Turkish politics, AK Party leader Recep Tayyip Erdogan, put improved relations with Greece high on his agenda. For its part, Athens quickly pledged to work with the new Turkish government and reemphasized a strongly positive view of Turkey's EU prospects. In sum, the atmospherics in the immediate wake of the November 2002 elections were very promising.

THE BIGGER PROBLEM: TURKEY AND ITS EUROPEAN FUTURE

The most worrisome menace from a Cyprus train wreck is the threat to Turkey's progress toward integration into Europe. If Cyprus talks founder, some foresee a backlash that could greatly strengthen the hand of anti-EU and reactionary forces inside Turkey.

Pessimists discern a real doomsday in the offing. Bulent Akarcali, deputy leader of the ANAP Party and known for flamboyant rhetoric, asserted in a March 2002 newspaper interview that Cypriot EU accession combined with denial of Turkey's membership would give rise to a situation comparable with that of Germany after Versailles. "[S]ensitive Turkish people," he said, "would embrace any kind of fascist development. This will lead to an armed struggle with Europe sooner or later."[6] His words are exaggerated for political effect, but they doubtless speak to underlying concerns of many in a worried country in troubled times.

Henri Barkey and Philip Gordon in an article written in 2001, titled *Cyprus: The Predictable Crisis,* foresaw a potential impact on Turkey in less cataclysmic, but still grave terms:

> The longer term cost for Turkey [of a crisis provoked by perceived intransigence over Cyprus] lies in Ankara's alienation or estrangement from the Western alliance. Turkey is not likely to join some other alliance system, nor will Turkish leaders actively court anti-American powers in their region or beyond. However, an inward-looking, increasingly nationalistic and autarkic Turkey could emerge, reversing the economic and political progress the country made during the 1980s and early 1990s.[7]

Few others might foresee such far-reaching internal change, but it cannot be precluded.

On the other hand, there are many astute Turkish leaders committed to a European vision for Turkey. They point out that as Turkey continues to modernize and its importance to the Western antiterrorist coalition becomes more evident, Europe can be expected to reevaluate its own interests and set things right with Turkey. There will surely be many such voices inside Turkey arguing for patience and against taking steps that will be self-defeating in the long run.

In any case, just how the Cyprus accession scenario will unfold is, of course, still uncertain. A settlement is possible and, short of that, the now likely course of serious negotiations on the basis of the UN's November 2002 proposals would permit Turkey's EU accession process to stay on track, perhaps even move to the next stage. Notwithstanding its tough talk, the EU has left itself maneuvering room with artful language in its presidency conclusions and could conceivably fashion some sort of bridging arrangement to allay confrontation. In the worst case scenario, much would depend on whether Turkey followed through with earlier threats to annex Turkish Cyprus if (Greek) Cyprus were to enter the EU before a settlement on the island.

Before examining the negotiating process, the determinants of policy, and the nature of the persistent stalemate over sovereignty and form of government, it is worth taking a closer look at why the UN framework for a Cyprus solution enjoys near-universal support.

THE UN'S FINAL PUSH: LAND FOR SOVEREIGNTY

UN Secretary General Kofi Annan's November 2002 proposal, which I take the liberty of referring to here as the Annan Plan, carried forward the basic framework from previous negotiations, with significant substantive changes and a plethora of new detail. Initial reactions from the parties focused on what was perceived to be its fundamental advance: an implicit trade-off that would on the one hand strengthen the sovereign powers to be given to Turkish Cypriots and on the other hand increase the land and property to be given to the Greek Cypriots. The following sections look at how the UN arrived at the Annan Plan, the competing visions it attempts to satisfy, and the interplay between Cypriots, Turks, and the EU that will determine whether it succeeds.

The Evolution of the UN Paradigm

After the debacle of 1974, the negotiating track for putting Cyprus, like Humpty Dumpty, back together again was initiated in 1977 when Archbishop Makarios and Denktash agreed that Cyprus would be reconstituted as, "an independent nonaligned bicommunal federal Republic."[8] Two years later Denktash and Makarios' successor, Spyros Kyprianou, signed a follow-on ten point agreement, stating *inter alia* that, "The independence, sovereignty, territorial integrity and non-alignment of the Republic should be adequately guaranteed against union in whole or in part with any other country and against any form of partition or secession."[9] Bizonality was not explicitly mentioned, but later became a part of the package.

Numerous UN Security Council resolutions elaborated on this beginning and ennobled the concept of a unique "bicommunal" and "bizonal" Cyprus. The crux of the matter is, obviously, to protect the much smaller Turkish Cypriot community from domination by the island's Greeks, while avoiding the meltdown that dissolved the first republic. The initial effort in 1960 to set up a western pluralistic democracy on Cyprus incorporated numerous provisions intended to give Turkish Cypriots an adequate role. The experiment was short-lived, as Greek Cypriots soon demanded change on grounds the government system was "unworkable." When the Turkish Cypriots refused to accept constitutional revisions, violence erupted and peaked in 1963, driving Turks into ghettos, spawning the UN peacekeeping force (UNFICYP) still in place on the island, and taking the country a giant step on the way to the disaster of 1974.

Until now, the apotheosis of the UN design was a semi-detailed blueprint known as "The Set of Ideas."[10] When presented by UN officials in late 1992 for high-level discussion at the UN, it had 101 paragraphs, a map with adjustments of territory for the two zones, and an appended program of early actions to promote goodwill and close relations between the two communities. The Greek-Cypriot president at the time, George Vassiliou, accepted it in its entirety but only as a basis for discussion (he shortly thereafter lost an election to current President Clerides, who promised to be a tougher negotiator), and Turkish-Cypriot leader Denktash, after criticism by the UN Security Council, asserted he agreed with ninety-one of the paragraphs.

In the Western public eye, Denktash has failed to justify his insistence on virtual independence for Turkish Cypriots. Nor has Turkey been able to make the case for its continued military presence, based on the Greek Cypriot pogroms against Turkish Cypriots in the 1960s and the ultranationalist Greek coup that was the proximate cause of Ankara's military intervention in 1974. Some Turks argue their Cyprus policy is parallel to U.S. military actions in, say, Panama or Grenada, but that begs the question of why Ankara's troops are still on the island in force. Few Europeans or Americans believe today's Greek community would resort to the violence of the past—cynics note the Greeks could doubtless rely on their greater wealth and population to buy or pressure Turkish Cypriots off the island.

Opinion in the West has seen the UN endeavor as a noble effort to reunify a nation that should never have split in the first place. It is widely believed that as a matter of principle a functioning democratic government not only can be re-cobbled together, but is the right thing to do. Moreover, not to do so would be to sanction ethnic separation and an undesirable reliance on force to solve disputes between neighbors.

Greeks and Greek Cypriots generally have perceived the UN as an ally. In the past, the UN has rejected Denktash's brand of separatism and hewed to a federal solution, which the Greek Cypriots have seen to be in their favor. Moreover, the international Greek community has cultivated world governments and exploited Western idealism to restore democracy and reverse the "illegal" gains made by force of Turkish arms. Greek immigrant communities have organized politically with considerable effect, nowhere more successfully than in the United States. The more than one million Greek Americans, who in 1974 induced Congress to impose an arms embargo against Turkey for several years, are a potent lobby supporting Greece and Greek Cyprus. Congress and the European Parliament, equally sensitive to the pressure from its ethnic Greek constituency, have periodically passed resolutions favoring Greek Cypriot positions and the UN federal model.

Officially the U.S. and European governments also have supported the UN Security Council resolutions and urged the parties to negotiate a settlement on that basis. This has become the "politically correct" stance in America, and any deviation would provoke strong Congressional reaction. In practice, Washington and most other capitals would be delighted with any agreement acceptable to the two Cypriot parties, but there has been virtually no public consideration of the alternative loose confederation advanced by the Turkish Cypriots.

Through most of 2002, the negotiating positions of both sides remained much as they had been, judging from periodic news leaks[11] and the apparent failure of Annan to budge the sides with his personal interventions in May and September. As the critical December European Council meeting drew closer, however, Annan was evidently encouraged by the Europeans and the Americans to put out his new plan in hopes of eliciting at least some sign of meaningful progress before the EU December summit.

One of the most significant new features in the Annan Plan is the inclusion of elements based on the unique governmental system Belgium has developed to function with its divided citizenry. The effect is to provide mechanisms that could give the Turkish-Cypriot entity (called "component state" in the Annan document) more extensive powers to deal independently on certain major issues, including the ability to deal directly with the EU or foreign governments.

THE BELGIAN MODEL

There is no exact model for the kind of governmental structure that has been debated in the UN bicommunal talks, although both the Swiss cantonal system and Belgium have come up as sources of ideas. Switzerland has fewer parallels than Belgium, which is deeply divided between its two main ethno-linguistic groups of Flemish and Walloon citizens. Until this year, however, Cyprus negotiators did not give much consideration to the Belgian model, in part because it is a parliamentary system as opposed to the presidential one carried forward in Cyprus from the 1960 constitution, and in part because it is only in the last few years that the devolution of power from the federal level in Belgium has become so extensive.

An in-depth analysis published in March 2002 by the Centre for European Policy Studies titled *Cyprus as Lighthouse of the East Mediterranean: Shaping EU Accession and Re-unification Together*[12] has called attention to the very strong relevance of the Belgian experience. As the study's subtitle indicates, both the Belgian government's internal power-sharing arrangements and its procedures for participating in EU councils could provide beacons for the Cyprus case.

While it is obvious the Belgian model could not be imported "as is" to Cyprus, its example could be a promising source of ideas to break the standoff of the past quarter-century. Belgium is a functioning democracy and a federal state, able to participate in EU councils with one voice. At the same time, it has achieved an extraordinary devolution of power from the national level. By the year 2000, Belgium had evolved to the point that it gave regional entities power over external trade and agriculture, in the process abolishing the federal ministry of agriculture. A number of mainland Turks, including a prominent think tank, the Turkish Economic and Social Studies Foundation, have taken a positive view of the potential applicability of the Belgian example.

Spurred, it appears, by the interest on the mainland, Turkish Cypriots in June 2002 proposed that some features of the Belgian system be discussed in the bicommunal talks. The Greek-Cypriot side demurred, later explaining it was prepared to "negotiate on the basis of [the Belgian constitution's] concept and not selectively on specific articles as Denktash wants."[13] The impression was left that neither side had much interest, but Belgium's relevance continued to crop up in the media. Most significantly, pending formation of a government after his party's electoral victory, Erdogan said on Greek television, "we support a solution based on the Belgian model."[14]

With the adoption of the Belgian concepts, the Annan Plan goes about as far as any plan could and still preserve a federal, as opposed to confederated, government structure. At the same time, it apparently seeks to maximize return of Greek-Cypriot properties taken over by Turkish Cypriots in the disaster of 1974. Both sides must now decide whether this proposed new fundamental balance is acceptable for their respective visions of what a future Cyprus should look like.

COMPETING VISIONS (1):
THE GREEK-CYPRIOT APPROACH

The Greek Cypriots will doubtless be prepared to negotiate on the basis of the Annan Plan. Nonetheless, the extensive devolution of power and the complicated decisionmaking procedures foreseen in Annan's proposals will surely raise concerns about the workability of such a government and whether over time it will produce a fair balance of power and benefit for the Greek Cypriot numerical majority. The new elements are a significant departure from the previous UN paradigm, which the Greek Cypriots embraced in principle.

President Clerides described the Greek-Cypriot outline in a May 14, 2002, interview with CNN TURK television: "a new constitution which will provide for two self-administered states or cantons. Each one will have its own executive, legislative and judicial organs for its civil service and the central authority will not have the right to interfere with their affairs." There would be a central government to represent Cyprus, with both sides participating and political equality ensured because neither side could take a decision unless it had "some support" from the other. Clerides said progress had been made on the security questions, but not on other issues.[15]

The Greek Cypriots may not have adopted the previous UN construct wholesale, but its framework carrying forward the unitary British model served their interests. Idealism aside, they stand to gain tangible benefit since they are not only the four to one majority but also are far wealthier, with per capita annual income above $13,000, as opposed to $3,500 or so across the Green Line. These would be powerful advantages in an open, democratic system, as long as it is not overly hobbled by minority veto powers.

The Greek team—Greece and Greek Cyprus—aggressively sought the backing of the international community to isolate Turkish Cyprus and brought pressure to bear for reunification of the island in line with UN proposals. It buttressed its case by stressing the unbroken legality and islandwide sovereignty of the government of Cyprus, branding the Turkish military action of 1974 a gross violation of international law that must be set right by reunification. They have been hugely successful, playing to Western idealism and exploiting émigré communities, as described above.

Western public opinion was further tilted toward the Greek position once EU membership became a concrete possibility. There is now an appealing image of a reunified Cyprus with the rights and personal safety of all its citizens fully protected by EU authority and institutions. European enforcement mechanisms would, in theory at least, provide an independent avenue for Turkish Cypriots to seek redress for maltreatment.

THE GREECE CONNECTION

Mainland Greece has identified its national interests with those of Greek Cyprus and has been an invaluable proponent of the Greek-Cypriot cause. The two are bound by close ethnic and religious bonds—the ties of "Hellenism"—although the idea of "enosis," or union between the two countries, has been a dead letter since the

Athens-inspired coup-attempt in 1974. In a multitude of international organizations, starting with the UN, Greek Cyprus and Greece can always count on each other's votes and lobbying help on any issue where they are crosswise with Turkey, which has to toil alone for both itself and Turkish Cyprus. Defense cooperation between Greece and (Greek) Cyprus directed against Turkey also reflects their unity of purpose.

Most importantly, the Greek Cypriots enjoy through Athens the obvious and enormous advantage of having virtually a seat of their own on the inner councils of the EU. Greece cannot call the tune on every occasion, but, by playing on the sympathetic ears of some colleagues and selectively exercising its veto threat, Athens has been able to shape EU positions concerning the latter's southeast corner.

Greek desires were surely the major factor in the EU's 1995 decision to put Cyprus in the line for membership. At the time, the United States and several EU member states were anxious to advance the EU's relations with Turkey and proposed doing so by establishing a formal customs union between the EU and Turkey. The approval of Cyprus accession was first and foremost a trade-off to ensure Greece's acceptance of the deal for Turkey. On the other side of the same coin, Turkey was constrained to mute its objections on the Cyprus aspect in order to preserve the customs union.

The EU's 1999 Helsinki decisions also bear the Greek stamp in that by virtually guaranteeing EU membership to Greek Cyprus they put extra pressure on Turkey with no corresponding push on the Greek Cypriots. That is not to say, of course, that the Greek Cypriots lack incentive or are negotiating in bad faith. While they have garnered extra chips in their pile from the EU's contribution, they have more to gain than to lose from a successful negotiation. Failure could put paid to dreams of reunification and, as indicated above, could in the worst case over time promote regional instability with incalculable risk to their future well-being.

Until the Annan Plan appeared, the Greek Cypriots were prepared to accept the basic UN concept, within which they had already accepted substantial concessions on power-sharing with the smaller Turkish-Cypriot community. Their stance was applauded by the EU and the UN Security Council, while Denktash found himself backed into a corner trying to defend his unpopular demand for a sovereign Turkish Cyprus. Now the Greek Cypriots must decide whether the Annan Plan goes past their bottom line on sovereignty aspects, or if it proves acceptable on that count, does it provide enough compensation with its formulations on territory, property return, and citizenship prospects for post-1974 Turkish settlers from the mainland.

COMPETING VISIONS (2):
THE TURKISH-CYPRIOT APPROACH

Greek-Cypriot championing of high-principled national integrity and Western democratic institutions rings hollow to many Turkish Cypriots. They look back to the ethnic violence that drove them into ghettos for self-protection from 1963 to 1974 and want iron-clad guarantees against its return. Joining the EU would not by itself suffice—their recollection of the years through 1974 is that Americans and Europeans, despite in the case of Britain explicit treaty obligations, stayed on the sidelines, unwilling to intervene when numerically superior Greeks were tyrannizing Turkish Cypriots. Nor did UNFICYP provide essential protections.

Until the new Annan Plan, Turkish Cypriots continued to resist the UN model, demanding an independent "partner state" fully equal to a counterpart Greek entity. Even if their physical security were somehow to be ensured, Turkish Cypriots have little doubt that Greek Cypriots would exploit majority voting and economic power to control political institutions, buy up land, and accumulate more wealth. Ethnic Turks would be left to fend for themselves as cheap labor and second-class citizens, if not eventually pressured or bribed to pack up and leave. Such is the legacy bequeathed by the excesses of both ethnic groups in the twentieth century.

The consummate spokesman for the Turkish-Cypriot position is Rauf Denktash, leader of the community since 1974. Some would challenge his credentials on grounds that he has used Turkish military support and the substantial number of Turkish mainland immigrants to squelch those Turkish Cypriots more inclined to accept a federal solution. The immigrant population is a particular sore point for Greek Cypriots, who see them as not only illegal but also more averse to reunification than native Turkish Cypriots.

Harassment, including arrests and jailing of journalists (the latest such case in August 2002), exists but has by no means completely stifled dissenting opinion in Turkish Cyprus. Opposition politicians have long attacked Denktash openly, and eighty-six nongovernmental organizations from Turkish Cyprus issued a "Common Vision" document in early August 2002 calling for a settlement by year's end to permit entry into the EU.[16] The words were carefully chosen and short on specifics but clearly constituted sharp criticism of Denktash for inflexibility.

Some foreign diplomats and close observers of the Cyprus scene are convinced that Denktash does not want a solution. It is perhaps more accurate to say he is unwilling to compromise on the principle of insulating Turkish Cypriots from the greater wealth and numbers of ethnic Greeks on the island. In either case, there seems no room under present circumstances in the UN-sponsored negotiations to meet his bottom line—hence the EU effort to get Ankara to use its leverage.

Whatever one thinks of Denktash, he has been a forceful leader of the Turkish-Cypriot cause since their ghettoization in 1963 and has won every election since 1974 on his side of the Green Line. No other Turkish Cypriot comes close to matching his stature, and, as long as he is active, it would be difficult if not impossible to put a settlement in place without at least his tacit agreement.

No Minorities

Denktash asserts that only full sovereignty for his community backed by mainland Turkey's military force can ensure the security and well-being of his community. He has steadfastly rejected the term "minority" and with it any notion of a majority–minority relationship. He has articulated in word and deed a Turkish-Cypriot demand for equal status with the Greek-Cypriot community.

In 1983, the Turkish Cypriots declared themselves the Turkish Republic of Northern Cyprus (TRNC). Denktash continues to lambaste the United States and the Europeans for ignoring his administration and recognizing the Greek-controlled government of Cyprus as representing all the island. Nonetheless, he stops short of insisting on creation of two completely separate independent states, and he accepts in principle the UN-adopted formulation that the future Cyprus should have "one international personality."

At the same time, however, Denktash's proposals, whether for a "confederation" or, most recently, a new "partner state," are tantamount to the creation of a virtually independent Turkish Cyprus with a superficial facade of linkage to a Greek-Cypriot affiliate. The parties are pledged to secrecy in the negotiations, but leaks have been skill-fully used by both sides, and an April 2002 news article described the recent expression of the Turkish-Cypriot position. Citing sources close to Denktash, the item reported he had offered his Greek counterpart a "vision of settlement" that included, among other points:

- [The] relationship between the two peoples of the island is not one of majority and minority but one between two equals. Neither party represents and/or speaks for the other and neither can claim authority or jurisdiction over the other.

- . . . [S]overeignty will rest with the two partner states and the new structure will have international legal personality in its areas of competence assigned to it by the two partner states.[17]

To craft a "bizonal, bicommunal" country, even one more bal-anced than Denktash's split-wide formulation, entails potentially con-tentious mechanisms and power-sharing rules. UN diplomats have been assiduously working on the task for two decades. Numerous imaginative devices, such as rotating offices from the presidency on down and weighted parliamentary voting, are still on the table. More crucial than the mechanics, however, is the extent of sovereignty and bizonality to be accorded the Turkish-Cypriot sector: words have not yet been found to satisfy both sides.

Denktash's terminology has moved from "confederation" to "part-nership," but he has not adapted his central vision to the context of Cyprus's membership in the EU. In essence, the conditions that he continues to advance for the Turkish-Cypriot zone-to-be run counter to EU ideals of internal EU harmonization and common freedoms.

The EU has provisions to accommodate special cases but strives to limit their scope and duration. EU officials have not objected to the assumption in the UN negotiating process that there will be extensive, ethnic-based arrangements in any Cyprus agreement. On the other hand, the EU has asserted the applicability of its core laws and regu-lations to Cyprus when it becomes a member state. While there will surely be exceptions for Turkish Cyprus in the event of settlement, legal challenges would likely generate early and strong pressures to move toward European norms.

THE TURKEY CONNECTION

Ankara has considerable leverage over its Cypriot cousins. Unlike Greek Cyprus, with its population of about 600,000 and vibrant economy, Turkish Cyprus has fewer than 150,000 people and remains dependent on its mainland big brother. Ankara props up the flagging Turkish-Cypriot economy, sponsors the TRNC's international presence, and maintains the thirty thousand Turkish troops stationed on the island for security against the Greek Cypriots.

Many Turks, especially political conservatives, want Turkey to retain a decisive role in the future of Turkish Cyprus. They stress the indivisible character of ethnic and religious bonds. Some also continue to maintain that, because of its physical proximity, Cyprus involves Turkey's own national security, although this consideration appears to have waned in recent years

Turkey is not, however, monolithic on the issue of Cyprus. There are voices that have quietly and persistently suggested Ankara should take a less ideological approach. Not every prime minister in Ankara has given Denktash unqualified support—in the early 1990s, Prime Minister Turgut Ozal manifested a more supple bent. In recent years, many in the Turkish business community have argued for greater flexibility, and in May 2002, wide media coverage was given to Deputy Prime Minister Mesut Yilmaz, leader of the governing coalition partner Motherland Party, when he called on Denktash to be more forthcoming. One newspaper referred to "heated discussion" at party-leader levels within the government.[18]

From 1998 through 2002, there was little daylight between the Denktash approach and that of Turkish Prime Minister Bulent Ecevit's government in Ankara. Ecevit, the prime minister who authorized the Turkish military invasion of Cyprus in 1974 during his first stint on the job, seems cut from much the same cloth as his Turkish-Cypriot colleague. His government came fully on board with Denktash in 1998, when it explicitly declared a common policy goal of confederation for Cyprus in angry reaction to the "slap in the face" dished out by the EU at the Luxembourg Council meeting. Also, in a strongly worded March 14, 2002, op-ed piece for the *International Herald Tribune,* then Foreign Minister Cem reaffirmed Ankara's official backing for Denktash, asserting the Turkish-Cypriot side has a "basic stance which it can never abandon." This reality, he said, requires for a settlement on the island "the confirmation of two equal separate states, each as a sovereign entity, forming through an agreement a new partnership state."[19]

Against this background, the Annan Plan appears at first blush to give as much sovereign power to the Turkish Cypriots as they can reasonably expect and the early commentary from Turkish political leaders, including former foreign minister Ismail Cem, was by and large favorable on this count. Their negative reactions focused primarily on the Plan's treatment of territory, property, and displaced refugees and settlers. The powerful military and state bureaucracies have generally embraced Denktash's maximum positions, and Turkish governments do not change such cardinal policies lightly. Nonetheless, Erdogan has obtained an exceptional personal mandate and could count on solid backing from the business community if he sought to compromise on Cyprus and accepted the Annan Plan at least in principle. In this context, the adaption of the Belgian experience is attractive not only on its merits, but because it is an alternative to what is seen in Turkey as a Greek-UN model. At the same time, much also depends on how the EU plays its Cyprus and Turkey membership cards.

THE EU: FORCING THE PACE

Taken at face value, the EU policy expediting Cyprus's accession since 1995 is intended to provide for the membership of a European state that qualifies in every respect, except that one-third of its territory has been hived off and quarantined. There is a legal government of Cyprus, which is recognized around the world as speaking for the whole island and is therefore an authoritative voice for accession negotiations. And Turkey's acceptance of its customs union in 1995 is still taken by some as tacit consent in principle to Cypriot entry; Ankara at the time voiced objections to membership for Cyprus before a settlement, but they were relatively mild and hence discounted.

The fact that Turkish Cypriots decline to take part in the negotiations is evidently seen by the EU as their choice. (Greek Cypriots insist the Turkish Cypriots can participate only as part of the delegation of the Greek-controlled government, but Denktash demands coequal status.) Were the Turkish Cypriots to opt in, the EU has put forth special financial provisions for the inclusion of Turkish Cyprus. In January 2002, Brussels announced that 106 million euros had been budgeted over the next three years to support development aimed at bringing Turkish Cyprus closer to parity with the considerably higher per capita gross domestic product level enjoyed by Greek Cypriots.[20] This kind of EU subvention would go far, not only to improve the lot of Turkish Cypriots but also to take the burden off Turkey's shoulders. It would simultaneously ease the adjustment pains of reunification for the Greek side, where concerns have been evoked by the example of the huge costs met by West Germany to absorb its economically backward East.

Some argue that, in these circumstances, it would be unfair to penalize Greek Cyprus by giving Turkish Cypriots the power to block the island's membership indefinitely. Underlying such reasoning is the evident belief that there is a proper Cyprus solution available—that is, through the UN negotiating process—and it is the Turkish Cypriots who are responsible for failure to achieve a settlement. Since economic carrots have not sufficed and Turkish Cyprus is protected by Turkey, the EU's leverage is being applied on Ankara.

For the EU, putting a Cyprus solution ahead of membership for Turkey goes beyond the ideal of settling the island's ethnic/religious dispute. The EU stance follows more from perceptions discussed above that Turkey has unreasonably relied on military force in Cyprus and has not done enough to promote the UN peace process. Getting a Cyprus settlement would make it politically easier to blunt the nettlesome Greek veto threat and help to support the case for Turkish membership throughout the EU. To this end, the Helsinki Presidency Conclusions document speaks of Turkey benefiting from "enhanced political dialogue, with emphasis on progressing towards fulfilling the political criteria for accession with particular reference to the issue of human rights, as well as [the Greek–Turkish bilateral disputes and the UN secretary-general's Cyprus effort]."[21]

QUESTIONABLE STRATEGY (1): TURKEY

The premise of the EU's strategy linking Cyprus talks and Turkey's membership seems to be that Turkey will not cut off its nose to spite its face by continuing to reject a solution brokered through the UN process and conforming to EU norms. One diplomat, who was close to the talks through the 1990s, summarizes the approach as: "The Turks may be stubborn, but they are not dumb." Turkey, the thesis runs, knows it simply cannot afford to foreclose its European option for the

sake of the small sacrifice needed to solve the Cyprus problem. But trying to quantify the strength or weakness of ethnic bonds is a difficult
proposition and dubious base for policy.

Moreover, it is far from clear what concrete EU membership benefits Turkey will get if it engineers concessions in Cyprus negotiations.
Reportedly, EU officials have suggested in private conversations with
Turks that initiation of formal accession negotiations with Turkey could
follow a settlement. But, as noted above, many Turks are already calling for this step on the basis of the legislation recently passed on the
death penalty and Kurdish rights. Turkish political leaders, under pre-
election pressure, regularly finessed the Cyprus angle by simply declaring it is not, or should not be, a factor for Turkish membership. This
approach blithely ignored the record of EU pronouncements, and the
new government in Ankara will have to do better if it wants a meaningful discourse with the Europeans.

In any case, even if Turkey jumped through all the current EU
hoops, many both inside and outside of Turkey are skeptical that the
EU will be in a position at the end of the day to deliver on the promise
of membership for Turkey. EU attitudes toward Turkey have been
ambivalent and appear still in flux. Governments of member states
have differing priorities when it comes to Turkey, and, more generally,
Europeans seem to have persistent reservations about the desirability
of accepting a large non-Christian nation into their bosom. Under-
scoring the point in mid-May 2002, Edmund Stoiber, then the front-
running candidate for chancellor in Germany's September national
elections, bluntly spelled out his strong objection to Turkey's membership, saying, "Europe cannot end on the Turkish-Iraqi border."[22]

The situation puts the Turks, as Morton Abramowitz has pointed
out, "in something of a Catch-22 situation."[23] If Turkey continues to
support Denktash, its EU bid may be set back for years, perhaps ended;
if it abandons Denktash's hard line, its EU bid may still be held back for
years. European public opinion and the governments beholden to it
have not yet reached a solid enough consensus to ensure acceptance
of Muslim Turkey. That is a fact of political life that hopefully will
change, but it will take time and almost certainly will not move far
enough to convince Turks before the Cyprus negotiations reach their
crunch point.

Moreover, the EU's posture leaves hanging the question of what
happens if Denktash does not sign on the dotted line and the Turks

stand by him to the bitter end. In such an event, does the EU have a plan to protect, in its own best interests, against the potential adverse developments discussed above?

The EU's campaign to move Ankara on Cyprus crossed the Rubicon at Helsinki. From some vantage points it may still appear more sensible to make a Cyprus solution a prerequisite for Cyprus EU membership or to impose other conditions, but the die has been cast. If not technically impossible, it is politically infeasible for the EU to reverse course on the accession procedure and the schedule it has laid down for the government of Cyprus. And Greece's veto inside EU councils is added insurance against back-pedaling.

Brussels will be "hoist by its own petard" if things go wrong. The imposition of artificial deadlines risks precipitating an irreversible division of Cyprus now, when there is still a chance that time could heal the wounds. In effect, the EU has taken pressure off the Greek Cypriots and signed on to their strategy of isolation and pressure. This has not worked for the past twenty-eight years. Throwing Turkey's EU membership onto the scales adds a substantial weight to be sure, but it also builds resentments that will carry forward if the balance is still untipped—or linger on to impede implementation of an agreement stuffed down unwilling throats.

In sum, the EU has articulated what it wants from Turkey but not what it will give in return. The accession process for Turkey itself should be more certain. The official EU stance, as formulated at Helsinki, is that "Turkey is a candidate State destined to join the Union on the basis of the same criteria as applied to the other candidate States."[24] The question therefore would seem not whether, but when. Brussels needs to move away from the confrontational tenor that has typified its relations with Ankara and give more concrete explanations of how Cyprus fits into the picture alongside the other ostensible sine qua non requirements for Turkish membership.

QUESTIONABLE STRATEGY (2): TURKISH CYPRUS

The EU should also shift gears to a more constructive tack that addresses Turkish-Cypriot concerns. Leaving the hard work to the UN, the EU has restrained its own contacts with Turkish Cypriots, meeting in unofficial venues on grounds that it does not recognize the Denktash administration. EU public pronouncements on the implications of membership for Turkish Cyprus have been limited to vague generalities. Enlargement Commissioner Guenter Verheugen, for example, speaking to the European Parliament in March 2002, said, "The Commission is keeping up its intensive contacts with the United Nations in order to ensure that any political solution is compatible with the relevant provisions of European law." How is the average Turkish Cypriot to interpret this declaration?

The EU's cautious approach to dealing with Turkish Cypriots keeps peace with Greeks inside the EU family, but risks giving up the opportunity to exert possibly decisive influence on the course of negotiations. As the Centre for European Policy Studies study mentioned above points out, the framework required for a reunified Cyprus to participate in the EU could supply "structures, guarantees and incentives that could hold together a bi-communal Cyprus," while the "Belgian laboratory" provides the practical demonstration of what works.[26] The EU needs to demonstrate concretely that membership for Cyprus and European institutions will be responsive to Turkish-Cypriot fears for their future security, well-being, and cultural identity.

A more positive EU strategy would proceed from the premise that Turkish Cyprus will come into the union, whether with, or after, the Greek side. The EU should make crystal clear its readiness to keep the doors open to Turkish Cypriots and spell out the elements of possible transition regimes. Ideally, the EU would persuade the two Cypriot parties to forego mutual isolation in favor of a new approach that opens the border, promotes exchanges and trade, immediately takes up property compensation for individuals, and relies heavily on confidence-building measures long advocated by the international community. These are the kinds of steps that would reduce mutual suspicion and provide incentive for change.

A further reality that must be addressed is the additional imbalance and bias that would be created by the unqualified entry into the EU of Cyprus without the Turkish Cypriots. Both Greece and (Greek) Cyprus would find it in their interest to exploit their combined votes inside EU councils whenever they could pressure Turkey for concessions to settle the Cyprus problem and bilateral Greek–Turkish differences. This is far more likely to produce rancor than cooperation unless the EU can find a way to treat Turkey and Turkish Cyprus on par with other aspiring members.

U.S. Interests and the Leadership Imperative

Tabling of the Annan Plan puts into play a crucial sequence that will set the tone for EU–Turkish relations on into 2003–2004. The Turkish Cypriots will in all probability accept the plan as a basis for negotiations. The EU Council in December could respond by setting a date for accession negotiations with Turkey, but it seems more likely and more consistent with the EU's recent pronouncements, that the council will propound a formula to set a date to set a date within the next year or two on condition that Cyprus and other developments continue to be favorable in EU eyes. Such a scenario can be cloaked in friendly language, but the end effect will be to kick the can down the road and tensions will build until the Cyprus issue is definitively settled or the EU recasts its approach.

The United States has traditional ties to the people of Cyprus and an abiding interest in seeing justice done by resolution of the island's division. This is so not just because of America's substantial Greek-American population but also in light of its global leadership responsibilities.

Although there have been zigs and zags, Washington has maintained generally good relations with both sides. The United States has taken the lead in the UN Security Council, named special envoys, contributed $305 million to Cyprus since the 1970s, and currently provides $15 million annually for bicommunal projects and scholarships to the United States. The United States is not loved on either side of the Green Line, but it has played a constructive role in keeping a peace process alive. And America's imprimatur remains vital for the credibility of any settlement.

From the U.S. strategic vantage point, the island itself, with a total population of about 750,000 and area about the size of Connecticut, is neither a big place nor a regional powerhouse in economic, political, or military terms. Its location is, of course, significant with reference to the Middle East, Central Asia, and Europe, but under foreseeable circumstances the sizeable British military base there will continue in operation. Close collaboration with the United Kingdom will work to shield crucial U.S. security interests.

The bigger question for Washington is Turkey, the more so now in view of the U.S. war against terrorism, conflict with Iraq, and engagement in the Middle East. In the overall scheme of things, most analysts agree that the compelling American national interest is not Cyprus per se but the broader framework of regional stability, for which Turkey is key. The Cyprus problem has a demonstrable capacity to cause trouble as a flashpoint between Greece and Turkey, a wedge between Turkey and the rest of Europe, a complication for NATO operations, and a contentious issue between U.S. administrations and Congress. It is also a divisive factor within Turkey, even more now that it is explicitly linked to EU membership.

For the past two decades, U.S. policy toward Greece and Turkey has been a balancing act to preserve American interests in the two countries by trying to help both while offending neither. Administrations have tended to lean toward Turkey and Congress toward Greece. September 11 and its aftermath shifted the middle point toward Turkey, but Greece remains high on the U.S. list of vital allies. Overall, the approach has worked reasonably well for NATO and U.S. bilateral relations, but it has not brokered a Cyprus solution.

In the past, if Cyprus talks foundered, life went on as before and negotiations could always be restarted after the dust settled. It is no longer that simple. Because the potentially irreversible consequences of a Cyprus breakdown are so profound, I had earlier argued that Washington should intervene in the near term to keep the process on track.[27] The United States has to do what it can to assure that the EU and Turkey work out an enduring mutual understanding on the fate of Turkish Cyprus and on the course to Turkey's own membership. If they fail, there will be little incentive for the Turkish side to make the compromises necessary to reunify Cyprus under one flag.

UN Secretary General Annan's initiative takes the pressure off Washington as long as his new proposals remain under positive consideration. As of mid-November 2002, cautious optimism is warranted. A strong government in Ankara is in the offing, and its leadership has set three priority objectives that auger well for Cyprus prospects: vigorous pursuit of EU membership, improved relations with Greece, and a Cyprus solution with elements of the Belgian model. The Annan Plan has realistic options for the Cypriot sides. EU leaders have welcomed the AK Party government and seem to be striving to assuage Ankara as best possible if the December European Council meeting does not set an unambiguous date for upgrading accession negotiations.

History, however, reminds one how quickly Greek–Turkish relations can go off the track. Powerful nationalist emotions can be energized overnight by misunderstandings or jingoistic appeals. And EU–Turkish relationships are also very fragile. The Europeans cannot hold Turkey at arms length much longer, but, perversely, they may not find a strong enough consensus in time to pin down membership for Turkey before frustration in Turkey starts to undermine coopera-tion, including on Cyprus.

WASHINGTON AND IRAQ VERSUS CYPRUS

Washington's prime concern as 2002 draws to a close is to sustain a solid bilateral partnership with Turkey and ensure Ankara's coopera-tion if and when the United States launches new military operations against Iraq. Having regained Republican control of Congress follow-ing the U.S. mid-term elections in November 2002, the Bush adminis-tration is well positioned to bolster its support for Turkey, although it will not be totally free of the constraints traditionally imposed by pro-Greek legislators and human rights activists.

Secretary of State Powell prominently supported Annan's initiative without taking a public position on substance. In the short term Washington can continue to work quietly for agreement based on the Annan Plan and for EU consent to an early date for starting formal membership negotiations with Turkey. The longer-term problem is to avert a breakdown that could prove virtually irreversible once Cyprus is inside the EU, and if European public opinion hardens against Turkish membership. From the U.S. viewpoint, it would obviously be ideal to act on the Annan Plan with an agreement in principle strong enough to ensure continuation of the negotiating process. The ques-tion is whether this can best be done by more forceful Washington intervention at this stage or by letting the UN keep the lead and wait-ing to see how its anticipated new proposal fares.

Twice in the past, the United States has taken the initiative to press the Cypriot communities to sign a framework agreement. The first such effort, the UN-sponsored 1985 High Level Meeting in New York, was brought about by strong U.S. diplomatic pressure. Greek-Cypriot President Kyprianou deemed the proposal far too favorable to the Turkish Cypriots and rejected it.[28] The second all-out UN push, also induced by U.S. maneuvering behind the scenes, produced the more balanced 1992 "Set of Ideas" noted above, which faltered when Denktash refused to sign on. Both these cases demonstrate that Washington can reenergize the process and refocus the agenda even if it cannot guarantee success at the end of the day.

As long as the possibility of war with Iraq hovers in the background, however, Washington will have little or no interest in shouldering a major, high-profile initiative on Cyprus. Its plate is too full with other foreign policy issues, and the new politics of Turkey is too untested for the United States to risk additional complications that could adversely affect its future military options in the area. On the other hand, a passive U.S. role reduces the pressures for progress and may allow opportunities to slip by. Washington can square this circle by doing its utmost behind the scenes to get the Cypriot sides, Turkey, and the EU locked into a negotiating process that can carry forward to 2004 and beyond if need be.

THE GORDIAN KNOT

Assuming there will be negotiations on the basis of the Annan Plan, the problem will be to establish some sequence or anchor. Otherwise, the two sides may find themselves going around and around in familiar circles as first one then the other finds itself unable to compromise under political or ideological pressures.

The logical starting point is agreement on the basic form of a government for the future nation of Cyprus. Until a common vision is hammered out, there is little solid ground for developing the specifics of governmental mechanisms and institutions. Conversely, if an outline, such as that proposed by Annan, can be accepted, negotiations could progress to the other key issues where agreement may hinge less on principle and more on compensation or provision of financial resources: territorial adjustments, return of property, housing for newly displaced persons, settlers from the Turkish mainland, and special arrangements to shield bizonality.

Former foreign minister Cem in the March 14 *International Herald Tribune* piece cited above declared, "I believe that an effort by the two leaders to reach a common vision for the future of Cyprus and to define the end result of the future that they want to achieve is the essential first step." Unless this can be done, he added, "the process will most probably be unsuccessful."

Although the Greek Cypriots have taken the position that it will be more productive to develop practical solutions to other core issues before taking on the overarching concept, their analysis of the negotiating problem is similar to Cem's. Greek-Cypriot ambassador to Athens Leonidas Pantelides wrote in an op-ed piece published by the Greek newspaper *To Vima* on January 20, 2002: "We can say that the Cyprus problem is composed—and hopefully its solution as well—of two elements: agreement on the basic form of the new political relationship between the two communities and, second, the concrete arrangements which will materialize from that agreed relationship." Like Cem, Pantelides continued in a grim vein, noting that the Turkish Cypriots insist on two separate states and the Greek Cypriots on one state. He concludes, "Unless one of the two sides gives way, agreement is not possible."[29]

Both sides agree only that the other has to give. Against this background of arid stalemate, the Annan Plan's incorporation of the Belgian experience has considerable promise. However, the Belgian model addresses primarily issues of dealing with the EU and, in certain cases, directly with other foreign governments. It does not provide a complete prototype for government structure appropriate to the Cyprus case, and the Annan Plan makes up with difference with a Swiss cantonal arrangement and complicated mechanisms for power-sharing executive and legislative bodies.

The outlook is for a series of difficult negotiations to finalize the Annan Plan well before Cyprus formally joins the EU in 2004. If negotiations fail to make demonstrable headway, or worse, threaten to fall apart, Washington should stand ready, sooner rather than later, to convoke all parties. In 1991 President George Bush on a visit to Ankara and Athens offered to host leaders from the two Cypriot communities along with those of Greece and Turkey. Disagreement on the Turkish side at the time killed the idea, but it could be revamped with roles for EU and UN representatives. The objective would be not to force a particular solution, which the United States cannot expect to do anyway, but to concentrate minds and proactively avoid the disastrous scenarios that would likely follow an acrimonious termination of bicommunal talks.

Beyond good offices, the United States should bring to the table a willingness to take the lead in forming a coalition to underwrite the security aspects of any bicommunal agreement. The form of government and the issues of physical security are bound together, especially for Turkish Cypriots, who predicate their case for sovereignty essentially on the ethnic troubles of 1963 to 1974. Until now, an

American commitment has been studiously avoided out of understandable concerns that the United States could find itself in the quicksand of interminable local ethnic contention. But that need not be the case, and only the United States has the stature and credibility to make a guarantee trustworthy; NATO is available to provide a multilateral framework, and it is illogical for the United States to be more deeply involved in the former Yugoslavia than in Cyprus.

Key to any breakthrough in the new circumstances is the EU, which was only marginally involved in previous Washington initiatives. Brussels holds the primary incentive packages for both Turkey and Turkish Cyprus. And the EU can provide for flexible transition regimes and targeted mechanisms to meet legitimate concerns of Turkish Cypriots as discussed above.

PULLING BACK FROM THE BRINK

If a common vision cannot be forged on future governmental structure, Washington should promote a transition plan with the straightforward objective of buying time without necessarily predetermining the final outcome. The challenge is to move away from the EU's near zero-sum confrontational strategy to a situation where the parties have incentives to keep working rather than follow through on threats to take retaliatory action. Europeans have to be convinced not to punish Turkey if Cyprus talks fail because the two communities on the island cannot overcome their differences, Turkey has to be convinced not to annex Turkish Cyprus because Greek Cyprus enters the EU, and all sides have to be convinced there is a better way forward than burning bridges.

Assuming entry of Cyprus into the EU before a settlement, a sensible transition plan to deal with the reality of Turkish Cyprus must recognize the existing division on the ground. Turkish Cypriots are no more ready to join a federation than Montenegrins, for whom the EU advanced a loose confederation with Serbia for a period of at least three years before a possible referendum on independence. The same logic argues for a temporary loose association between the Cypriot sides pending negotiated settlement of Turkish Cyprus's future, however long that may take.

If possible as well, a start should be made on the questions of territorial adjustment and the fate of properties taken from their respective owners in the upheaval of 1974. The sides have to agree on what method will be followed to determine which properties will be returned, which will be compensated, and how properties will be valued for this purpose. The continuing failure of the leadership to come up with some agreement in principle on these issues is allowing false expectations to become articles of faith, especially on the Greek side, while depriving owners of just compensation and magnifying the difficulty of fair evaluations. American and European property settlement mechanisms used in the wake of World War II and expropriations by Communist regimes provide appropriate experience and models. Until now in Cyprus, the language of negotiating tactics has masked the lack of political will to confront unpopular choices.

Finally, in any transition arrangement every effort should be made to implement the confidence-building measures that have long been on the UN table, in particular the return of Varosha (a Greek-owned suburb held by the Turkish side but virtually unused since 1974) and the opening of the Nicosia airport (closed since 1974). By the same token, there should be a vigorous expansion of current bicommunal activities, which have been restricted in practice by administration policies on both sides of the Green Line. As shown by the experience of Eastern Europe, promotion of contact, exchange, and commerce is a more effective engine of reconciliation than enforced isolation.

If all else fails and the worst-case scenario of a deep rupture between the EU and Turkey materializes, Washington has to be prepared to step in with whatever allies it can find to substantially upgrade relations with Ankara. Turkey has to do its part—such a development will not be possible if it is perceived outside the U.S. administration as passive acceptance of Ankara's intransigence on Cyprus. In the final analysis, if Washington has the courage of its conviction that Turkey's future lies with the West, it has to ensure that there is enough substance in the total political and economic relationship to make this a meaningful reality for both sides.

CHAPTER EIGHT

THE ENDLESS PURSUIT
IMPROVING U.S.–TURKISH RELATIONS

HENRI J. BARKEY

> *Soon after we started our new jobs, [Marc] Grossman in Ankara and I in Washington, we sat down to discuss what Turkey meant for us in the post–Cold War era. We developed a new concept which was fully backed by the White House and Pentagon, that Turkey was the new front state for the West, and in that sense, she had taken up the role of Germany during the Cold War.*
>
> —Richard Holbrooke[1]

> *The events of 11 September seem to have led the Bush Administration to a conclusion that took the Clinton Administration eight years fully to digest—that in today's world the Turks are good people to have in our corner.*
>
> —Mark R. Parris[2]

Does every new administration in Washington at some point in their tenure "suddenly" rediscover Turkey, as the above quotes seem to suggest? In fact, Turkey has loomed and continues to loom very large in Washington's foreign policy calculations. This was the case during the cold war, when Turkey earned its keep by facing numerous Soviet divisions. After the Soviet Union's demise, its strategic currency was highly valued because of its proximity to many different troubled regions: the Balkans, the Caucasus, the Middle East, and Central Asia. The September 11, 2001, attacks on the U.S. mainland and the launch of the global war on terrorism served once again as a reminder of Turkey's enhanced geostrategic significance because of its proximity to the war zone, its own concern with terrorism, and the symbolism of its role as a successful and secular Muslim state. What has changed in recent years is the U.S. approach to this important ally. The incoming Bush administration adopted the classical approach, which emphasizes the strategic importance of Turkey and limits U.S. involvement to state-to-state relations. Another approach, which the Clinton administration tried—not always with complete success—is to engage Turkey at all levels, societal and state, and encourage change.

The United States has always had an enduring interest in making this relationship work as smoothly as possible. If every administration—sooner or later—is cognizant of Turkey's importance and in need of its "services," either as a strategic partner or "model" Muslim country, then why do U.S.–Turkish relations appear so troubled at times? Why is Turkey's role in the North Atlantic Treaty Organization (NATO) and aspirations for membership in the European Union (EU) a contentious issue in U.S.–European relations?

Ankara's take on the relationship is contradictory. On the one hand, Turks believe that Washington sells them short because it does not fully appreciate Turkey's contribution to the Western alliance and the difficulties it faces in its neighborhood and in domestic politics. Turkish explanations for what they often perceive to be lackluster U.S. support are quite simple: U.S. domestic politics, influenced by inherently anti-Turkish Greek, Armenian, and human rights–oriented lobbies, casts a shadow over the executive branch's ability to carry out pro-Ankara policies. On the other hand, Turks also believe that they are much too important for Washington not to support Ankara's objectives and respond to its needs. Turkey recognizes that Washington, especially in the past couple of decades, has been a much more reliable ally than the Europeans, who, in Ankara's view, have proved time and time again to harbor few warm feelings for the Turks. But whether it is U.S. support for EU accession, economic bailout packages, or arms sales, Ankara believes all are naturally due to it because in its view its strategic location is worth its weight in gold.

This chapter argues that U.S. government policymaking toward Turkey has become freer of intense involvement by ethnic lobbies or sustained congressional engagement that could derail administration initiatives, as was the case in the 1970s, 1980s, and early 1990s. The sophistication and diversity of the U.S.–Turkey relationship have increased dramatically. Congress, despite the single-issue focus of some members, has come to finally realize this. This diversity and complexity also means that not everyone in the U.S. government will always agree with Ankara's preferences or with those of their own colleagues. There is a greater divergence of views on policy within the executive branch, though not on overall aims. To be sure, lobbies and other interest groups are still a lively part of the system, although the atmosphere that characterized the debate over the Turkish arms embargo in the late 1970s is deep in the past. Congress and the lobbies' influence, especially now that the days of military assistance are over, are more a function of the general state of Turkish–American relations. With the advent of the Bush administration, especially after September 11, Turkish policy has found its old niche, as security concerns are emphasized at the expense sometimes of global political and economic goals.

WASHINGTON'S STAKE IN TURKEY

U.S. interests and objectives in Turkey have steadily expanded since 1990. The cold war's straightjacket has given way to many new considerations. The primary U.S. foreign policy vision after the cold war was based on preventing regional disputes from threatening its own and its allies' interests and on globally expanding market reforms and democratic principles and practices. With no serious Russian threat to European security, U.S. attention has shifted to mid-level powers such as Iran and Iraq with ambitions to acquire nonconventional weaponry and the means to deliver them. This policy vision lacks the simplicity of containment, but it has impacted Turkey significantly. Turkey's proximity to many regions in flux or in conflict together with Ankara's long-standing adherence to the NATO alliance helped Washington reinterpret this country's geostrategic importance.

Simply put, Turkey is important for the United States for four reasons. First, it serves as a potential platform for the projection of U.S. power, as the 1991 Gulf War demonstrated. Saddam Hussein's resilience in the aftermath of the war has made Ankara essential to sustaining the United Nations (UN) sanctions regime. From the Incirlik base in Turkey, U.S. and British airplanes routinely patrol the no-fly zone over northern Iraq in an effort to keep Saddam Hussein's forces away from Kurdish-controlled parts of Iraq. It is difficult to see how the United States could have sustained its policy of sanctions, regime isolation, and protection of the Kurdish population without Turkey's cooperation.

Second, Turkey is also different and valuable because it is a NATO ally that takes security seriously. Its need for military modernization notwithstanding, Ankara has large numbers of troops under arms that are deployable, and it is committed to maintaining its spending on defense given its location in a "bad neighborhood."

Third, Turkey is a bulwark standing in the way of revisionist regimes like Iran intent on changing the regional landscape. Turkey's strong links to the United States, NATO, and the West in general are in direct opposition to some of Iran's regional preferences, if not designs. Hence, even in the event of cordial relations with Ankara, no Iranian government can ignore Turkey's reaction in its regional calculations. The improving relations between Turkey and Israel throughout the 1990s have changed the strategic setting in the Middle East—although much exaggerated by Arab countries—which helped Washington perceive Ankara as a more balanced regional player.

Finally, for Washington, Turkey represents an alternative and successful example for many countries in the Middle East and Central Asia. It is a model to be emulated as the only Muslim NATO member and EU candidate. In addition to its historical ties to the West, Turkey has had a vibrant, albeit flawed, democratic political system and in the 1980s embraced economic liberalization—well ahead of Latin America and, save for Israel, the only one in the Middle East.

Ankara's actual contributions to Washington's challenges have gone well beyond the Middle East. Turkey collaborated with the allies in both Bosnia and Kosovo. It steadfastly improved relations with Bulgaria and Romania, took the lead in organizing Black Sea regional institutions, and thus proved to be a source of stability throughout the Balkans. Both the Bush and Clinton administrations in the 1990s encouraged Turkey's efforts to reach out to the Turkic Central Asian countries and to the Caucasus to provide them with technical and economic know-how, not to mention political leadership, all designed to counter growing Iranian and Russian influence in the region. Turkish forces at Washington's request also took part in the ill-fated Somalia operation. Similarly, in April 2002, Washington prevailed upon Ankara to take over the leadership of the Afghan peacekeeping force in Kabul, the International Security Assistance Force.

It was Prime Minister and later President Turgut Özal who solidified Turkey's image in Washington after a decade of turbulence. He made himself a valued interlocutor during the Iran–Iraq war and decisively maneuvered his country in support of U.S. and allied action against Iraq in 1990. While often drawing attention to his own Muslim identity and Turkey's unique role in NATO, Özal nevertheless succeeded in convincing Washington of his deep commitment to the West and its values. Despite his traditional upbringing and religious roots, Özal was by far the most pro-American leader Turkey has ever had. He shared none of the suspicions of the United States of his left- and right-wing contemporaries. Having engineered the most far-reaching restructuring of the Turkish economy, he strongly believed in Turkey's ability to become an economic powerhouse of its own and a U.S. ally. With Özal, Washington could envision in Turkey a more democratic, stable, and prosperous ally and, as a result, also a better commercial partner.

Turkey's growing strategic value made its internal stability an even more important concern for U.S. policymakers. Instability in Turkey could potentially lead to the ascendancy of anti-Western forces, be they Islamic or nationalist in orientation, which could in turn lead to the denial of U.S. access to crucial military facilities and change the whole environment in the Middle East. Moreover, the Turkish political system has not found its equilibrium; electoral change could bring about a significant reorientation in the country's foreign and domestic policies and thereby undermine the four reasons the United States attaches importance to Turkey. To paraphrase Heinz Kramer, instability in Turkey has the ability to transform the country from an asset to a liability.

In the 1990s, Turkey—a Muslim country and the successor to a great empire—found that it was not immune to the revival of ethnic claims and religiously based ideological movements that gained currency after the collapse of Communism. These new movements undermined two principles of the post–World War II order: the inviolability of state boundaries and secularism. The reemergence of Kurdish activism and Kurdistan Workers' Party (PKK) insurgency in the 1980s raised anxieties in Turkey about the viability of the state and its territorial integrity. Turkey's established order was also challenged by the resurgence of Islamist politics: the pro-Islamic Welfare Party won a narrow plurality in the 1995 elections and succeeded the following year in forming a coalition government with the secularist, right-wing True Path Party. This coalition government triggered a backlash from the dominant military, which succeeded in engineering its downfall.

The Turkish elite perceived these claims of ethnic and religious orientation as existential challenges, but many in Washington during this period worried that the severe methods used to deal with them could, in the long run, undermine Turkey's stability. Moreover, the perceived overreliance on repressive means and curtailment of basic freedoms were incompatible with the importance Americans attach to democracy and free speech. In an era when the Clinton administration was intent on enhancing democratization worldwide, such fundamental problems in an important ally cast a shadow on the global democratization process. Turkey could not serve as a "model country" if it banned the use of Kurdish, the mother tongue of a significant segment of its population, or simple expressions of religious piety and restricted basic freedoms in the name of safeguarding the republic. U.S. officials, unsympathetic to the demands of extremists among the Kurds and the Islamist Welfare Party and even supportive of all of Turkey's actions against the PKK and its sympathizers, were nevertheless worried about the long-term spillover effects of delegitimizing moderate opposition movements. Deputy Secretary of State Strobe Talbott most clearly articulated this concern when he argued that "we believe that limiting avenues for legitimate political activity—whether by putting people on trial or in jail for what they write or say or by banning political parties or by shutting down NGOs [nongovernmental organizations]—carries with it the risk of an unintended consequence: it may turn moderates into extremists, who will then provoke further curtailment of freedom and undermine the health of democracy itself."[3]

The challenges posed by Kurdish and Islamic activism were accompanied by a weakening of the Turkish economy and an erosion of the status of the political elite, which had virtually abdicated its decisionmaking powers to the military establishment. This in turn gave rise to another problem for Washington: the disproportionate role of the military in political decisionmaking contradicted basic democratic norms. During the cold war this was tolerated, but in the emerging world vision the military's influence was anathema to America's other allies, the Europeans.

These shortcomings in Turkish policymaking interfered with the improvement in Turkish–American relations. The violations of human rights, the prosecution of journalists and politicians for what many in the United States would consider freedom of speech transgressions, the prevalence of torture, and the cruel nature of the conflict in the Kurdish-inhabited Southeast enabled the Greek and Armenian Americans to link up with human rights NGOs to oppose numerous arms sales to Turkey. U.S. decisionmakers were caught between the need to work with Turks on daily matters and their desire to address issues that threatened Turkey's stability. Too much interference risked alienating the Turks, while ignoring Turkish political reform would undermine longer-term U.S. goals.

THE CLINTON YEARS: HELPING TURKEY HELP ITSELF

The focus of U.S. policy after the cold war became making Turkey politically and economically more stable and above all seeing it integrated into Europe. Gone were the days when the sole emphasis was on security issues, arms sales, and managing the Greek–Turkish dispute. Turkey was to be nurtured to consolidate and expand its economic gains of the 1980s and its market system, deepen its democracy, and increase its regional influence, all the while being assured of U.S. support to deal with domestic challenges. Turkey was much too important to be left to its own devices, and, as administration officials often reiterated, the United States would help Turkey help itself.

U.S. policy toward Turkey in the 1990s was based on five pillars: (1) the traditional security relationship, including arms sales; (2) support for democratization and political reforms; (3) expansion of the Turkish economy through the realization of such projects as the building of an oil and gas pipeline network from the Caspian Sea to Turkey; (4) managing the Greek–Turkish relationship and especially the sensitive Cyprus issue; and (5) support for Turkey's application for the customs union with the EU and eventually for full EU membership. These pillars reflected general mid-term policy guidelines for the administration and were interlinked. For example, improved Greek–Turkish relations and democratic conditions in Turkey would reduce opposition to arms sales. Similarly, the EU process, with its strict admission requirements, would help reduce tensions with Greece and resolve the Cyprus problem as well as improve democratic practices and expand the economy.

In this vein, Washington undertook a number of policy initiatives. It actively supported the construction of major oil and gas pipelines from Central Asia through Turkey at a time when the oil companies were not convinced of either the economic feasibility of such a venture or of the quantities of oil available in the Caspian—oil giants much preferred simply to use existing Russia-based pipeline networks or build new ones through Iran. The United States had strategic reasons as well for pursuing these ventures in Turkey: reducing dependence on Middle Eastern oil, preventing Iran from becoming a conduit for Central Asian resources, and also lessening dependence on Russia and the former Soviet republics.

As a signal to Turks and the international capital markets, Washington designated Turkey as one of the ten big emerging markets, alongside South Korea, India, Brazil, and Indonesia. These were countries that the United States expected would grow rapidly in the near future and constituted credible markets for U.S. investments and commercial dealings. In the case of Turkey, this largely symbolic designation did not help much;[4] domestic economic problems and the archaic legal system alienated would-be investors. Ironically, mindful of its own ailing domestic textile industry, Washington rebuffed continuous Turkish efforts at getting the textile quota rescinded or reformulated. But more importantly, the Clinton administration became very attentive to the broad economic needs of the Turkish economy. The assistance of the U.S. administration was vital in securing International Monetary Fund (IMF) loans, the most important of which came in November 2000, for Ankara to sustain Turkey's faltering economy.

The five pillars notwithstanding, three issues came to dominate U.S.–Turkish relations during the 1990s: Turkey's candidacy for EU membership, Iraq and human rights, and problems in Turkey's democratization process. Of these, Turkey and the United States had fairly complementary positions on the first, much less so on the second, and had serious differences on the third. Although not strictly a core issue, Iraq acquired a special place in the bilateral relationship.

THE EUROPEAN UNION

Supporting Turkey's quest to further its integration with Europe was an easy choice for the United States. It mostly required only intense diplomatic activity, since the United States would incur none of the costs associated with the potential inclusion of Ankara. European and U.S. visions of the EU clash at a fundamental level. For the United States, as much as the EU is an instrument of economic and political integration it is also viewed as an extension of the Western security infrastructure. The Europeans, while conceding the spillover into security, view the EU more as a community of like-minded states linked by a common set of values. Turkey's accession to the EU in U.S. eyes, therefore, is a natural outgrowth of long Turkish participation in the "Western" club of nations, primarily through NATO. It would also be a sure way of insulating Turkey from the forces of Islamism. In 1995, Washington lobbied hard with the EU to conclude a customs union agreement with Ankara—a first, though not necessary, step on the way to EU membership. Following the customs union agreement, Washington focused on getting the Europeans to give Turkey a chance for membership by including it on the list of future candidates. Washington also thought that the process of customs union and candidacy negotiations would in the long run provide an avenue to resolve the Cyprus problem.

Europeans demurred: they were afraid of Turkey's large population, its relative underdevelopment, and its distance from the European cultural mainstream. Islamic immigration into Europe also raises all sorts of domestic political problems. Europeans also have severe reservations about Ankara's treatment of its Kurdish minority, the weakness of its democratic institutions, and the Cyprus problem. Moreover, Turkey's membership would dramatically alter the EU's borders and, by extending them to Iraq, Syria, and Iran, would invite new political, economic, and security challenges for which the EU is unprepared.

Washington, however, was relentless in its advocacy for Turkey. It redoubled its efforts after the ill-fated December 1997 EU Luxembourg Summit at which Turkey was clearly shunted aside by the Europeans, triggering a crisis in EU–Turkish relations. After the summit, Turks boycotted all political dialogue with Europeans and significantly hardened their position on a gamut of issues, including Cyprus. European officials visiting their U.S. counterparts were lectured at length by the Americans on the injudiciousness of denying Turkey a chance to join the EU. Washington argued that excluding Turkey was a strategic mistake that risked not just the future direction of Turkey's foreign policy but also of its economic well-being. Ultimately, the harsh Turkish reaction and especially the importuning of the United States succeeded in convincing the Europeans to reverse their Luxembourg stance at the 1999 Helsinki Summit, and Ankara was included in the list of candidate countries. But accession itself would not be a possibility for many years to come.

What stimulated the United States to be a strong advocate of Turkey's EU membership was the radical transformation of Turkey that the process of EU integration promised. The United States does not want to be solely responsible for the Turkish economy. Current trade patterns and geography, not to mention traditional commercial relationships, militate against a strong economic role for the United States in Turkey. More than 50 percent of Turkish trade has consistently been with European countries. Also, the United States expects that the desire to join the EU would more likely succeed in democratizing and reforming the Turkish political system than any U.S. effort; the EU's preconditions for even beginning accession talks with any candidate, codified as the Copenhagen criteria, include a series of political reforms.[5] Hence, Turkey's aspiration to join the European Union was a win-win proposition for the United States. It not only relieved the United States from a certain amount of responsibility for ensuring Turkey's future economic welfare but also promised a more prosperous Turkey, even a member of a competing economic bloc was likely to be a more stable, reliable, and better future economic partner of the United States. The alternative was to relegate Ankara to the edges of Europe, where the chances of it becoming a liability in the future were not insignificant. In sum, Washington was shifting much of the burden for transforming Turkey into a strong, stable, democratic, and prosperous society onto the Europeans; the easiest, fastest, and surest way of getting there.

Iraq

In the 1990s, Saddam Hussein's regime in Iraq became a principal American preoccupation. The Clinton administration enunciated a policy of "dual containment" against both Iran and Iraq, although in the case of the latter it would translate into more than simple containment. Because Saddam's rule presented the most immediate threat and necessitated the protection of the Kurds, Iraq emerged as Washington's priority. The United States supported UN arms inspectors' efforts to find and destroy Iraq's weapons of mass destruction—the basis for the

UN sanctions regime. By implementing a no-fly zone patrolled by coalition planes over both northern and southern Iraq, Washington made sure that Saddam did not deploy forces against either Kuwait or the Kurds. Finally, Washington kept probing Baghdad's weaknesses to see if it could effect political change without committing its own forces. Turkish cooperation was crucial to all of these efforts since U.S. access to northern Iraq could only be ensured by Turkey and not Syria or Iran, Iraq's other neighbors. Iraq led to an unprecedented level of cooperation between the United States and Turkey and simultaneously created a constant source of irritation and acrimony.

The linchpin of the cooperation was Operation Provide Comfort (OPC, renamed and restructured as Operation Northern Watch in 1997). Under this operation, an allied force patrolled the Iraqi northern no-fly zone to deter Saddam's troops. OPC had come into being with active Turkish cooperation following the 1991 Gulf War, when half a million Kurds fled to the Turkish border after their uprising failed and created a humanitarian crisis. OPC enabled the Kurds to reclaim much of their territory and allowed Kurdish refugees, including a million camped in Iran, to return home. Many Turks, however, believed that, with OPC, the United States was intent on building a Kurdish state in northern Iraq, no matter how many times U.S. officials publicly or privately repeated American fidelity to Iraq's territorial integrity. At the very most, the U.S. effort had given life to a Kurdish political entity in Iraq, which began receiving aid from international NGOs and, later under the oil-for-food deal struck with Baghdad, substantial amounts of goods from Iraqi oil revenues. Fierce U.S. support for UN sanctions on Iraq, the Turks complained, caused them huge commercial losses, which, they argued, in turn fueled the Kurdish insurgency within their own territory. The absence of Iraqi authority in northern Iraq, Turkey also argued, allowed for the Turkish-Kurdish insurgency group, the PKK, to establish bases on Iraq's border and cross at will.

As Turkey's anti-insurgency campaign gathered steam in the 1990s, Turkish troops routinely crossed the border into northern Iraq and eventually set up semipermanent bases there. In the early 1990s, the Turkish parliament waited until the eleventh hour to approve the biannual renewal of OPC. The Turkish military often tried to limit both the rules of engagement for U.S. pilots and the frequency of flights over Iraq. After allowing NGOs relatively free access to northern Iraq, Ankara clamped down and closed its borders to them in 1994. Turks also explored ways of improving relations with Baghdad, announcing in 1998 the upgrading of relations with Iraq to the ambassadorial level, for instance. In 2001, Ankara, despite vigorous U.S. objections, announced that it would build a second border gate with Iraq, bypassing the Kurdish enclave and thus facilitating Turkish–Iraqi trade, much of which is contraband and beneficial to the regime in Baghdad. So far, however, the Turks have not shown any hurry to complete this project.

U.S. policymakers have had to constantly maneuver around Turkish sensitivities on Iraq. By and large, Washington has offered uncritical support for Turkish actions against the PKK, including Turkish military incursions in northern Iraq, even when they cause civilian casualties among the Kurds. It also has provided political support at all international gatherings and, among other things, made it illegal in the United States to raise funds for the PKK. When Turkey threatened Syria militarily in 1998 to force Damascus to expel PKK leader Abdullah Öcalan, Washington, despite its worries about a new conflagration in the Middle East, was supportive of Turkey. Moreover, when Öcalan fled Damascus in search of new havens in Europe, the United States put pressure on various governments to arrest him. Eventually, when Öcalan found a brief respite in the Greek ambassador's residence in Kenya, the United States was instrumental in having him handed over to Turkish authorities.

U.S. support for Turkey in this area could not have been more different than Europe's. European countries condemned terrorism but gave equal importance to much-denied Kurdish rights in Turkey. Sensitive to human rights, Europeans also feared the spread of the conflict in Turkey to the Kurdish and Turkish communities in Europe, especially in Germany. Still, Washington's approach, anchored in global concerns about international terrorism and apprehension for Turkish stability, was not always sufficient to buy off Turkish acquiescence in northern Iraq. When a fight between different Kurdish factions endangered U.S. policy in Iraq in the mid-1990s, Washington worked hard to reconcile them, despite lukewarm support from Ankara. The Turks, instead, feared the demonstration effect the Iraqi Kurds might have on Kurds in Turkey and played off one Kurdish faction in Iraq against the other. In 1998, Secretary of State Madeleine Albright brokered an agreement between the two Kurdish factions, the Kurdistan Democratic Party (KDP) and the Patriotic Union of Kurdistan (PUK). The so-called Washington Accords called for a democratic, unified, federal Iraq; the Turks were not only embarrassed to be left out[6] but were resentful that the agreement made any reference to the concept of federation.[7]

U.S. officials also feel they helped Ankara by convincing the UN Security Council to mandate that Iraq export at least 50 percent of its oil through Turkey as part of the oil-for-food program. Despite its fervent wish to tighten the noose around Saddam, the United States also sided with Ankara during the discussions relating to UN Security Council Resolution 1284, a later iteration of UN Security Council Resolution 986, to exclude Turkey's trade with Iraq through the Kurdish areas from the sanctions regime. Still, arguing that they were the most affected by the Gulf War and the ensuing sanctions regime, the Turks resented Jordan's special status, which allowed Amman relatively free access to Iraq.

The Kurdish zone was the source of hostility in Turkey to U.S. efforts in Iraq. Two politicians spearheaded the opposition to the United States in Iraq, but both ultimately had to retreat: the Islamist Necmettin Erbakan and the nationalist and center-left politician Bulent Ecevit.[8] Erbakan, who had bid OPC goodbye on the night of his election victory, ultimately renegotiated the extension of OPC, albeit under its new name, Operation Northern Watch (ONW). Ecevit had never disguised his disapproval of the Gulf War, the sanctions regime, and the protection offered to Kurds in Iraq.[9] But if Ecevit had any intention of improving relations with Baghdad after coming to power, he had to quickly backtrack. In 1999, soon after Congress had passed the Iraq Liberation Act, which directed the Clinton administration to remove Saddam from power, Ecevit invited Tarik Aziz, Iraq's deputy prime minister, to Ankara over Washington's opposition. Unfortunately for Aziz, his visit coincided with the capture and return to Turkey of Öcalan with U.S. assistance, and he received a cold shoulder from Turkish authorities. Ecevit also retreated on a number of other issues, including an agreement to expand the rules of engagement of ONW for aircraft, giving them greater leeway to respond to missile firings. The fact that both of these die-hard opponents of U.S. policy in Iraq had to back down was due to the mutual dependency Iraq had created between Washington and Ankara. As much as Iraq was Ankara's ace in its dealings with the United States, Turks understood that the vital importance of this issue for Washington made it a double-edged sword. Any serious Turkish break with the United States on Iraq would have resulted in a major firestorm in Washington, and especially in

Congress. Despite serious disagreements, both parties recognized their mutual dependence and limitations.

HUMAN RIGHTS AND DEMOCRATIZATION

Turkey's rediscovered importance coincided with the reemergence of its twin domestic threats—Islamists and Kurds—and the resulting deterioration of its human rights performance. The PKK-led Kurdish insurrection, which peaked around 1992, was ultimately defeated through the application of sheer brute force and extra-legal methods.[10] Especially under Prime Minister Tansu Çiller, the police and other paramilitary forces were given a free hand. As a result, hundreds, if not thousands, of villages in southeast Turkey were destroyed or evacuated, people disappeared, incidents of torture multiplied, and the government imposed restrictions on freedoms of speech and association. This put the United States in an uncomfortable situation, especially when political parties were banned and avenues for a peaceful dialogue reduced. At the height of the cold war, Washington was more tolerant of interruptions in the democratization process, such as the 1980 Turkish coup that stopped regime-threatening left–right violence. With the end of the cold war and the new democratization wave of the early 1990s, Turkey's turnabout—considering its NATO status—was disconcerting to Washington. The administration also understood that human rights abuses and the democratic deficit in Turkey interfered with its ability to advance other items on Washington's agenda with Ankara.

The primary dilemma for the United States in this instance was how to reconcile its support for the fight against the PKK with its concern for deteriorating human rights conditions in Turkey. Understandably, the administration was divided internally as to how to approach this issue, and few missed the irony of the situation: while the United States was militarily protecting Iraqi Kurds, its ally, Turkey, was engaged in a campaign of repression against its own Kurds. Washington tried to square the circle by criticizing Ankara's behavior and its shortcomings on democratization and using the bully pulpit as well as quiet entreaties with Turkish officials. When it saw reason to congratulate the Turks for tangible improvements, no matter how minor, Washington was effusive with its praise.

A trickier problem for Washington was the sudden rise of the Islamist movement in Turkey. Islamist political parties, unlike their Kurdish counterparts, had a definite anti-American agenda. The everyday discourse of the Islamist Welfare Party's leader, Erbakan, was replete with anti-American diatribes. He and his party had advocated the end of OPC[11] and the reorientation of Turkish foreign policy away from the EU and the United States toward the Islamic world.

In the December 1995 elections the Welfare Party won a plurality. Divisions within the center-right culminated in a Welfare-led coalition with Çiller's center-right True Path Party. Erbakan's premiership exacerbated the confusion about Turkey in Washington. On the one hand, it was difficult to argue against a legitimate and constitutionally formed government; on the other hand, there were serious misgivings about where Erbakan was capable of taking Turkey. The United States went about its business with Turkey as if Erbakan was not there; it had other interlocutors in the foreign policy establishment, including the much more reliable military.[12] Despite his rhetoric against OPC, Erbakan signed off on another renewal soon after taking office. Most of Erbakan's foreign policy initiatives were harmless, but costly. For instance, he tried to construct a "rival" to the G-7, the D-8 (standing for the developing 8), composed of large Muslim countries such as Indonesia, Nigeria, Iran, and the like. His other ventures, such as an early, much-heralded trip to the Muslim countries of Iran, Libya, Indonesia, and Malaysia, proved his inexperience.

It was only when the Turkish military decided to embark on a public campaign in February 1997 to oust the Erbakan-led government that the United States was faced with the unpleasant choice between the "secular" military and a government that professed to have democracy on its side. Washington instead remained on the sidelines, as Alan Makovsky remarked, contenting itself with "Delphic remarks for a secular, democratic Turkey."[13] The Turkish general staff caused the government's collapse in June 1997. The U.S. government in effect stood by for what was a coup in everything but name only— or, as journalist Cengiz Çandar aptly named it, "a post-modern coup." If the U.S. government did not stand up for the Welfare Party in 1997, it compensated when it strongly criticized the authorities for the party's ban in 1998 (as it had likewise done in the case of the pro-Kurdish parties earlier). Moreover, when Tayyip Erdogan, a Welfare Party member and a popular former mayor of Istanbul, was convicted and

sentenced to a prison term and lifetime ban on politics in 1998, ostensibly for reading a poem by a renowned Turkish nationalist poet, the
U.S. consul general in Istanbul visited him in his office. The visit caused
an uproar; the United States was accused of interfering in the domestic affairs of the country.

The United States used a variety of approaches to encourage the
Turks to improve their human rights performance. These included
public diplomacy, quiet diplomacy, and efforts at strengthening
Turkish civil society and NGOs. The most visible element of public
diplomacy was the annual State Department human rights reports, the
one instrument most resented by Ankara.[14] Turkey, as many Turks
would complain, was not only unfairly treated, but it also often ended
up with a chapter second only to China's in length. These reports provided the basis for much of the criticism levied at Turkey by NGOs,
Congress, and unfriendly lobbies. In addition, high-ranking U.S. diplomats were careful to maintain a public rhetoric of encouraging reforms
in Turkey. Deputy Secretary of State Talbott detailed the reasons for
U.S. anxieties over Turkish human rights practices by giving the most
comprehensive speech of any incumbent high-ranking U.S. official.[15]
Secretary of State Albright criticized Ankara for the persecution of journalists.[16] If public diplomacy upset the Turkish establishment, it also
conveyed an important message to those who labored for reform in
Turkey—politicians, journalists, academics, and NGOs—and looked to
Washington for moral support and even protection.

These public efforts at diplomacy were often buttressed by quiet
approaches. The State Department and the White House negotiated a
list of seven criteria with the then Turkish prime minister Mesut Yilmaz
in 1997 by which the United States would judge Turkish progress on
the human rights front. This list was then shared with the NGO community and manufacturers in an effort to get them to cooperate and
help the process along. It consisted of the following: "1) decriminal-
ization of free speech; 2) releasing of journalists and parliamentarians
who had been imprisoned for political reasons; 3) ending torture and
police impunity; 4) reopening of non-governmental organizations that
had been shut down by Turkish authorities; 5) democratization and
expansion of political participation; 6) lifting of the state of emergency
in southeastern Turkey; and 7) resettlement of internal refugees displaced by the civil war."[17] This exercise in defining a road map was as
much an attempt to encourage Turks to reform as an expression of
unwillingness by the administration to pass up a deal of this magnitude

in order to insulate itself from congressional criticism over a controversial arms deal.

Arms sales became the most direct means of pressure available—
the reason why Congress scrutinizes deals—as the United States has a
commanding lead in both sheer market size and technology. At the
end of the 1990s Turkey had emerged as one of the prized markets
for arms exporters, with its thirty-year plan to spend as much as $150
billion on modernizing its armed forces. The size of the Turkish market, in turn, provided Ankara with some leverage against Washington,
and Turks openly voiced their criticisms of the United States as an
unreliable supplier.[18]

THE U.S. DECISIONMAKING ENVIRONMENT

The proliferation of issues, the multiplicity of actors, and the need to
balance short-term needs against long-term considerations complicate
the American decisionmaking process. It is not surprising that the U.S.
government is often criticized for either doing too much for Ankara
or too little. This section analyzes three interrelated factors influencing
the making of U.S. policy on Turkey: internal U.S. government considerations, the role of Congress and nongovernmental bodies, and
the Turks themselves.

THE EXECUTIVE BRANCH

The executive branch starts with a pro-Turkish disposition. Turkey's
importance to the United States and the challenges and opportunities
it represents mean that officials at the State Department and the
Pentagon perceive postings to Ankara or Turkey-related positions as
far more important and career enhancing than those in most European
capitals. As Morton Abramowitz points out, Turkey is one of the few
countries where the U.S. ambassador exerts "real and a continued
influence in Washington," in large measure because of the complexity
of the country's internal politics and the general lack of knowledge
among senior U.S. officials of that country.[19] If sailing is not always
smooth it is because the multiplicity of salient issues and geographical
areas in which Turkey is active naturally give rise to turf battles and

lead to a lack of focus. Policy on Turkey often appears to be a sum of disjointed parts.

There are two important sources of division within any U.S. administration on Turkey. The first revolves around simple geographically driven bureaucratic considerations: administratively, Turkish policy is the responsibility of European bureaus, whereas many of the issues in which Turkey plays a crucial role are located in the Middle East. Consider, for instance, the exigencies of Iraq policy at the White House, the Pentagon, and the State Department. It is not uncommon, therefore, to find Near East-related officials attempting to exert maximum pressure on Ankara to comply better with the Iraq sanctions regime while others in the European division are cajoling the Turks to be more forthcoming on the Cyprus dispute. Another source of tension within the executive branch originates from the proliferation of congressionally created bureaucratic mandates, such as the special Cyprus coordinator, or global directives requiring reports on a variety of topics, from human rights to religious freedom and, most recently, trafficking in persons (TIP). The 2002 TIP report, which was highly critical of Turkey, elicited strong, indignant reactions from Ankara at a time when the Bush administration is constantly showcasing Turkey as a role model.

A far more important source of conflict within the U.S. government recently has been the emergence of two distinct policy camps on Turkey. Both start with the same premise: Turkey is crucial to U.S. security. One school of thought believes that Turkey's strategic importance to the United States should not be compromised by any other consideration. They argue that antagonizing Ankara risks emboldening anti-American, Islamist, and nationalist movements and pushing Turks away from the United States. Some officials counsel that any criticism of Turkey, especially on democratization, be done privately or not at all for fear of embarrassing allies. With its roots in traditional statecraft, this mode is by the far the most dominant. The other school advocates active involvement in Turkey at all levels and not just security-related concerns. More global in orientation, this approach argues that the United States ignores Turkey's internal problems in an age of greater transparency, at its own peril. Unless the United States tends to all of Turkey's requirements, including assistance in the democratization process, the likelihood of internal instability and anti-American movements increases. Without U.S. help to Turkey to close its democratic and human rights deficits, it is unlikely to become a member of the EU, which would mean the failure of a cardinal U.S. policy objective. Ironically, both schools are concerned about the long-term bilateral relationship and the possibility of "losing Turkey" because of its internal instability.

As distinct as these two approaches may appear, U.S. policy has come to reflect a mixture of what both advocate. The strength each has at any one point in time is a function of the administration's vision and priorities and, within these broad parameters, the relative strength of individuals, departments, and bureaus. In the State Department, not surprisingly, those in favor of engagement are concentrated in the least influential bureaus with global mandates, such as the Bureau for Democracy, Labor and Human Rights (DRL). DRL under Harold Koh in Clinton's final years, however, was quite successful in articulating an agenda, building alliances inside and outside government, and exerting a disproportionate influence. In the case of Turkey, Koh was successful in keeping his issues visible, not just in the department but also in Turkey, and maintaining the pressure for reform. Regional bureaus control the day-to-day implementation of policy. What bureaus such as DRL can hope to accomplish through sheer perseverance and, especially in the post–cold war era, by invoking the "high moral ground," is to force the regional bureaus to push for change, however small. As in many bureaucratic organizations, the war between bureaus and departments is at times intense, with each side accusing the other of either being too critical of Turkey or not reporting and hiding the facts.

THE POLICY IMPACT OF CONGRESS, THE LOBBIES, AND NGOS

For the past few decades, Turks have habitually complained about the negative influence exerted on the executive branch by Congress, lobbies, and NGOs. Turkish diplomats routinely refer to "alien influences" and the Turkish press talks of evil lobbies.[20] Perhaps no other U.S. ally has had to endure the crossfire of such an eclectic alliance of interest groups, consisting of Greek and Armenian Americans (Turks also perceive the existence of a separate Kurdish lobby) and human rights groups and their congressional allies. The concentration of Greek and Armenian Americans in crucial electoral states such as New York, New

Jersey, and California has served to amplify their political clout. Human rights groups are unlike their ethnic allies in that the latter pursue a zero-sum approach that seeks to punish Turkey.

Human rights NGOs want the administration to use its powers to push for greater democratization, and they are willing to work with the Turkish government to this end. To be effective, they cooperate with others in Congress to block arms sales. In addition, organizations such as Human Rights Watch and Amnesty International have a natural constituency within the U.S. government's pro-engagement forces.

The most profound change in Turkey's fortunes on Capitol Hill was caused by Turkey's decision to improve relations with Israel. Unable to match Greek and Armenian Americans with an equally effective Turkish-American lobby, Ankara made a calculated decision to shop for a constituency in the United States. The conversion of the Jewish-American groups is one of Ankara's great foreign policy successes of recent times. The process started in the 1980s under Prime Minister Özal, who turned to the leadership of Turkey's small Jewish community for help in Washington. Turkey has continuously tried to score points by displaying its tolerance for Jews and, in the 1990s, used its burgeoning relationship with Israel to win over Jewish Americans. Especially on the Armenian genocide question, even if not all Jewish congressmen were won over, the fact that many Jewish-American organizations supported Turkey on a topic sensitive to Jews was influential in staving off further embarrassments for Ankara.[21] Jewish-American cooperation extended beyond the Armenian genocide issue; it greatly assisted Turkish diplomatic efforts on other fronts as well. For instance, American Jews could also be counted on to rally around basic Turkish ideas such as secularism or to help Ankara's ally Azerbaijan in Congress.

American-Jewish groups make up for the absence of a strong, broad-based pro-Turkish business lobby. China, by contrast, while not an ally of the United States and with a terrible human rights record, has succeeded in mobilizing American industry to be its voice in Washington. Turkey's inability to attract sizeable quantities of foreign direct investment has meant that no blue chip companies, except for defense contractors, come forward to do Turkey's bidding. Even though the defense industry has strongly supported Turkey, defense procurement remains as the most controversial of all commercial relations. Whereas military contractors have generally lobbied the U.S. administration against strict requirements for export licenses, human rights groups, especially during the years of the Kurdish insurgency, sought to limit arms sales to Ankara.

It would be premature to argue that the American-Jewish community's support for Turkey has permanently leveled the playing field. Jewish groups are careful not to run afoul of other ethnic groups with which they have collaborated over the years. Moreover, Jewish-American members of Congress are generally more liberal than their colleagues, especially on human rights and democratization. Jewish support could well be tested by Turkish reactions to the ongoing violence between Israel and the Palestinians. In April 2000, hostile Turkish reaction to Israeli retaliations to terrorist incidents undermined much of the good feelings that had developed, especially after the 1999 Istanbul earthquake when Israelis figured prominently in rescue operations. This change in atmosphere might have gone unnoticed had it not been for Prime Minister Ecevit, who, in a prepared speech to his parliamentary group, accused Israel of genocide in the West Bank. While Israeli reaction to the Ecevit statement was muted, American-Jewish reaction—Ecevit's subsequent efforts at clarifying his statement without apologizing notwithstanding—was one of shock.[22] The controversy quieted down as leading members of the Jewish community and the Turkish government engaged in damage control.

Turkey's improving image in the United States also has helped Ankara enlist new supporters, among them the influential but departing Republican senator Jesse Helms. Nevertheless, Turkey continues to face difficulties in Congress. On the eve of what was expected to be a close 2000 congressional contest, in an effort to court Armenian-American voters, it was still possible for the Republican leadership in the House to propose a nonbinding resolution recognizing the Armenian genocide so as to help one lone, beleaguered Californian colleague; it took President Clinton's direct intervention to avert a crisis with Turkey, which threatened to retaliate by measures such as closing the Incirlik airbase and canceling $11 billion worth of energy contracts. At times, laws passed by Congress—unrelated to Turkey—have interfered with arms sales and create a crisis in relations between the two countries. For instance, the Leahy amendment to a 1996 law prohibiting U.S. financing of equipment to security forces involved in human rights violations became a major stumbling block in the sale of armored personnel vehicles to Turkey in 1999. Although the State Department had issued an export license, the amendment prohibited the use of U.S. loan guarantees, which almost proved to be a deal breaker.[23]

TURKISH EXCEPTIONALITY

Turkey presents some unusual challenges to U.S. decisionmakers because of the imbalance between its civilian and military authority. The weakness of civilian political leaders has contributed to a decisionmaking vacuum, which the officers have filled. This has complicated dealings with the Turkish government, as civilian leaders have to make sure that the Turkish general staff is on board. The military's ascendancy has contributed to a policy of brinksmanship in its foreign relations.

Unlike in any other NATO state, the Turkish military, since the 1960 coup, has emerged as a singularly powerful domestic and foreign policy actor. Weak civilian elites have progressively abdicated larger and larger swathes of decisionmaking authority to an institution that has little, if any, accountability to other public authorities. By the same token, the military's dominant presence has often rendered Turkish politicians irresponsible and seemingly irrelevant. The lack of confidence in civilian authority permeates all levels of society, from the man in the street to business leaders and civil society institutions. The military determines national security policy and decides on the size of its own budget and how it is allocated. No significant national security decision can be taken without the general staff's consent. This power has expanded concurrently with the perceived domestic threats to include a wide array of domestic social issues as well. The military's clear emergence as Turkey's most powerful actor has meant that it has become an impediment on the road to EU accession.

Whether the issue is progress toward EU membership—the EU requires that Turkey eliminate the political role of the military as a precondition—or Iraq, or human rights and democratization, U.S. foreign policymakers have to take into account the preferences of the Turkish military. Heinz Kramer argues that there is no Turkish "grand strategy" for its role in the post–cold war order. Instead, decisionmaking is quite ad hoc, even rigid and one dimensional. Ankara combines its inflexibility in what it believes is "its rightful and legitimate position" with "open or disguised military threat."[24] Turkey has successfully pursued a very risky and forceful foreign policy that has emphasized threats and sometimes its military power, whether toward its allies in Europe and the United States or its foes, such as Syria. For example, after the European Union's 1997 Luxembourg Summit, Turkey suspended all political dealings with the EU until the latter relented and, in the 1999

Helsinki Summit, offered Ankara the prospect of candidacy. When the Cypriot government disclosed that it would import long-range Russian anti-aircraft missile batteries, Ankara threatened the island with dire consequences if it went ahead with the shipment and left it to the United States to convince the Cypriots to rescind their deal. Similarly, to dissuade the EU from inviting Greek Cyprus into the EU, Ankara threatened to counter any such move by annexing the northern part of the divided island. Ankara seemed to put even its relations with Washington on the line when it tried to dissuade the U.S. House of Representatives from adopting a nonbinding commemorative resolution on the Armenian genocide by denying access to military bases in Turkey.[25] In 2002, it punished one of the Kurdish groups in northern Iraq for making claims on an oil-rich town by cutting the lucrative diesel fuel trade between Iraq and Turkey.[26]

Turkey has been remarkably successful with this approach, but consistently using it with allies and friends also sows the seeds of future disputes. In the current debate on European accession, the anti-EU musings of even those who claim to want Turkey to become a member exude the sense that Ankara must have applied for membership in an enemy alliance. The Turks, to the extent that they resort to brinkmanship tactics because the national consensus on the EU is fragile, risk alienating the one constituency with decisive power: the European public and their representatives.

The challenges presented by the preeminence of the military may not be immediately apparent to Washington, where some would prefer to interact with straightforward officers instead of feeble politicians. Doing business with the military on foreign policy matters when interests and preferences coincide is indeed easy. It is when the reverse occurs, especially in situations where the officers stake out a strong ideological perspective, that bargaining with an institution unaccustomed to the give-and-take of everyday political life leads to a different set of complications. Negotiations on the future of the European Security and Defense Policy (ESDP), for instance, were prolonged by the disagreement between the Turkish military and the Turkish ministry of foreign affairs. U.S. policymakers may, in principle, object to dealing directly with the military, but they too have learned to solicit implicitly or explicitly the Turkish general staff's preferences on important decisions.[27] Just like the Turkish public, U.S. leaders have at times preferred the easy route and hoped for the generals to take a decision quickly, efficiently, and, naturally, along U.S. interests. Ironically, this

attitude undermines the very messages that the United States has tried
to convey on democratization.

U.S.–TURKISH RELATIONS ON THE EVE OF SEPTEMBER 11

When President Bill Clinton left office, U.S.–Turkish relations were
enjoying an unprecedented period of harmony. This was capped by a
very successful five-day presidential trip to Turkey in November 1999,
when for the first time an American president addressed the Turkish
parliament. A number of developments in Turkey enabled this change
in policy for an administration that had been accused of being exces-
sively critical of Turkish policies. These included the rapprochement
between Greece and Turkey, especially after the devastating earthquakes in the summer of 1999 in both countries; the consolidation of
the Turkish–Israeli relationship and the concomitant lessening of pressures on Turkey in the U.S. Congress; collaboration in Kosovo and
southeastern Europe; and the end of the PKK insurgency following
the capture of Öcalan, which raised hopes for political liberalization
in Turkey. As a result of U.S. and EU pressure, Turkey did introduce a
modicum of change in its laws. Additionally, there were no big-ticket
arms transfer items in recent years to engender a dispute. Despite the
human rights community's decision to make the sale of attack helicopters a litmus test of the government's arms export policy and the
general lack of progress on the seven points agreed to by Prime
Minister Yilmaz in 1997, the administration was confident that it could
successfully push the sale through Congress. Still, the Turkish government did not feel secure enough in this commitment and delayed its
purchasing decision until after the 2000 presidential elections in the
United States.

From Ankara's perspective, Washington had delivered on two
major Turkish concerns: the capture of Öcalan—which had propelled
an interim prime minister, Ecevit, to win the 1999 elections—and the
EU's Helsinki decision in the same year. Both of these increased
Turkish cooperation, especially on Iraq. Political and economic
reforms, even if exaggerated, were seen as a vindication by the administration that its policy of putting pressure on Ankara while simultaneously assisting the latter in every possible way was proving

successful, albeit quite slowly. In his speech to the Turkish parliament, President Clinton outlined a vision for Turkey that fit well with his administration's overall policies:

> There is another vision—one that requires a strong Turkey playing its rightful role at the crossroads of the world, at the meeting place of three great faiths. It is possible to see that brighter future: one of rising prosperity and declining conflict; one in which tolerance is an article of faith, and terrorism is seen, rightly, as a travesty of faith; a future in which people are free to pursue their beliefs and proclaim their heritage; in which women are treated with equal respect; in which nations see no contradiction between preserving traditions and participating in the life of the world; a future of growing respect for human rights that protect our differences and our common humanity; and, specifically, a future in which nations that are predominantly Muslim are increasingly partners with nations that are not, acting in concert in ways, large and small, to realize the shared hopes of their people.[28]

By the end of his term, especially after his trip, Clinton had become the most popular U.S. president in Turkey ever. Still, many Turks preferred George Bush to Albert Gore in 2000 because of their expectation that a Republican administration would underemphasize issues of democracy in favor of more traditional security concerns.

The Bush administration came to power with a set of foreign policy priorities that were in stark contrast with those of its predecessor. Gone was the emphasis on globalization—economic and political—democratization, and the expansion of a community of shared values. The new Bush team focused instead on new security threats; weapons of mass destruction and ballistic missile defense topped its agenda at the expense, critics argued, of many of the multilateral arrangements its predecessors had entered into. Moreover, during the campaign Bush was dismissive of Clinton's "nation-building" approach and, just as previous Republican presidents, he preferred to stay away from interfering in the domestic affairs of U.S. allies.

It was clear from the election campaign that Iraq would loom large in the early years of the administration. The hardening of the U.S. position on Iraq was an unwelcome development to Turkey. Even Secretary of State Colin Powell's smart sanctions proposal, an early effort at molding Iraq policy, would have required stiffer controls of illicit Iraqi revenues along the Turkish, Syrian, and Jordanian borders, significantly reducing the income of the three countries from their dealings with Baghdad.

Well before the new administration had time to formulate its Turkish priorities, it faced its first Turkey crisis. This was the financial collapse of February 2001, the worst economic crisis in the republic's history. Unlike Clinton, who in November 2000 had moved quickly with the IMF to restore confidence in the Turkish economy, the Bush administration hesitated at first. The treasury department under Paul O'Neill's leadership was inclined not to bail the Turks out because the administration had intended to put an end to the Clinton-era practice of rescuing countries that had not sufficiently reformed themselves. In the case of Turkey, O'Neill had to be persuaded that strategic consideration had come into play and that Turkey was entitled to another chance and ultimately deserved a combined IMF/World Bank package of $31 billion. Not only did the administration fear that, left to its own devices, Turkey could follow Argentina into chaos, but also it felt that it needed to pay closer attention to domestic developments in Ankara. The brush with calamity made it easier for the Turkish government—with its hardcore nationalist elements—to accept Kemal Derviş, a World Bank vice president, as its new economic czar. Throughout 2001, Derviş painstakingly began to implement long-ignored economic reforms, often relying on his Washington connections to move recalcitrant politicians and bureaucrats to implement the program. The Bush administration's initial reluctance to come to Turkey's aid had some payoff; it forced the reluctant Turkish leaders to take the economic reform package much more seriously.

September 11 and the New Bush Administration

September 11 changed U.S. priorities. In addition to combating terrorism, the administration's determination to induce regime change in Iraq was strengthened. The post–September 11 atmosphere in the United States is increasingly beginning to resemble the cold war era in the form of the mobilization of resources, the reorganization of government structures and institutions, and, most importantly, the

singleminded focus on and determination needed to defeat an enemy.
Hence, the Bush administration's relationship with allies and foes
alike is also being redefined. The war on terrorism has propelled
Turkey, once again, to the front lines, given its borders with Iran and
Iraq. Turkey was quick to offer support to the United States in the
war against terrorism; it opened its air space and bases to U.S. forces
moving to Afghanistan and cooperated on intelligence, anti-money-
laundering operations, and maritime interdiction efforts. The Turkish
military was reluctant to commit forces to an Afghan peacekeeping
operation without adequate NATO support for fear of failure and
thereby damage to its reputation at home and abroad.[29] The United
States ultimately prevailed—also providing $280 million in aid—and
the Turks agreed to replace the British as head of the International
Security Force in April 2002.

The Turkish government has strong incentives to cooperate with
the U.S. anti-terrorist efforts. For the Turkish establishment, civilian
and military, the war on terrorism validates two strongly held basic
positions: that Turkey has been a prime and misunderstood victim of
terrorism (in this case Kurdish terrorism) and that extremist Islamic
movements, including Turkish ones, constitute a major threat to world
peace. September 11 and the subsequent war on terrorism thus have
served to legitimize the Turkish state's hardline policies against the
PKK, recently rebranded as KADEK, which has tried to recast itself as
a political movement since it abandoned the armed struggle following
Öcalan's capture. The new atmosphere helps the Turkish government
maintain its uncompromising attitude to Kurdish political parties and
movements. Ankara, with abundant U.S. support, has pushed the EU
very hard to declare both the PKK and KADEK illegal terrorist organizations throughout Europe. Similarly, in the mind of the government,
the Taliban's harsh rule and al-Qaeda's violence have served to remind
average Turks of the dangers of Islamism and have put similar Turkish
movements and parties on the defensive.

Ankara's prime worry is the expansion of the war on terrorism to
Iraq. As the Bush administration increasingly signals that it will attempt
to overthrow Saddam Hussein's regime in Baghdad, Ankara is appre-
hensive about potential chaos in Iraq after Saddam's overthrow and the
possibility that the Kurds in northern Iraq will seek to set up an independent Kurdish state.[30] Ankara finds even the prospect of a federated Iraq with a Kurdish entity as one of its constituent parts
unacceptable, although it will be hard-pressed to object to such an

arrangement should the Iraqi people freely decide on it. Recently, Ankara has warned the Kurds not to cross their red lines by seeking to incorporate the Iraqi town of Kirkuk, which Turks consider to be a primarily Turkoman-inhabited town, in a post-Saddam scramble for territory.[31] The danger for Turkey in a post-Saddam era is that, in its zeal to prevent the Kurds from crossing red lines, it will find itself drawn into an adventure in northern Iraq.

This jockeying is also part of a bargaining process with the United States. Turkey is likely to suffer financially from a U.S. war against Iraq; in the aftermath of the 2001 economic crisis, tourism revenues have loomed large in Turkish plans to engineer an economic recovery. With an estimated $11 billion in projected tourism revenues for 2002, Ankara wants to be ensured by Washington that any action against Saddam is swift and does not coincide with its peak tourism season. In addition to protecting tourism revenues, Turks will want assurances that IMF loans will continue and will ask for foreign military sales loan forgiveness. Ankara is also likely to bargain hard and resort to brinkmanship tactics to ensure a role for Turkomans in a post-Saddam Iraq. The Turkoman issue is mostly a weapon in Turkey's arsenal largely deployed to prevent the formation of a strong Kurdish federated entity in Iraq. Similarly, Turkey will expect to be closely consulted on the United States's policy toward the Kurds. The Turks have been offered high levels of assurances. Some in Turkey hope that American dependence on Turkey for an Iraq operation will permit Ankara to drive a hard bargain on other issues, such as Cyprus.

The Bush administration knows that it cannot mount an effective anti-Saddam operation without the cooperation of Turkey. Ankara's passive participation by acquiescing to the use of its air bases, use of transit facilities for U.S. troops provided they are not stationed on Turkish soil for any extended period, and the possible resupply of ground and other forces operating in Iraq will be militarily decisive as well as politically crucial in legitimizing an American-led multinational coalition. The current unwillingness of Saudi Arabia to align itself with the United States on Iraq reduces the United States's maneuverability and highlights its reliance on Turkey and Kuwait. Iraq topped the agenda during Prime Minister Ecevit's January 2002 trip to Washington. Soon after his return from Washington, Ecevit distanced himself from Saddam and even warned him about his noncompliance with UN resolutions.[32] Ecevit has since reiterated that he prefers the United States not to remove Saddam by force. The United States has, in 2002, picked up the pace of high-level consultations with Ankara to demonstrate its determination to oust Saddam and to reinforce the atmosphere of cooperation with Ankara.

Still, as strong as the Turkish card appears to be, both the Bush administration and the Turkish government are cognizant that Ankara cannot afford to alienate Washington. If Turkish objections were to prevent a U.S. move against Saddam, Turks fear a political backlash in Washington could undermine Turkey's economic recovery and reverse all the diplomatic gains of the past decade. Because of the current economic crisis, the United States today has a great deal more leverage over Turkey than it did in the Clinton years. In effect, Washington and Ankara find themselves in the same situation that they were in throughout the 1990s over Iraq, except that the stakes are much higher now. Should the United States intervene militarily in Iraq, there would still be a great many reasons why Turkish and American interests would diverge during and after the operation, particularly if the U.S. effort is longer and bloodier than expected. With the Turkish population overwhelmingly opposed to a military intervention, there still are many unpredictable events or outcomes that could create serious disagreements between Ankara and Washington. The most immediate uncertainty comes from the upcoming elections scheduled for November 3, which could dramatically alter the Turkish political landscape should a coalition of pro-Islamist and nationalist parties succeed in forming a government.

With a U.S. administration focused on terrorism, Turkey, like many other countries, expects that Washington will not want to scrutinize human rights conditions or lack of progress in democratization closely. This also applies to ethnic politics. The advent of a Republican administration, together with September 11 and Greek–Turkish rapprochement, has reinforced the general trend toward the diminution of ethnic influence in the White House. With the administration emphasizing traditional strategic concerns within the context of the war on terrorism at the expense of other issues, Armenian- and Greek-American groups may find it much more difficult to make their points. The administration is in the process of articulating a new doctrine that will rely heavily on preemption; even if the Iraqi regime is replaced, Iran and Syria, which still figure prominently among states supporting terrorism and developing weapons of mass destruction, are likely to remain in American crosshairs. As Deputy Secretary of Defense Paul Wolfowitz put it, "in the United States, we understand that Turkey remains on the frontlines of the war on terror. And we also understand that Turkey is a model for those in the Muslim world who have aspirations for democratic progress and prosperity. Turkey gives us an example of the reconciliation of religious belief with modern secular democratic institutions."[33]

The Bush administration's approach to Turkey in general and EU–Turkish relations in particular is different than Clinton's, in great part because the terrain has radically changed. Clinton focused on promoting liberal democracy in Turkey and not going to war with Iraq. Bush, on the other hand, is more interested in a stable, even if imperfect, Turkey that will support the United States in a war against Iraq. Bush will seek to build on the existing foundation, avoid interfering in domestic matters, and not take great risks. Republicans have traditionally been reluctant to preach democracy to allies—even illiberal ones—preferring to use this form of discourse for American ideological enemies such as Cuba and, more recently, Iran. Fundamentally, the difference between the two administrations is in the short- and long-term perception of stability. While both have wanted stability in Turkey, the Clinton administration perceived this in a more dynamic way—a country had to change and adapt to be stable. The Bush administration perceives Turkey as already having all the ingredients for a stable society; what is important is to consolidate them.

The Bush administration did not devote the energy its predecessor did to Turkey's European quest until 2002. The strongest endorsement of Turkey's EU aspirations came from Wolfowitz, who, visiting Turkey in July 2002, articulated for the first time a clear position on behalf of the administration.[34] Following this visit, State Department Undersecretary for Political Affairs Marc Grossman visited Brussels and strongly encouraged the Europeans to consider Turkey's case seriously. The administration's previous reticence notwithstanding, the Turks had achieved little in the way of political reforms that could be lauded for coming close to European requirements. Suddenly, in August 2002, the Turkish parliament introduced provisions allowing for Kurdish broadcasting and education, the limitation of the death sentence, and other changes. However, while a step in the right direction, these reforms are unlikely to satisfy the Europeans. Ankara will expect Washington not to leave any stones unturned in getting the Europeans to give Ankara a date first to begin EU accession negotiations and second for facilitating the process itself. Much will depend on the outcome of the November 3 elections. U.S. leverage is limited in any event, but it will be affected by both how well Turkey does and the state of transatlantic relations. Any widening of the Atlantic divide will diminish the Bush administration's influence on this issue.

Another potential impediment on Turkey's road to Europe is Cyprus, which will be invited to become an EU member at the December 2002 EU summit. Cyprus will be invited even if it remains divided because Greece has threatened to block all enlargement if no invitation is made. Turkey has threatened dire consequences if and when that event occurs, and the United States will have to choose sides. Ankara, again, may expect Washington to do its bidding in EU corridors. The Bush administration is unlikely to try to block Cyprus's entry, not because such a course of action would likely fail but rather, as important as Turkey may be to its calculations, the United States does not want to jeopardize EU enlargement, which it regards as crucial to the stability of Eastern Europe. Still, a crisis over Cyprus can not only set EU–Turkish relations back but also undo much of the progress on Greek–Turkish relations. Turkish actions seen as being aggressive can also revive congressional passions. The administration has so far taken a backstage approach to this looming problem, hoping that a solution will be forthcoming from the ongoing bicommunal negotiations under UN auspices. Here again Iraq comes in: any crisis over Cyprus before the beginning of operations against Saddam is likely to affect the operations negatively.

BUILDING TOWARD THE FUTURE: A STRATEGIC PARTNERSHIP?

For over a decade, Turkish and American diplomats have openly discussed elevating their relationship to a "strategic partnership." Neither side has ever explicitly defined the term, but from time to time it gets bandied about in the Turkish media. From the U.S. perspective this would probably have to mean more than cooperation in the cold war (or a war on terrorism for that matter) entailed; it implies a strong and more persuasive relationship with a democratic, prosperous, and stable Turkey, a member of NATO and ultimately of the European Union.

One possibility, suggested in a RAND study, is a strategic relationship that would focus on three areas of future cooperation: energy security, countering the threat of weapons of mass destruction and missiles, and an effective integration of Russia into the West.[35] In the post–September 11 era one can easily add terrorism to this list. In the same study, Ian Lesser argued that the United States, in order to widen its influence in the Middle East, should also take advantage of newly created relationship clusters, such as Turkey-Israel-Jordan, as examples of what he calls the "new 'security geometries' or alliances in critical regions." Such a regional approach might represent the beginnings of a new strategic partnership, which would be all the more important in the aftermath of a possible intervention in Iraq. This would require that Turkey and the United States come to some understanding on regional differences. Iraq and Iran are the most obvious test cases, where Turkey and the United States share the assessment of the threat but still espouse divergent policies on how to tackle it.

A strategic relationship in which Turkey is the new front-line state for the West does not just relate to the regions where Turkey is influential but has a wider, international focus. It would require closer military-to-military relations, greater Turkish participation in U.S. arms manufacturing, and, more importantly, discussing, sharing, and coordinating approaches on key issues. This conceptualization of strategic partnership is more sophisticated than one informed by cold war exigencies, in which the operative concern was access to bases and power projection. In fact, the changing nature of NATO is likely to alter the U.S.–Turkish relationship. The larger and more unwieldy NATO becomes, the greater will be the United States's reliance on key partners, such as the United Kingdom and Turkey, for specific undertakings by the three or to convince other members to go along with initiatives and for military operations. Turkey is likely to continue to invest in defense, and its military bases offer the United States forward-positioning that few other countries can match. By their own admission, however, in NATO and other defense-related venues, Turks have not paid much attention to issues that did not concern them directly.[36] Hence, a strategic partnership would require a change in focus by Ankara. Finally, such a relationship could not flourish without a booming Turkish economy to support defense requirements and provide the United States with nonsecurity interests. This may explain Wolfowitz's recent comment that "President Bush has raised our economic relations with Turkey to a strategic level; we are pursuing every effort to increase our trade and investment from a base that is currently too low."[37]

Turkey's fortunes with the EU will ultimately help define any possible strategic partnership with the United States. There are three possible avenues along which the EU–Turkish relationship can develop. Turkey can decide not to join the EU, the EU may decide to reject Turkey's candidacy despite fulfillment of the requisite criteria, or Turkey could finally succeed in joining.

TURKEY REJECTS THE EU

In the event of the ascendancy of anti-EU forces in Turkey who are unwilling to meet the political criteria for EU membership because they fear the democratization of the Turkish political spectrum, the diminishing role of the military, and the easing of restrictions on individual liberties and Kurdish expression, EU accession could be put off perhaps for decades. Although parliament passed legislation in haste to help fulfill the EU's Copenhagen criteria in August 2002, the fact remains that Turkish elite opinion is increasingly polarized on both the desirability and the feasibility of becoming a member of the EU. Any number of events could trigger a backlash against EU membership, including Cyprus's accession without the Turkish Cypriots, the transformation of Iraq following a U.S. invasion, or election victories by hardcore Turkish nationalists. Some of the alternatives suggested in the past, such as turning East toward the Islamic world, have been thoroughly discredited. When the secretary general of the powerful National Security Council, four-star general Tuncer Kilinç, suggested at an Istanbul conference in spring 2002 that Turkey ought to look in the "direction of Russia and, without antagonizing the United States, Iran" as an alternative to the EU, the remark received attention but was roundly condemned by the Turkish media, which are not usually known for their temerity to take on the military.[38] Still, Kilinç's and other high-ranking officers' comments questioning the EU's sincerity vis-à-vis Turkey indicate that there are divisions within the military and severe doubts about implementing reforms needed to fulfill the Copenhagen criteria. A Turkey that rejects the EU is likely to be nationalist, politically and economically inward-oriented, and highly reliant on its military for day-to-day management of its affairs.

The trade-off for the United States in such circumstances is an imperfect democracy in exchange for a potent actor willing to use its power in tandem with Washington.[39] In such an eventuality, would Turkey jettison its customs union agreement with Europe and conclude a free-trade agreement with the United States? Turks are not the only ones who have entertained such notions: Euroskeptic American proponents of a Turkish–American axis believe that the European project is increasingly diverging from the principles that sustained the Atlantic alliance and point to the U.S. need for more reliable global allies such as Turkey. However, a free-trade agreement with the United States cannot be a substitute for the EU, nor is the United States willing to shoulder the burden of the Turkish economy on its own for the foreseeable future. Alternatively, the Europeans, relieved by Turkey's decision not to seek membership at this time, would be inclined to look for ways to support Turkey. One way would be to conclude a compact with Ankara that enhances the customs union beyond industrial trade to include agriculture and services.

Would a Turkey that turns its back on the EU really be an acceptable strategic partner for the United States? Much of the answer depends on the trajectory of the Atlantic Alliance. Should the paths of Europe and America further diverge, the United States may want an Ankara willing to cooperate in the region. By contrast, if U.S.–EU relations overcame the difficulties emanating from the war on terrorism with all its manifestations including Iraq, the Arab-Israeli conflict, and divergent perspectives on defense expenditures, the United States would not benefit much from a Turkish partner unwilling to conform to Western norms. Unlike Israel, which has a strong democracy and historical and political bonds, or India, which is in the process of quickly establishing economic, strategic, and political attachments to the United States, an introverted Turkey is unlikely to find deep support beyond the argument that it occupies a key strategic location in the globe. In this case, Turkey would be condemned perpetually to offering its location in exchange for resources and recognition; or, as George Soros put it bluntly, "the only thing Turkey can export is its army." In short, without the EU, Turkey would suffer from its inability to play any negotiating card in its dealings with the West other than the geostrategic one. With Cyprus unresolved, Turkey would create a permanent thorn in the side of the EU and, by extension, the United States. In fact, this Turkey would be a step back to the time of concern that its assets could turn into liabilities.

THE EU REJECTS TURKEY

The second, more likely scenario is one in which Turkey fulfills the Copenhagen criteria but for a variety of reasons is denied membership in the EU. This could come about as a result of an overburdened, overextended, and internally divided EU unwilling to shoulder the complexities of Turkish membership. There is no question that a Turkey that genuinely adopts all the EU-required reforms would be deeply disappointed by the European rejection. In the short run, anti-European forces would have the upper hand, but the transformation that a full implementation of the Copenhagen criteria would bring is unlikely to be reversed easily. Despite its disappointment, it is unlikely that such a Turkey would turn its back on the West or retaliate in the same fashion it did after the less important Luxembourg decision. A rejection would not be seen as a permanent setback but a temporary one.

A Turkey, transformed by the EU accession process, that is democratic, prosperous, and stable would, however, be a better partner for the United States. At the very least, it would over time be free of the kind of problems, such as human rights and democratization, that marred the U.S.–Turkish relationship in the 1990s. This was what Özal envisioned: a unique place for a Turkey well entrenched in Western economic and political institutions. Outside the EU, Turkey would look to the United States not only as its main ally; it would very much need a closer relationship with the United States to overcome some of the disadvantages of having been excluded from Europe, such as being outside the ESDP. As a result, Turkey's regional politics would more likely approximate America's. Washington, in other words, would be Turkey's closest confidant, just as it is today, with the difference that, having institutionalized economic and political reforms, Turkey would be a more confident and richer power, able to sustain defense commitments and economically engage other parts of the world.

For the United States, a European-like Turkey that is not a member of the EU has certain advantages. The growing divergence in transAtlantic relations is unlikely to affect U.S.–Turkish relations but, quite the contrary, may strengthen them. More importantly, such a Turkey would not be constrained by European membership in its dealings with the United States or for that matter the adjacent regions. Hence, outside the EU, Turkey would be likely to invigorate its efforts at regional leadership in the Middle East and beyond, in Central Asia and the Caucasus, in tandem with the United States. The Middle East is likely to remain volatile for many years to come, even if an Israeli–Palestinian agreement were to be achieved. The expected demise of Saddam's regime will increase Turkish involvement in Iraq, not just economically but politically and militarily. More importantly, if a truly democratic government in Iraq replaces the Saddam regime, this development would undoubtedly have tremendous consequences for the rest of the Arab world. What had previously hampered Turkish activism in part had been the fact that it was resource poor. A non-EU member but prosperous Turkey could easily make inroads in a transformed Middle East and beyond.

Turkey: A Member of the EU

From the American standpoint, an enhanced U.S.–Turkish strategic partnership is compatible and even preferable with Turkey as an EU member. The disadvantages of Turkish membership revolve around two issues: the United States would lose a big, prosperous market to the EU; and, politically, Ankara in the EU would have to adopt Brussels's policies and preferences on many contentious points separating the two sides of the Atlantic, including reduced attention to defense-related issues. However, there is little reason for the United States to worry about these outcomes.

On the economic front, closer integration with Europe may mean that a larger number of contracts, say for commercial airplanes and other big-ticket items, will go to Europe. However, the fact remains that a smaller U.S. share of an expanding Turkish economic pie is likely to mean many more commercial opportunities over time than there are at present, when economic mismanagement and arcane laws have discouraged investors from entering the Turkish market. Just as Greece and other southern European countries had to implement deep structural, irreversible economic reforms to enter the EU and the euro zone, Turkish entry into Europe would ensure the creation of a stable economic environment.

Similarly, on the political front, the European institutions are the best protection against political instability—including the emergence of political Islam—one of Washington's prime concerns in Turkey. In the past, political instability and concomitant economic mismanagement have brought the soldiers to the fore. To be sure, just as in every other

European society, there will be those who remain opposed to membership in the EU; in Turkey this may be accentuated by cultural differences. Still, it is in the interests of Europe and the United States to see Europe evolve into a more multicultural society. From the American point of view, membership in the EU is by far the fastest path to Turkish prosperity and democracy and, for the United States, the least costly means of achieving it.

Turkey's geography will continue to dominate its security concerns and, more than any other country, it is the United States that will be attentive to them, not to mention to have the continued wherewithal to operate in far-flung places. Turkey's contribution to the EU as a strategic partner of the United States could potentially very much look like that of the United Kingdom on the other side of the continent. The United Kingdom and Turkey represent the bookends of Europe, and if Turkey joined the EU, both would have special relationships with the United States. In the end, it is far more preferable to the United States to have Turkey as a member of the EU; just as in other European countries, EU membership transforms a country and institutionalizes the gains in political democracy and economic well-being. In the meantime, with its large military no longer involved in political affairs, Turkey would continue to contribute to European security.

POLICY RECOMMENDATIONS

The primary long-term challenge for the Bush administration in Turkey is not different from the challenges its predecessors faced: how to get Turkey to become a reliable, stable, and democratic partner. However, short-term considerations, primarily the possibility that the United States will soon engage in military operations to depose Saddam Hussein, are very much in play. Beyond Iraq, the administration will have to tackle the more fundamental problems posed by Turkey. The recent economic and political crises in Ankara have demonstrated once again how difficult it is for policymakers in Washington to approach Turkey piecemeal. Turkey today has earned the distinction of being the largest recipient of IMF funding in history. Most of the country's economic woes can be directly attributed to the malfunctioning political system, in which leaders have refused to assume responsibility and accountability.

Besides Iraq, the U.S. administration may be faced with two other difficult challenges in Turkey. The Islamist-leaning Justice and Development Party (AK Party) is leading in the polls for the November election. An AK victory (outright majority or plurality) could lead to a repeat of the events of 1996, when the Islamist Welfare Party and the center-right True Path Party formed a coalition government. Although AK has moved toward the center and is not as radical as Welfare was, it nonetheless is viewed with great suspicion by the military and a significant segment of the civilian establishment. Already, AK's leader, Tayyip Erdogan, has been prevented from participating in the elections. Even if the United States wants to treat this as a domestic affair, Turks are likely to look to Washington for signs of approval or disapproval. The United States should not be seen as sanctioning another coup: an AK government may not be what Washington desires, but the fact remains that America should show that its relationship transcends parties.

Ankara will use the pending U.S. military operations against Iraq to obtain as much as it can from Washington in exchange for its support. The Bush administration will understandably do its utmost to assure itself of complete Turkish cooperation. Ankara's laundry list of demands will range from getting a say in post-Saddam Iraqi affairs, especially regarding the Kurdish region and the fate of the Turkomans in Iraq, to assurances that it will not suffer economically as it did in 1991, to loan forgiveness, a share of post-conflict rebuilding contracts, and even help with the EU accession process and the Cyprus issue.

Striking a balance will be difficult. Washington undoubtedly will be mindful of Turkish economic needs, the parlous state of the economy, and especially the potential damage to the tourism sector; it will almost certainly support more IMF funds if that proves necessary. Like Turkey, the United States opposes the creation of a separate Kurdish state in northern Iraq, but U.S. and Turkish interests can diverge when it comes to the structure of a future Iraq. Whereas Ankara would loath to see a federal arrangement that allows for one or more Kurdish areas, the United States cannot easily oppose such an arrangement if the people of Iraq consent to it. What the United States can insist on, however, is that the new Iraqi regime gets rid of the remaining armed PKK presence in the North (Turkey also can be helpful by promising amnesty). The United States will want to pursue a policy that minimizes the likelihood of a direct and armed Turkish intervention in the north. The Turks have promised to intervene in the case of Kurdish independence or in the event that the Kurds incorporate the oil-rich city of Kirkuk into their federal domain. It is important to the United States that a Turkish military intervention—one that Turks can achieve with great ease—is avoided. Prolonged Turkish military engagement in northern Iraq would undermine the cardinal goal of the U.S. administration to establish a new democratic regime in Baghdad. Moreover, it may lead Turkey into an involvement from which it will find it difficult to extricate itself. Turkish–American cooperation on Iraq should continue past the end of any operation. In any event, rebuilding and stabilizing the new Iraq will take some time; Turkish bases, its border with Iraq, and goodwill will be important to the success of this effort.

Iraq, as argued earlier, is a double-edged sword. Turkey has every incentive to make the United States dependent on it while combining forces with Washington. The 2001 economic crisis exposed Turkey's vulnerabilities; Ankara too has few options in this matter. Washington, therefore, should be able to set reasonable parameters around Turkish involvement and demands without the fear of alienating Ankara. The United States in providing support for Turkey must not lose sight of other priorities, such as Turkey's economic reform program. Any economic support it promises should not come at the expense of the internal consistency of the IMF-instituted program.

Whatever happens in Iraq, Ankara will still be dealing with the ramifications of its economic crisis and its quest for EU membership. Turkish expectations that the EU will give a date for the beginning of the accession negotiations have been heightened following the vote in parliament to allow for Kurdish broadcasting and education and limiting of the death sentence. These, however, are preliminary steps and are not likely to satisfy the Copenhagen criteria as understood by the Europeans. Moreover, Turks in the past have not followed through on their major reform programs by passing enabling legislation.

Although the United States might be tempted to push the Europeans to go along with the Turkish request, it is not in Washington's interest to do so. Washington was right in supporting Turkey's candidacy status, especially after the 1997 Luxembourg debacle. However, short-circuiting the process by pleading the exceptional nature of the Turkish case does not advance Washington's goals. It is true that some Europeans may not be disposed to admit Turkey into the EU for cultural reasons, but Ankara's and, indirectly, Washington's positions would be much strengthened if Turkey genuinely fulfilled the Copenhagen requirements. Cutting corners or the perception that

Washington may do Ankara's bidding in Brussels plays into the hands of those in Turkey who are unwilling to go all the way with the reforms. This applies not just to getting an accession date but also to the future when Turkey, having gotten a date, will embark on these negotiations. The United States should join the EU in encouraging Turkey to persist in economic and political reform. There are also practical reasons for the United States not to invest its prestige in getting a non-EU-ready Turkey into the EU. Turkey has demonstrated time after time that it will only introduce reforms only when it is pressured by outside forces or when all other options have been exhausted. There is no other explanation for the sudden changes introduced by the Turkish parliament this August. Also, unlike the candidacy status, membership is a far more crucial step and the Europeans are unlikely to be as accommodating of American wishes as they were in the earlier case.

U.S.–EU cooperation on getting Turkey ready for the EU is the best possible policy option. Because of the economic crisis, the United States has already had to engage in shaping economic policy in Turkey and preventing any backsliding on economic reform. The same has to be done with political conditions, the process of democratization, and improving human rights. The United States has to step out and encourage political reforms. It is difficult for an administration that is focused on Iraq to contemplate these policies, but the fact of the matter is that the sooner the Turks implement them, the stronger the relationship between the two allies will be.

POSTSCRIPT

The political earthquake of November 3 has the potential to transform Turkish–American relations. The victorious Justice and Development Party's (AK Party) stated goals, especially concerning the European Union, the democratization of Turkey, and the expansion of human rights, are what the United States had been advocating for Turkey since the end of the cold war. Still, the ascendancy of a pro-Islamist party may not have been what Washington wanted to see in one of its most important allies, especially at a time when the United States is engaged in a war on fundamentalist Islamic terror. The election victory of Tayyip Erdogan, the former Istanbul mayor, and his party also coincides with Washington's heightened activity to implement regime change in Iraq.

It would be natural for American leaders to look at the AK Party with unease. Despite the considerable distance the AK Party has traveled toward the political center and its efforts at fashioning an Islamic-democratic party, the fact remains that the leadership of the party has had a long history of hostility toward the United States. They were part of a series of parties founded by the veteran Islamicist leader Necmettin Erbakan whose anti-Americanism and anti-Westernism writ large dominated his political worldview. The difference between this election and the 1995 one in which Erbakan's Welfare Party won a narrow plurality has been striking. Whereas Erbakan told the crowds that his victory represented the end of Operation Provide Comfort and U.S. influence, Erdogan's tone was vastly different. He unequivocally anchored his party's and future government's policy on reaching an accommodation with the European Union on membership criteria and speeding up the process of democratization.

The AK Party's moderation is due in large part to the military's decision forcing the Erbakan-led coalition government out of power and the subsequent banning of the Welfare and its successor Virtue parties, Erdogan and the new prime minister, Abdullah Gul, decided to break with Erbakan and the more radical elements of the Islamist movement. Their journey to the center and toward a policy of close cooperation with the European Union is driven in large measure both by their desire to avoid the mistakes of the past that riled the powerful secular military establishment and their belief that the military's future role in a Turkey closing in on EU membership will be severely constrained. Even if the AK Party's motivation for integration with Europe is derived from self-preservation, this can only be good news for Washington. First and foremost, if the AK Party succeeds in further democratizing Turkey by applying the Copenhagen criteria, it will pose a challenge to the EU, which hitherto had hidden behind Ankara's recalcitrance in extending a date beginning accession negotiations.

The taming of what was a powerful anti-American Islamist movement in a vital NATO ally provides the United States with additional benefits (the more strident remnants of Erbakan's followers fared poorly with their Felicity party only receiving some 2 percent of the votes). Successive U.S. administrations had touted the "democratic, pro-Western, and secular" Turkish model to the Arab world with little result. Arabs saw in Turkey a radical secularist regime buttressed by a military prone to interventions. The resounding victory of a moderate Islamist government in Turkey that remains pro-Western and genuinely seeks to deepen its links with Europe finally will provide Washington with the model that it really needs for the Arab world. Erdogan stepped into this role himself after the election when he said that he hoped to provide an example to the Arab world.

Improvements in Turkey's European perspective and its democratization agenda will not completely smooth Washington's relations with Ankara. AK Party leaders, who for decades have labored as part of Islamic parties, are uncomfortable with the tone of the post–September 11 U.S. foreign policy. Their discomfort over a divide that increasingly looks like one of East (Muslim) versus West (Christian) is shared by a wide segment of Turkish society. This is likely to complicate the dialogue between Washington and the new government over issues such as Iraq. In the end, a new AK Party government will defer to the military on a matter of such vital import to national security. They will also be cognizant that their political well-being is very much a function of the health of their economy, which, in turn, has been kept alive by the massive Washington-supported IMF bailout plan. Still, the new leadership in Ankara will want to see the Iraq operation done under United Nations cover with minimum Turkish participation and collateral damage.

Washington's three concerns in Turkey will revolve around the Iraq operation, the continued improvements in the Turkish economy, and domestic stability. On Iraq, especially if the war were to take place soon, the new government will be able to ride off the storm with greater ease as it settles itself to confront the principal economic challenges. A prolonged war with large numbers of casualties will strain Turkish–American relations. The AK Party does not have the same worries that the outgoing government had about the future of Iraq and the role the Kurds are likely to play in it. For one, its leaders have a better grasp of the Kurdish southeast than Ecevit or his nationalist allies. The AK Party is unlikely to oppose a federated Iraq that provides for a Kurdish federal region.

The Turkish economy remains in frail state; the AK Party has promised to keep to the IMF plan with some slight modifications. Yet, the problem for the Washington, which has been instrumental in "investing" some $31 billion in Turkey's economic future, will continue to be the management of the stabilization plan. The AK Party's economic cadres do not have the depth of experience that Kemal Dervis had provided during tenure as economic czar. The likelihood of mistakes, which can help unravel the program is, therefore, much greater.

Finally there is the question of stability. The fact that the AK Party government will be able to count on an impressive parliamentary majority in parliament—itself a first in fifteen years—should not raise concerns regarding governmental stability. Moreover, the AK Party's intentions all point in the direction of greater stability: the recognition that Turkey has to graduate to becoming a country that takes the rule of law seriously will also help political stability. Yet, some 45 percent of the Turkish electorate remains disenfranchised as the parties they backed failed to pass the 10 percent threshold needed to make it into parliament. This and the fact that radical secularists in the media, civilian, and military bureaucracies continue to see the AK Party as a danger to the secular order established by Ataturk give rise to the possibility that these forces will band together to polarize the body politic to trigger another military coup. In the past, Washington had succeeded—though not completely—in pursuing a policy that supported democracy in Turkey. It had criticized the banning of the Virtue Party and, perhaps more importantly for this AK Party leadership, had on numerous occasions demonstrated its dislike for the sentencing of Erdogan to a prison term and the resulting ban on his participation in political activity. Now more than ever Washington will have to pursue a policy that does not show any ambivalence on the question of democracy.

The AK Party's victory heralds a new era in Turkish-American relations. On certain issues—Europe, democratization, and aspects of the Iraq problem—there will be a greater meeting of the minds between Washington and Ankara. On another level, Washington will have to be a great deal more careful in its dealings with the AKP government, which will analyze U.S. policies from a perspective that is still heavily influenced by an Islamist worldview.

CHAPTER NINE

AFTERWORD
TURKEY'S 2002 ELECTIONS: A POLITICAL EARTHQUAKE AND ITS AFTERMATH

CENGIZ ÇANDAR

Turks went to the polls November 3, 2002, and produced a seismic event. The AK Party (the Turkish initials of the Justice and Development Party), one with strong Islamist roots, won a landslide victory. In the history of Turkish democracy, the 2002 elections have been compared only to the 1950 elections in the magnitude of its consequences. The 2002 election liquidated a whole generation of politicians, including former prime ministers ranging from Bülent Ecevit to Mesut Yılmaz and Tansu Çiller. Another former prime minister, Necmettin Erbakan, the godfather of political Islam in Turkey, shared a similar fate. The 2002 election result could also be seen as a disgruntled people's attempt to "throw the bums out." Ninety percent of the seats in parliament changed hands, a breathtaking number. The Turkish mainstream media exuberantly hailed the result.

The AK Party, a moderate spin-off of the previously banned Islamic Virtue Party, won approximately 34.2 percent of valid votes (10.8 million out of 31.5 million votes cast), but captured almost two thirds of the parliament, 363 of the 550 seats. These figures gave the party an outright parliamentary majority and left them only four seats short of the two-thirds majority needed to change the constitution.

The election result produced a two-party parliament for the first time since 1946 and the first single-party majority government since 1987. The Republican People's Party (CHP), which was frozen out of parliament in the preceding 1999 elections, became the only opposition bloc in the parliament, winning 178 seats. Independent candidates, some of whom seem to ally themselves to the AK Party, won the remaining nine seats.

Turkey has a new and unique experiment indeed and how it will unfold remains to be seen. Never before has a party with Islamist roots legitimately claimed the center of Turkey's political stage. The AK Party has been successful in dispelling the negative perceptions of Turkish public opinion to the party's Islamic origins. While it is true that the AK Party is a direct descendant of the Refah (Welfare) Party, the fundamentalist party of the Turkish political scene in the late 1990s, it is also true that by conscious design it has represented the more modern, much less dogmatic branch of that lineage. By rejecting the Islamist label, Tayyip Erdogan's AK Party was able to reach well beyond the Islamist electoral base of 21 percent of the vote in 1995, which had elevated Erbakan's (also Tayyip Erdogan's) Welfare Party in 1995 to be the lead party in a coalition government. In this election the other, more traditional branch of the Islamist movement, Saadet (Felicity) Party, ran on a different platform and collected less than 3 percent of the vote.

However, it is far from certain that the AK Party can persuade Turkey's ardent secularists, including the powerful military, that it has changed its Islamist skin, that it does not have a "hidden agenda," which remains a principal concern of those circles. The public manifestation of Islamist symbols—from the headscarf worn by the wives of Turkey's new prime minister, the new speaker of the parliament, and more than half of the ministers of the new government, to the daily prayer ceremonies of senior officials—carry the deep political and cultural tensions of Turkish society. The speculation over whether the military would allow the AK Party a free hand in ruling Turkey is not over and will not be for some time. That speculation is also put forward by Turkey experts in the United States as in the following appraisal: "Finally, there is the possibility that the secularist forces will try to polarize the political scene as a way to undermine the government and, thereby, hope to trigger another military coup. Indeed the military itself, even if it decides not to overtly block the new government from power, may try to discredit the latter and make it fail."[1]

In Turkey itself, it has become something of a basic belief among the cognoscenti that unless AK Party rule attempts to erode the pillars of Turkey's secular edifice and fails to pursue a pro-Western policy, the military will not intervene. The initial signs of the post-election period suggest this to be so.

One valid question is whether the AK Party rank and file and the party constituency will allow the party leadership to accommodate itself to the system against which the popular support for the AK Party developed, since the party became perceived as the vehicle to change the system? AK Party has strong Islamic underpinnings. Many party loyalists are members of previous, more radical movements, and it remains to be seen whether they will go along with the noncon-frontational attitudes espoused by the current leadership.

There is no simple answer to that question. Much will depend on the evolution of AK Party rule. As the traditional (formerly mainstream) political parties have a very slim chance of a comeback and as the opposition CHP (Republican People's Party) is identified with the bureaucratic elite and thus without bright political prospects, AK Party, for the foreseeable future, will occupy a unique dominant position in Turkey's political scene. It will function as the central governmental authority but it will also be expected to act as an instrument of change representing the interests of the periphery vis-à-vis the political center.

That periphery includes a variety of discontented. What ensured the AK Party's massive victory in the polls was, by and large, a protest, a popular response to the chronic inability of a fragmented political system to deal effectively with fundamental challenges facing Turkey. It is a widely shared view that the AK Party's success in the 2002 election has less to do with the party's Islamic roots and more to do with the abject failure of all the other main parties to overcome their reputations for corruption, economic mismanagement, political infighting, and entrenched clientelism. According to a post-election survey conducted by Tarhan Erdem (who has credibility because of his accurate forecasting of the 1999 and 2002 election results, when compared with 1999 elections), AK Party received the votes of 69 percent of Fazilet (Virtue) Party electorate, 38 percent of MHP (nationalists), 28 percent of ANAP, 21 percent of DYP (both parties of center-right) and 14 percent of DSP (Ecevit's pseudo-leftist party), which meant that it managed to win votes from just about every electoral bloc. These figures indicate that AK Party voters were drawn not only from the ideologically motivated Islamists or the underclass that has suffered most from the recent economic crisis, but also from conservative, middle-class professionals and intellectuals, resentful of the incompetence and bad governance of the political class that long dominated Turkey's political scene.

Although representing broad and diverse segments of Turkish society, the AK Party leadership is aware of its limitations in exercising power, and they know that membership in the EU is the best insurance policy for the party's continued existence. Furthering democratization in Turkey will both pave the road to the EU and simultaneously present the best bulwark for the party to resist the pressures of the Turkish secular civilian-military establishment; this process is regarded as the first priority in AK Party's domestic agenda. The EU goal also explains the vigorous pro-EU campaign of the AK Party leader following his party's election victory. With dizzying speed, Erdogan toured all fifteen EU capitals as well as Brussels and Strasbourg, the seats of the European Commission and the European Parliament, before the fateful European Enlargement Summit at Copenhagen, December 12, 2002.

To the surprise of many pro-West Turks and Europeans alike, Erdogan succeeded in developing a good rapport with European leaders from Silvio Berlusconi of Italy to Tony Blair of the United Kingdom, and a close relationship with Kostas Simitis of Greece. He declared his happiness being in Athens, which he described as "a beautiful city where democracy was born and where Plato and Socrates have lived," an atypical manner even for a moderate Islamist politician. He also described Greece, to the satisfaction of the Greek leaders, as "not Turkey's eternal rival but closest ally and future strategic partner."

Seeing Erdogan on the road to European capitals only a few days after his election victory has been a striking and comforting picture for the pro-EU Turkish secularist elite, and a stark contrast to former Islamist prime minister Erbakan, who made two initial visits abroad, first to Iran, Pakistan, Malaysia, and Indonesia, then to another set of Islamic countries, Egypt, Libya, and Nigeria. His aim was to establish a competitor Islamist bloc against the Western-dominated G-7. As a matter of fact, he created a short-lived D-8 (developing 8, that some called M-8 as Muslim-8). Erdogan took a completely different route than his former mentor Erbakan; he moved toward Europe and the Western world.

Erdogan, the party chairman, and the deputy leader Abdullah Gül, who replaced Ecevit as Turkey's prime minister, now define their party not even as moderate Islamist but as a conservative democratic one. Earlier, Erdogan had described himself as a Muslim democrat, which led some observers to characterize the AK Party as a counterpart of the Christian Democrats of Europe. Bülent Arınç, the AK speaker of the parliament and one of the three main leaders of the party, even objected; he insisted that the AK Party is not a center-right but a centrist party, filling the vacuum created by the devastation of the two traditional parties of the center right, Motherland (ANAP) and True Path (DYP). Quite possibly the AK Party will undergo at some early point an identity crisis, which might further complicate its organizational integrity and political fortunes.

Nevertheless, the AK Party's survival under the watchful eye of the Turkish military and other secularists will depend more than anything else on its success in finding practical solutions to Turkish economic problems, in playing its cards well concerning Iraq so as to dispel the doubts that Washington may harbor about its reliability ruling as a key U.S. ally, and, above all, in leading Turkey into the European Union. Whereas one might expect a party with Islamic roots to be even more opposed than other Turks to a U.S. intervention in the Muslim world, AK Party leaders in fact have always stressed their abhorrence of Saddam and his regime. Erdogan and other AK Party leaders had remarked on several occasions that from a moral standpoint, Muslims could not condone a tyrannical regime. Privately, they have indicated that they will consult with, and even defer to, the Turkish military leadership on questions of national security, including Iraq.

The strongest asset that AK Party and its leadership possess is self-confidence. That derives not only from its huge election victory. Subsequently, the unexpected blank check accorded to the AK Party government by some prominent members of the Turkish secular elite, and especially the warm reception of Erdogan in many European capitals as well as the perceived friendly attitude of the United States, are the major sources of that self-confidence. Erdogan has been encouraged to formulate an ambitious aim, making Turkey under AK Party rule an example of the compatibility of Islam and democracy.

He and other AK Party leaders are aware that Turkey as a role model in achieving the "harmony of civilizations" in contrast to the "clash of civilizations" that has haunted the international system in the post–September 11 period, will have an enormous international appeal and give the AK Party an excellent opportunity to win widespread support. It would reconcile Turkey's Islamic roots with its secular democracy and Western orientation. Should the AK Party experiment prove successful, with American and European support, the result will be a powerful message to a democracy-deficient and economically deprived Muslim world.

The 2002 elections heralded a radically new era in Turkey. The election results generated the scarcest commodity in the country: optimism. It has prevailed in Turkey in the autumn of 2002. But Turkey has an incredibly difficult agenda, domestically and internationally. It would be impossible to solve the immediate issues without optimism and self-confidence and with a proven incompetent and corrupt political class. The 2002 elections, for the moment at least, changed all that.

| Notes

Chapter Two

1. The author is vice chairman of Tekfenbank, former vice governor of the Central Bank of Turkey (1988–93), and a columnist in the daily newspaper *Hurriyet*. Views expressed in this chapter do not imply those of the institutions with which the author is affiliated.

2. Heath W. Lowry, "Betwixt and Between: Turkey's Political Structure on the Cusp of the Twenty-First Century," in Morton Abramowitz, ed., *Turkey's Transformation and American Policy* (New York: The Century Foundation Press, 2000), p. 25.

3. For a more detailed analysis of developments in the 1980s, see Ercan Kumcu and Sevket Pamuk, *Artık Herkes Milyoner* (Now Everyone is a Millionaire) (Istanbul: Dogan Kitap, 2001).

4. For a comprehensive survey of financial market liberalization in the 1980s, see I. Atiyas and H. Ersel, "The Impact of Financial Reform— The Turkish Experience," in Gerard Caprio Jr., Izak Atiyas, and James A. Hanson, eds., *Financial Reform: Theory and Experience* (New York: Cambridge University Press, 1996). See also, Isik Inselbag and Bulent Gultekin, "Financial Markets in Turkey," in Tevfik F. Nas and Mehmet Odekon, eds., *Liberalization and the Turkish Economy* (New York: Greenwood Press, 1988).

5. In many respects, Turkey's achievement in liberalizing its economy in the 1980s was well ahead of those of other emerging-market economies at that time. See, for example, *Central Banking Issues in Emerging Market-Oriented Economies,* symposium sponsored by the Federal Reserve Bank of Kansas City, Jackson Hole, Wyoming, August 23–25, 1990.

6. A standby agreement between the International Monetary Fund and a member state enables the member to arrange for immediate drawing rights in addition to its normal drawing rights in cases of emergency as in a temporary balance of payments crisis.

7. See I. M. D. Little et al., *Boom, Crisis, and Adjustment: The Macro-economic Experience of Developing Countries* (New York: Oxford University Press, 1993).

8. For a full treatment of deteriorating public finance in the 1990s, see Ercan Kumcu, *Istikrar Arayışları* (In Search of Stability), 2d ed. (Istanbul: Dogan Kitap, 2002).

9. See also Z. Onis, "The Turkish Economy at the Turn of a New Century: Critical and Comparative Perspective," in Abramowitz, *Turkey's Transformation and American Policy.*

10. Since 1970, the average real growth of GNP has been 4.6 percent in Turkey. Over the past thirty years, the Turkish economy has never continuously grown longer than two consecutive years above this average, the 1995–97 period being the only exception.

11. Among the reasons for insufficient flow of foreign direct investment are uncertainty created by high inflation and, in parallel, depreciation of the currency, frequent changes in tax laws, and administrative difficulties in obtaining foreign investment permits.

12. For a more comprehensive treatment of the program, see Ercan Kumcu, "Where Did Turkey Go Wrong? A Tale of Two Crises," paper presented at the conference on International Financial Architecture: Recent Issues and Alternatives of Reform, Rio de Janeiro, June 25–26, 2001.

13. Morton Abramowitz made similar points in "Introduction and Overview," in Abramowitz, *Turkey's Transformation and American Policy.*

14. The IMF suggested that the preannounced exchange rate regime be abandoned immediately and the exchange rate be left to float in November 2000. See interviews with bureaucrats and other government officials by Okan Müderrisoğlu, *Sabah,* February 19–22, 2002.

15. This was the point raised in Ercan Kumcu, "The IMF's Blunder in Turkey," *Financial Times,* March 13, 2001. Michael Deppler's response (Letters to the Editor, *Financial Times,* March 18, 2001) to that article totally missed this point. See also Mahfi Egilmez, Letter to the Editor, *Financial Times,* March 17, 2001. For a more comprehensive critique of the IMF's handling of the crises in Turkey, see M. Egilmez and E. Kumcu, *Ekonomi Politikası: Teori ve Türkiye Uygulaması* (Economic Policy: Theory and Application in Turkey), 2d ed. (Istanbul: Om Yayinlari, 2002).

16. In retrospect, the IMF preferred that Turkey abandon the foreign exchange rule as soon as its sustainability was questioned so that new

funds would not be used to make the otherwise unsustainable foreign exchange rule sustainable for some time, as experienced in the case of Argentina over the past few years. It is reported that IMF officials also insisted that the foreign exchange rule should have been abandoned immediately after the November crisis.

17. According to the IMF's statistics, duty losses accumulated at public banks increased from $2.7 billion in 1995 to $19.2 billion in 1999, roughly 13 percent of GNP.

18. See Hasan Ersel and Mete Mercan, "Exchange Rate and Uncertainty," unpublished manuscript, Yapi Kredi Bankasi, 2002. The uncertainty created by the freely floating exchange rate regime since February 2001 is higher than that in the 1994 crisis and during the Gulf War.

19. Instead, a form of managed floating exchange rate regime as pursued during the Asian and Russian crises could have been adopted to smooth out exchange rate fluctuations so that uncertainty created by volatility in exchange rates would have had a smaller effect on output and inflation. See M. Egilmez and E. Kumcu, *Krizleri Nasıl Çıkardık* (How Did We Create the Crises?), 2d ed. (Creative Yayıncılık, 2001). The IMF refused such a strategy on the ground that any commitment by the central bank to any preannounced exchange rate movement would have meant risking international reserves. In fact, that would not necessarily have been the case since the stability in exchange rate changes would have reduced currency substitution and would probably have prevented financial markets from shrinking as a result of the outflow of funds by domestic residents. Hence, international reserves would have more likely increased after a stable exchange rate policy had some credibility, as observed after the 1994 crisis.

20. In the eyes of the public, the central bank governor and the undersecretary of the treasury basically carried out the program implemented in the year 2000. As the program was abandoned, both left their posts. In fact, these were the only public officials who assumed responsibility for the failure. The present program is known to be Derviş's, allowing the politicians once again to disassociate themselves from any shortcomings of the program while still claiming success if it is realized.

21. The prime minister is already complaining that the BRSA, as well as other independent regulatory agencies that have been recently established, is a "government within the government" that cannot be controlled by elected officials.

CHAPTER THREE

1. Feroz Ahmad, "Politics and Islam in Modern Turkey," *Middle Eastern Studies* 27 (1991): 6.

2. Elisabeth Özdalga, *The Veiling Issue, Official Secularism and Popular Islam in Modern Turkey* (Surrey, U.K.: Curzon Press, 1998), pp. 19–20.

3. Nakschibendi religious order is an illegal sect banned in the 1920s by Atatürk that has exerted significant political influence since the foundation of the republic. Turgut Özal and his family are known to have had close relations with this order and the personification of political Islamism in Turkey. Erbakan is also a member of this sect.

4. Özdalga, *The Veiling Issue, Official Secularism and Popular Islam in Modern Turkey*, pp. 19–20.

5. Nuray Mert, "Cami Gölgelerinden Gölge İnsanlara: Kültürel İslâm Edebiyatı," Tezkire 14–15 (1998): 50–51.

6. Tanıl Bora, Türk Sağının Üç Hali (İstanbul: Birikim Publications, 1999), p. 125.

7. Ticanis were an especially militant sect in Turkey. They committed numerous vandalist activities against Atatürk's monuments in protest of secularism. Throughout the 1950s, there were many trials for their anti-state activities.

8. Ümit Cizre, *Muktedirlerin Siyaseti* (İstanbul: İletişim Publications, 1999), pp. 92–95.

9. Cizre, *Muktedirlerin Siyaseti,* p. 96.

10. Mert, "Cami Gölgelerinden Gölge İnsanlara," p. 50.

11. Mert, "Cami Gölgelerinden Gölge İnsanlara," p. 51.

12. Yalçın Akdoğan, Siyasal İslâm (İstanbul: Akdogan, 2000), p. 161.

13. One of the issues of the journal *Girişim,* published by Islamists Kurds, included articles on the Kurdish problem as its cover story. This was the first time that Islamists publicly prioritized the Kurdish issue.

14. Cizre, *Muktedirlerin Siyaseti,* p. 153.

15. There was a similar division between Turkish and Kurdish communists in the 1970s. While the former thought that nationwide reforms and provision of rights would implictly improve the Kurds' situation in Turkey, the latter wanted to protect the Kurds' rights explicitly. This disagreement triggered the foundation of the PKK.

CHAPTER FOUR

1. For the best and most up-to-date books on Turkey's Kurdish challenge, see Henri J. Barkey and Graham E. Fuller, *Turkey's Kurdish Question* (Lanham: Carnegie/Rowman & Littlefield, 1998); Kemal Kiriçi and Gareth M. Winrow, *The Kurdish Question and Turkey* (London: Frank Cass, 1997).

2. For a discussion of earlier missed opportunities for addressing the Kurdish issue in Turkey, see Philip Robins, "The Overlord State: Turkish Policy and the Kurdish Issue," *International Affairs* 69, no. 4 (1993): 657–76.

3. Such an approach is closely associated with the Turkish academic Serif Mardin. See, for example, his "Center-Periphery Relations: A Key to Turkish Politics?" in Engin D. Akarli and Gabriel Ben-Dor, eds., *Political Participation in Turkey: Historical Background and Present Problems* (Istanbul: Bogazici University Publics, 1975).

4. The PKK said that it would end its fifteen-year guerrilla insurrection but that it would continue to strive for Kurdish rights within a "framework of peace and democratization." Harmonie Toros, "Kurdish Rebels Make New Peace Overture to Turkey," Associated Press, Istanbul, September 2, 2000.

5. It was even suggested during the last parliament, 1995–99, that there were between 150 and 170 members of parliament of Kurdish origin, making Kurds overrepresented as a group. See Report of the Euro-Turkish Dialogue, Tegernsee, December 4–6, 1998, p. 1.

6. For a fuller discussion of likely Kurdish ethno-nationalist numbers in Turkey, see Philip Robins, "Turkey and the Kurds: Missing Another Opportunity?" in Morton Abramowitz, ed., *Turkey's Transformation and American Policy* (New York: The Century Foundation Press, 2000).

7. An estimated fifty-four different ethnic and religious groups in Turkey in the mid-1920s were successfully assimilated into a Turkish national ethos. Report of the Euro-Turkish Dialogue, p. 1.

8. The council includes Cemal Bayık (also known as Cuma), whom some Kurdish commentators believe would become leader in the event of Öcalan's demise. Other important members of the council include Murat Karayalın and Mustafa Karasu.

9. The delegations, which returned on October 1 and October 29, were made up of long-standing members. The leader of one, Ali Sapin, was a well-known figure within the ERNK in Europe.

10. PKK, "Our Extraordinary 7. Congress Is a New Beginning for Our Party and People," February 9, 2000, p. 4.

11. "New Era in Kurdish Politics," press release on the 8th Congress of the PKK, April 20, 2002.

12. See, for example, "PKK Changes Name—Only," *RFE/RL Iran Report 5,* no. 14 (April 22, 2002): 6.

13. KADEK Executive Council, "A New Era of Historical Development Has Begun for Our People and Our Movement with the 8th Congress of the PKK," Resolution on the 8th Congress of the PKK, April 15, 2002 (official translation).

14. This formed part of an agreement forged among Turkey's three-party coalition whereby the government would refrain from taking the Öcalan death sentence to the Turkish Grand National Assemby for confirmation until the European Court of Human Rights has ruled on his appeal. Conditions for a policy couched in terms of restraint included Öcalan ceasing to issue "threatening statements" through his lawyers. See *Briefing,* no. 1276, January 17, 2000, p. 3.

15. Öcalan's lawyers visit his island jail every fifteen days, thereby providing his only communications link with his supporters.

16. In the words of one student, he organized resistance to assimilation and projected demands for cultural fulfillment. Conversations in Diyarbakır, April 1, 2000.

17. Interview with member of the Executive Council of the Kurdistan National Congress, May 13, 2002.

18. For example, on hearing that the PKK had changed its name, Turkish prime minister Bülent Ecevit accused the organization of deception, saying that it had not abandoned its separatist goals. *Briefing,* no. 1390, April 22, 2002, p. 4.

19. For example, Dr. İsmet Şerif Vanlı, the president of the Kurdistan National Congress (KNK), a PKK-dominated umbrella-grouping purporting to represent Kurds from throughout the Middle East and the diaspora, continues to speak of the establishment of a bizonal, federal state in Turkey. See his speech in the Grand Committee Room of the House of Commons, London, January 23, 2001, reprinted in *Kurdistan Report,* no. 31, Autumn 2001, pp. 3–9.

20. For a discussion of the emergence and early prospects for HADEP, see Henri J. Barkey, "The People's Democracy Party (HADEP): The Travails of a Legal Kurdish Party in Turkey," *Journal of Muslim Minority Affairs* 18, no. 1 (1998): 129–38.

21. A case was opened at the Constitutional Court in 1999 seeking the closure of the party on the grounds that it had provided a focus for anticonstitutional activity. Some three years later the case was still pending. See *Briefing,* no. 1383, March 4, 2002, p. 2.

22. These range from the arrest of supporters holding peaceful demonstrations, through periodic harassment of HADEP officials and party activists, to the initiation of court cases against its leaders. The trial of Murat Bozlak and other party officials in connection with a demonstration of support for the PKK at the 1996 party convention was still pending in 2002.

23. Contemporary accounts suggested that the meeting had gone well and there was an atmosphere of cooperation. The meeting generated little criticism in the local press or from other sources in the country. *Briefing,* no. 1255, August 16, 1999, p. 8.

24. Cem declared that people should be able to enjoy broadcasts in their own languages.

25. See declaration by international writers and artists in *Kurdistan Report,* no. 29, March–April 2000, p. 22.

26. For example, an Amnesty International report, *Turkey: An End to Torture and Impunity Is Overdue!* EUR 44/072/2001, October 2001, p. 24, details the arrest and abuse of the deputy mayor of Diyarbakır, Ramazan Tekin, in January 2000.

27. The two men have not been seen since they were summoned to the gendarmerie station in Silopi, though the authorities later claimed that they had been released, kidnapped by the PKK and taken to northern Iraq. See ibid., p. 12.

28. Gül Demir, *Turkish Daily News,* February 26, 2001.

29. The outcome of the April 18, 1999, election was: DSP, 22.19 percent, 136 seats; MHP, 17.98 percent, 129 seats; Fazilet Partisi (FP; Virtue Party), 15.41 percent, 111 seats; Anavatan Partisi (ANAP; Motherland Party), 13.22 percent, 86 seats; DYP, 12.01 percent, 85 seats; Independents, 0.87 percent, 3 seats.

30. For example, only one out of the five parties represented in the Turkish Grand National Assembly was prepared to argue openly in favor of the complete abolition of the death penalty because of the Öcalan factor. *Briefing,* no. 1383, March 4, 2002, pp. 1, 3.

31. *Briefing,* no. 1378, January 21, 2001, p. 8.

32. *Briefing,* no. 1371, December 3, 2001, p. 2.

33. *Briefing,* no. 1379, January 28, 2002, p. 4.

34. *Briefing,* no. 1380, February 4, 2002, p. 2.

35. The package was unexpectedly tabled and adopted following an extended twenty-two-hour debate, but one that largely presented the country with a legislative fait accompli.

36. In July 2002 the NSC decided to reduce the number of provinces covered by the emergency rules from four to two, with just the governorates of Diyabakır and Şırnak remaining.

37. Amnesty International, *Turkey,* p. 22.

38. *Briefing,* no. 1386, March 25, 2002, pp. 7–8.

39. For the Presidency Conclusions of the Helsinki European Council, December 10–11, 1999, see http://www.ue.eu.int/newsroom/LoadDoc.cfm?MAX=1&DOC=!!!&BID=76&DID=59750&GRP=2186&LANG=1.

40. The precedent of Slovakia was relevant to Turkey's position, since accession negotiations with Bratislava were delayed for political reasons relating both to the quality of the country's democracy and its position on human and in particular minority rights. See European Commission DG 1A, "Accession Partnership: Slovakia," http://www.europa.eu.int/comm/dg1a/enlarge/...ss_partnership/slovakia/slovakia_ap.htr.

41. Unlike the political criteria, however, the economic criteria are not a sine qua non for the opening of accession negotiations, although they are a sine qua non for accession to full membership.

42. For example, of the eight paragraphs dealing with "minority rights" in the House of Commons Foreign Affairs Committee report on Turkey, published on April 30, 2002 (Sixth Report of Session 2001–02, HC606), every one is dominated by the Kurds, though one (paragraph no. 51) emphasizes the importance of Turkey granting cultural rights to other minorities, such as the Alevi and the Laz (p. 18).

43. It was perhaps with this in mind that the *Economist* was able to say that "many in the EU reckon that it could still take decades before the Turks are able to meet crucial political demands, such as full respect for the rights of the Kurdish minority." See "Europe's Magnetic Attraction: A Survey of European Enlargement," *Economist,* May 19, 2001, p. 17.

44. All references made to "the National Programme for the Adoption of the Acquis," unofficial translation, also known as the national plan, March 19, 2001, accompanied by press release of the Turkish Embassy, London, March 19, 2001.

45. The Luxembourg summit has become a notoriously black moment in bilateral relations between the EU and Turkey. Though the summit communiqué recognized Turkey as "eligible for membership," it failed to confer candidate status on Ankara, leaving Turkey in a minority of one, alone among all the other EU aspirant members of the time.

46. Vanlı speech.

47. The Turkish side had been urged to delay the publication of their national plan until the accession partnership had been adopted for fear that any shortcomings might elicit a Greek veto.

48. The conclusion of a briefing on the EU's accession partnership and Turkey's national plan from Lehman Brothers, "Turkey: Easing Towards the EU," *Global Weekly Economic Monitor,* March 16, 2001, p. 1.

49. The Germans were, for example, the Europeans most supportive of the United States's decision that the International Monetary Fund should put together another bailout for the Turkish economy.

50. For an official clarificatory defense of the amended articles, see Secretariat General for European Union Affairs, "Constitutional Amendments," Ankara, October 4, 2001.

51. Amnesty International, "Turkey. Constitutional Amendments: Still a Long Way to Go," January 2002, p. 1.

52. Ibid., p. 10.

53. Oxford Analytica daily brief, "Turkey: Constitutional Changes, Part 2," December 28, 2001, p. 16.

54. Evidence for this ranges from the banning of the organization in Germany in 1992 to the d'Alema government's refusal to deal with Öcalan during his brief stay in Rome in 1998.

55. The reference was to the 1923 Treaty of Lausanne, which addressed the future status of Turkey without mention of the Kurds. Radical Kurds hold Britain and France responsible for Lausanne, which they see as having created the Kurdish problem. See Osman Öcalan, edited excerpts from a speech to Medya TV, "To Include the Kurdish Freedom Movement in the New EU Terrorism List Is a Declaration of War," April 15, 2002.

56. Ibid.

57. Ibid.

58. An early manifestation of this reply was that the Swedish foreign minister, Anna Lindh, had been obliged to cancel a visit to Diyarbakır because local Kurds had refused to meet her.

59. See, for example, Desmond Fernandes, "The Targeting and Criminalisation of Kurdish Asylum Seekers and Refugee Communities in the UK and Germany," Peace in Kurdistan and the Ahmed Foundation for Kurdish Studies, London, 2001.

CHAPTER FIVE

1. Çağrı Erhan, "USA and NATO Relations," in Baskin Oran, *Türk Dış Politikası* [Turkish Foreign Policy], vol. I (Istanbul: İletişim Publishing, 2001), pp. 681–715.

2. Ibid.

3. Metin Toker, Demokrasimizin *İsmet Paşalı Yılları 1944–1973* [Democracy at the time of İnönü] (Ankara: Bilgi Publishing, 1991), pp. 195–211.

4. Erhan, "USA and NATO Relations," pp. 702–703.

5. Baghdad Pact was a peace and security collaboration agreement in the region, signed by the United Kingdom, Iraq, Pakistan, and Turkey.

6. Erhan, "USA and NATO Relations," p. 794.

7. Interview with journalist Yalçın Doğan.

8. Interview in *Daily Radikal,* May 6, 2002.

9. Mehmet Altan, *On Yıl Önce Bugün* [Ten Years Ago Today] (Istanbul: İyiadam Publishing, April 2002), p. 36.

10. Although the military indeed generally speaks with one voice, there are commonly perceived differences between the more "liberal" officers of the navy and the air force relative to those of the army. Various recent conversations of the author with retired officers have confirmed this belief.

11. The TUSIAD leadership recently met with the military and stated that their views were similar on EU issues. That was later somewhat contradicted by an ambiguous chief of staff statement declaring that this was not the case and military views are expressed only through official statements.

12. Ian Lesser, "Bridge or Barrier: Turkey and the West after the Cold War," Rand Corporation, Santa Monica, Calif., 1992, p. 3.

13. Stephen J. Blank, "Turkey's Strategic Engagement in the Former USSR and U.S. Interests," in Stephen J. Blank, Stephen Pelletiere, and William Johnson, eds., *Turkey's Strategic Position at the Crossroads of World Affairs* (Carlisle, Penn.: Strategic Studies Institute, U.S. Army War College, 1993), pp. 55–56.

CHAPTER SIX

1. Cengiz Çandar, "Çılgın bir kaos dünyas?na doğru" [Toward a Crazy World of Chaos], *Yeni Şafak,* September 12, 2002.

2. Timothy Garton Ash, "A Moment That Will Define the 21st Century," *The Independent,* September 13, 2001.

3. Dışişleri Bakanı Sayın İsmail Cem'in, ABD'ye yönelik terörist saldırılar hakkında basın mensuplarına yaptığı açıklama [Statement of the minister of foreign affairs, Mr. İsmail Cem, to the pressmen, Foreign Ministry Diary], September 13, 2001, http://www.mfa.gov.tr.

4. Özdem Sanberk, "A Dangerous Myth That Distorts Islam," *Financial Times,* September 18, 2001.

5. Ira Lapidus of the *New York Times* formulated it as follows: "Turkey has political parties, free elections and a parliament, but it is actually run by a parallel government, the military. The army considers itself the heir to the principles of Atatürk, promoter of secularism and a European-style modernity, defender of the unity of the nation and the state. Young officers are imbued with a sense of personal responsibility for the future of the country." Ira M. Lapidus, "Trying to Outrun Its Own History, Turkey Stumbles," *New York Times Book Review,* September 19, 2001.

6. Tasnif Dışı, "Genel Kurmay IInci Başkanının Açış Konuşması" [Unclassified, The Opening Speech of the Deputy Chief of General Staff], September 26, 2001.

7. Ali Çarkoğlu and Kemal Kirişçi, "Türkiye Dış Politika Araştırması" [Survey on Turkey's Foreign Policy], Bosphorus University, Department of Political Science and International Relations, Istanbul, March 2002, pp. 10, 12, 14.

8. Ankara Sosyal Araştırmalar Merkezi [Ankara Social Research Center], "Mayıs 2002 Türkiye Gündemi Araştırması" [May 2002 Survey on Turkey's Agenda], Ankara, May 2002.

9. "İsrail soykırım yapıyor" [Israel Is Committing Genocide], *Radikal,* April 5, 2002.

10. Barbara Lerner, "The Turks, Too: Joining Anti-Israeli Left?" *National Review Online,* April 19, 2002.

11. "Kıvrıkoğlu: Medya yalan haber yazıyor" [Kıvrıkoğlu: Media Is Distorting News], *Yeni Şafak,* April 24, 2002.

12. Genelkurmay Başkanlığı, *Güncel Konular* [Main Issues] (Ankara: Genelkurmay Başkanlığı [General Staff Publishing House], 1999), pp. 10–11. See also Evren Değer, "TSK'ya göre ABD 'sabıkalı'"

[According to the Turkish Armed Forces/The USA Is the Culprit], *Radikal,* November 23, 1999; Fehmi Koru, "Change Little by Little," *Turkish Daily News,* November 25, 1999; Nazlı Ilıcak, "Türk Silahlı Kuvvetleri Broşürü" [The Turkish Armed Forces Brochure], *Yeni Şafak,* December 1, 1999.

13. Devrimci Halk Kurtuluş Partisi/Cephesi [People's Liberation Party/Front] (DHKP/C) is the current one of successive organizations with Marxist-Leninist rhetoric and is believed to be Alevi-oriented by Sunni Turks in Turkey. They have been in collaboration with the PKK and other leftist organizations in their militant anti-state activities. Most recently, DHKP/C militants, in and out of prison, along with other organizations organized numerous uprisings and hunger strikes against the introduction of single prison cells in 2000–2001.

14. "Türkiye yeni bir arayışa girmeli" [Turkey Should Be Searching New Alternatives], March 7, 2002, http://www.ntvmsnbc.com.

15. Morton Abramowitz, "Introduction and Overview," in Morton Abramowitz, ed., *Turkey's Transformation and American Policy* (New York: The Century Foundation Press, 2000), p. 15.

16. "Ecevit'ten Bush'a Karar Ver!" (From Ecevit to Bush: Make Up Your Mind!), *Milliyet,* October 22, 2002.

17. "Ecevit Milliyet'e Açıkladı: Savaşa Sürükleniyoruz" (Special from Ecevit to *Milliyet:* We Are Being Dragged into War), *Milliyet,* October 13, 2002.

18. "Ecevit: Çok gencimiz ölür" (Ecevit: Many of Our Young May Die), *Radikal,* October 14, 2002.

19. "Turizm kayb? 10 milyar dolar" (Loss for Tourism 10 Billion Dollars), *Radikal,* October 14, 2002.

20. Ibid.

21. "Turkey Tells the United States to Discuss Any Action against Iraq," *Reuters,* December 27, 2001.

22. Kılınç Paşa'dan ilginç mesajlar, "Kürt devletine müdahale ederiz," [Interesting messages from General Kılınç: "We will intervene in a Kurdish state], *Hürriyet,* June 14, 2002.

23. "ABD Saddam'ı Devirmekte Kararlı" [The United States Is Determined to Overthrow Saddam], *Milliyet,* July 16, 2002.

24. "Turkey and America: Partners at the Crossroads of History," Paul Wolfowitz, Turkish Economic and Social Studies Foundation, Istanbul, July 14, 2002.

25. *Hürriyet,* July 16, 2002.

26. "ABD Saddam'ı Devirmekte Kararlı."

27. "Sivil toplum AB dedi," [Civil Society Say: Yes to the EU], *Radikal,*
June 6, 2002.
28. "Ufuk Turu" [Tour d'Horizon], *Habertürk TV,* June 15, 2002. (Ufuk
Turu is a weekly talk show on Monday nights with three contributors:
Özdem Sanberk; Emre Gönensay, a former foreign minister; and
Cengiz Çandar.)
29. Paul Wolfowitz, "Turkey and America."

CHAPTER SEVEN

1. Since the truce in 1974, Cyprus has been divided into two zones,
separated by a buffer zone comprising about 4 percent of the territory
monitored by the UN Peacekeeping Force in Cyprus. The Greek-
Cypriot zone, administered by the government of the Republic of
Cyprus, has about 59 percent of the territory of the island with about
595,000 people—or 78 percent out of a total population of 763,000.
The Turkish-Cypriot zone, which in 1983 declared itself the Turkish
Republic of Northern Cyprus but has not been recognized by any government except Turkey, has about 37 percent of the island's territory
and 18 percent of the population or about 140,000 people. All but 1.3
percent of the ethnic Turks live in the Turkish zone; all but 0.5 percent
of the ethnic Greeks live in the Greek zone. Figures are estimates for
2001 from the CIA Factbook, available at http://www.cia.gov.
2. Luxembourg European Council, "Presidency Conclusions,"
December 12, 1997, paragraphs 28 and 35, available on the official EU
website, http://www.europa.eu.int/council/off/conclu/index.htm.
3. Helsinki European Council, "Presidency Conclusions," December
11, 1999, available on the official EU website, http://www.europa.eu.
int/council/off/conclu/index.htm. Paragraph 9 b) reads, "The European
Council underlines that a political settlement will facilitate the accession
of Cyprus to the European Union. If no settlement has been reached by
the completion of accession negotiations, the Council's decision on
accession will be made without the above being a precondition. In this
the Council will take account of all relevant factors."
4. At the end of 1995, a small Turkish freighter ran aground in the
Aegean just off the Turkish coast on uninhabited rocks called Imia by
Greeks and Kardak by Turks. The incident escalated over the next several weeks as the two governments vigorously disputed sovereignty
over the islets and media coverage inflamed public opinion. Tensions

rose and military forces confronted each other until interventions by President Bill Clinton and U.S. ambassador Richard Holbrooke helped restore the status quo ante. The official websites of the Greek (www.mfa.gr) and Turkish (www.mfa.gov.tr) foreign ministries set forth their respective, strongly differing, views on the matter.

5. Helsinki European Council, "Presidency Conclusions," paragraph 4.

6. Interview with *Turkish Daily News,* March 4, 2002, available at http://www.turkishdailynews.com.

7. Henri J. Barkey and Philip H. Gordon, "Cyprus: The Predictable Crisis," *National Interest,* no. 66 (Winter 2001): 83-93.

8. Denktash-Makarios High Level Agreement of February 12, 1977, available on the official Republic of Cyprus website, htpp://www.pio. gov.cy/docs/proposals/agreement1977.htm. Its four main points or guidelines are: "1. We are seeking an independent, non-aligned, bi-communal, Federal Republic. 2. The territory under the administration of each community should be discussed in the light of economic viability or productivity and land ownership. 3. Questions of principles like freedom of movement, freedom of settlement, the right of property and other specific matters, are open for discussion taking into consideration the fundamental basis of a bi-communal federal system and certain practical difficulties which may arise for the Turkish Cypriot community. 4. The powers and functions of the Central Federal Government will be such as to safeguard the unity of the country, having regard to the bi-communal character of the State." Also archived by the United Nations as paragraph 5 of UN Document S12323.

9. Denktash-Kyprianou 10 Point Agreement of May 19, 1979, available on the official Republic of Cyprus website, http://www.pio. gov.cy/docs/proposals/agreement1979.htm.

10. UN Set of Ideas 1992, text archived on the official Republic of Cyprus website, http://www.pio.gov.cy/docs/un/ideas.htm.

11. See in particular Yusuf Kanli, "Less Meeting, More Substance in New Round of Cyprus Talks," *Turkish Daily News,* February 28, 2002; Ralph Boulton, "Round Two: Let the Wrestling Begin," Cyprus Mail, March 1, 2002.

12. Michael Emerson and Nathalie Tocci, *Cyprus as Lighthouse of the East Mediterranean: Shaping EU Accession and Re-unification Together,* Centre for European Policy Studies, Brussels, 2002.

13. Cyprus News Agency: News in English, press release quoting government spokesman Michael Papapetrou, June 26, 2002, archived on http://www.cyna.org.cy.

14. "Papandreou: Greece Will Stand By Cyprus Even if It Rejects Plan," *Cyprus Mail, News Articles in English* 02-11-06, posted November 6, 2002 on www.cyprus-mail.com. See also "Abdullah Gul Explains How the JDP Understands the Belgian Model," NTV broadcast November 6, 2002, translated into English by the Cyprus Press and Information Office, released as Item 7 in its bulletin, "Turkish Press and other media No. 211/02," November 6, 2002; A. Kourkoulas, "Turkey's Erdogan Backs Improved Ties with Greece; Cyprus Solution," *Athens News Agency,* Istanbul, September 28, 2002, from www.ana.gr.

15. Interview by Mehmet Ali Birand, broadcast by CNN TURK May 14, 2002, available on the official Republic of Cyprus website, http://www.pio.gov.cy, link to Turkish Press and Other Media no. 90/02 02-05-15.

16. Reported in the Turkish-Cypriot newspaper Kibris, August 10, 2002; news item translated and summarized by the Cyprus Public Information Office and posted at http://www.hri.org/news cyprus/tcpr/2002/02-08-12.tcpr.html.

17. Yusuf Kanli, "Comprehensive Reconciliation," *Turkish Daily News,* April 12, 2002.

18. "Annan in Cyprus to Salvage Direct Talks Process," *Turkish Daily News,* May 15, 2002, available at http://www.turkishdailynews.com/FrTDN/latest/for.htm.

19. Ismail Cem, "A Common Vision for Cyprus," *International Herald Tribune,* March 14, 2002.

20. European Commission, "Commission Offers a Fair and Solid Approach for Financing EU Enlargement," press release IP/02/170, Brussels, January 30, 2002.

21. Helsinki European Council, "Presidency Conclusions," paragraph 12.

22. Quentin Peel and Anton Notz, "Stoiber Warns against Continual EU Enlargement," *Financial Times,* May 16, 2002.

23. Morton Abramowitz, "Face-to-face-to-face in the Aegean," *Time-Europe* 159, no. 4, January 28, 2002.

24. Helsinki European Council, "Presidency Conclusions," paragraph 12.

25. Guenter Verheugen, speech to the Plenary Session of European Parliament, Strasbourg, March 13, 2002, archived as EU document number SPEECH/02/104 on the official EU website, http://www.europa.eu.int RAPID reference service. Note also Commission president Romano Prodi's earlier speech to the Cyprus parliament,

October 25, 2001, archived as document number SPEECH/01/495, when he stated, "Let me stress that the European Union, with its acquis, will never be an obstacle to finding a solution to the Cyprus problem. . . . I am confident that the European Union can accommodate whatever arrangements the parties themselves agree to in the context of a political settlement."

26. See Emerson and Tocci, *Cyprus as Lighthouse of the East Mediterranean*, "Executive Summary—Conclusions," as well as their excellent discussion in Chapter 5, "Preparing for Accession to the European Union."

27. M. James Wilkinson, "The Cyprus Drama: The Last Act" (New York: The Century Foundation Press, 2002)

28. Marios L. Evriviades, "The US and Cyprus: The Politics of Manipulation in the 1985 U.N. Cyprus High Level Meeting," occasional research paper no. 3, Panteion University, Athens, October 1992. In this paper, Evriviades, a Greek-Cypriot diplomat who participated in the UN talks, called the exercise a "US high-handed and cynical attempt" to neutralize the Cyprus problem as an impediment to the Reagan administration's expanding strategic military agenda with Turkey.

29. Leonidas Pantelides, "A Chronological Perspective in the New Talks about Cyprus," *To Vima,* January 20, 2002, author's translation.

CHAPTER EIGHT

1. Interview with Richard Holbrooke in Yasemin Congar, "The State of Turkish-American Dialogue: Do You Understand What I'm Saying?" *Private View* (Spring 1999). Holbrooke gave the interview soon after stepping down as assistant secretary of state for European and Canadian affairs.

2. Mark R. Parris, "Turkey and the U.S.: A Partnership Rediscovered," *Insight Turkey* 3, no. 4 (October–December 2001): 3. Mark Parris is a former U.S. ambassador to Turkey.

3. Strobe Talbott, "U.S.-Turkish Relations in an Age of Interdependence," 2d Turgut Özal Memorial Lecture, Washington Institute for Near East Policy, Washington, D.C., October 14, 1998, http://www.washingtoninstitute.org/media/talbott.htm.

4. The brainchild of the secretary of commerce, Ron Brown, this initiative lost its most important supporter with his untimely death.

Brown, who had planned to visit all ten emerging markets with large business delegations, never made it to Turkey.

5. Birol Yesilada, "Turkey's Candidacy to Join the European Union," *Middle East Journal* 56, no. 1 (Winter 2002): 100–106; also see Ziya Onis, "An Awkward Partnership: Turkey's Relations with the European Union in Comparative-Historical Perspective," *Journal of European Integration History* 7, no. 13 (Spring 2001).

6. Heinz Kramer, *A Changing Turkey: The Challenge to Europe and the United States* (Washington, D.C.: Brookings Institution Press, 2000), p. 124.

7. Turkey decided in retaliation to "upgrade its diplomatic relations with Baghdad to full ambassadorial level. Deputy Premier Bulent Ecevit said the dramatic move was in response to the agreement between the two Kurdish factions which had accelerated a process aimed at perpetuating the de facto partition of Iraq." *Mideast Mirror,* October 1, 1998.

8. For more on Erbakan's and Ecevit's relations with Saddam Hussein, see Henri J. Barkey, "Hemmed in by Circumstances: Turkey and Iraq Since the Gulf War," *Middle East Policy* 7, no. 4 (October 2000).

9. In a very revealing set of interviews and meetings with Saddam Hussein in the early 1990s, Ecevit shared with the Iraqi leader his anxieties regarding Western designs over Iraq and Turkey, the negative role of human rights organizations, and the activities of the Kurds in Northern Iraq. See Derya Sazak, *11 Eylul Golgesinde Saddam* [Saddam in the Shadow of September 11] (Istanbul: Dogan Kitapcilik, 2002), pp. 123–41.

10. Some two hundred thousand Turkish troops and special police forces as well as sixty thousand village guards were deployed in the Southeast to combat the PKK.

11. Among the many outlandish claims made by Erbakan were accusations that the United States supported the PKK and transported equipment to Armenia's nuclear power plant. *Milli Gazete,* June 29, 1995.

12. Erbakan was completely shunned by the U.S. administration. Two high-ranking U.S. officials met with him soon after he took office; only Peter Tarnoff, state department undersecretary for political affairs, and then U.S. ambassador to the UN Madeleine Albright came through Ankara.

13. Alan Makovsky, "U.S. Policy toward Turkey: Progress and Problems," in Morton Abramowitz, ed., *Turkey's Transformation and*

American Policy (New York: The Century Foundation Press, 2000), p. 225.

14. General Cevik Bir remarked that "regarding human rights, we told our counterparts that the Turkish Armed Forces are far ahead compared to many European nations. Unfortunately we are facing double standards in human rights." Ugur Akinci, "General Bir: 'We are ahead of Europe in Human Rights,'" *Turkish Daily News,* November 27, 1997.

15. Talbott, "U.S.-Turkish Relations in an Age of Interdependence."

16. She made a point of singling out a Turkish journalist, Nadire Mater, who was being prosecuted for a book of interviews she published with soldiers who served in the Southeast in the conflict with the PKK. Albright's reference to Mater made the front-page headline in the daily *Milliyet,* took the Turkish establishment by surprise, and drew attention to her book, Mehmedin Kitabi [Mehmed's Book], which had been banned by the authorities. *Milliyet,* October 15, 1999; Sabah, October 18, 1999.

17. Tamar Gabelnick, William D. Hartung, and Jennifer Washburn, "Arming Repression: U.S. Arms Sales during the Clinton Administration (Washington, D.C.: World Policy Institute and Federation of American Scientists, October 1999), p. 6.

18. See for instance the comments of Lieutenant General Batmaz Dandin, chief of the planning and principles division of the Turkish general staff, who argued "that the United States was becoming 'an unreliable defense source for Turkey day by day.'" He warned that U.S. weapons contractors will not be able to win Turkish tenders if that attitude continues. *Turkish Daily News,* May 15, 1999.

19. Morton Abramowitz, "The Complexities of American Policymaking on Turkey," in Abramowitz, *Turkey's Transformation and American Policy,* p. 176.

20. Congar, "The State of Turkish-American Dialogue."

21. Sukru Elekdag, "Sorular," *Milliyet,* October 9, 2000.

22. Murat Yetkin, "Ankara'da Soykirim Panigi" [Genocide Panic in Ankara], *Radikal,* April 6, 2002. Interestingly, recriminations in Ankara against Ecevit's statement were focused on his imperiling Turkey's relationship with an important ally and not on whether his was a correct description of events.

23. Dana Priest, "New Human Rights Law Triggers Policy Debate," *Washington Post,* December 31, 1998, p. A34. In the end, the issue was resolved through a compromise that allowed EXIM Bank to provide loan guarantees for units vehicles that went to Turkish provinces

where there was no discernible evidence of human rights violations and denied them where there was.

24. Kramer, *A Changing Turkey*, pp. 204 and 212.

25. Henri J. Barkey and Philip H. Gordon, "Cyprus: The Predictable Crisis," *National Interest* (Winter 2001–2002); Mehmet Ali Birand, "Herkesi Tehdit Ediyoruz" [We Are Threatening Everyone], *Posta,* April 12, 2002.

26. *Financial Times,* August 17, 2002.

27. Most recently, Vice President Dick Cheney, on a tour of the region to drum up support for a campaign against Saddam Hussein's regime in Iraq, requested that the chief of staff also be present in his discussions with senior Turkish leaders.

28. Accessed at http://clinton3.nara.gov/WH/New/Europe-9911/remarks/1999-11-15d.html.

29. Interviews with Turkish officials, Ankara, March 2002.

30. The secretary general of the National Security Council, General Tuncer Kilinç, told the Lebanese daily an-Nahar that Turkey would militarily intervene in the event the Kurds set up a separate state. *Hurriyet,* June 14, 2002.

31. *Turkish Daily News,* June 12, 2002.

32. See Cengiz Çandar, "Bagdat'tan Washington'a U donus?" [A U-Turn from Baghdad to Washington?], *Yeni Şafak,* January 23, 2002; Hürriyet, January 24, 2002.

33. Paul Wolfowitz, Turgut Özal Lecture, Washington Institute for Near East Affairs, March 13, 2002.

34. "As profound as our friendship with Turkey may be, it is even more profound when added to Turkey's fundamental relationship with Europe. Turkey's full integration into the European institutions is in the best interests of the people of Turkey, the people of Europe and of the United States." TESEV, Istanbul, July 14, 2002, http://www.defenselink.mil/speeches/2002/s20020714-depsecdef.html

35. Zalmay Khalilzad, "A Strategic Plan for Western-Turkish Relations," in Zalmay Khalilzad, Ian O. Lesser, and F. Stephen Larrabee, *The Future of Turkish-Western Relations* (Santa Monica, Calif.: RAND, 2000), pp. 79–93.

36. Guven Erkaya and Taner Baytok, *Bir Asker Bir Diplomat* [A Soldier a Diplomat] (Istanbul: Dogan Kitapcilik, 2001), p. 27.

37. Acessed at http://www.defenselink.mil/speeches/2002/s20020714-depsecdef.html.

38. Sami Kohen, "Akademide Alternatif Tartismasi" [Discussion of Alternatives at the Military Academy], *Milliyet,* March 8, 2002; Mehmet

Ali Birand, "Pasalar Konustukce, TSK'ye Bakis Degisiyor" [As the Generals Speak, People's View of the Turkish Armed Forces Changes], Posta, March 15, 2002; Murat Yetkin, "Kilinç'in Konusmasi ve Avrokuskuculuk" [Kilinç's Talk and Euroscepticism], *Radikal,* March 15, 2002.

39. For a discussion of these issues, see Ihsan Dagi, "Kritik Karar: ABD ya da AB," *Radikal,* March 12, 2002.

CHAPTER NINE

1. Henri J. Barkey and Philip H. Gordon, "Turkey's Elections and the United States: Challenges Ahead," CSIS Europe Program congressional hearing, Washington, D.C., November 4, 2002.

INDEX

Abramowitz, Morton, 164, 196

Afghanistan: Turkey's peace-keeping forces in, 2, 129, 152, 211, 233; Turkish support of U.S. effort in, 104, 152

Air control, dispute with Greece, 181

Akbulut, Yildirim, 114

Akincilar, 72

AK Party: ban of, 74, 84; characterization of, 10, 73, 255; on Cyprus, 16; development of, 9, 69–71; on EU admission, 13, 82, 247; future of, 83–84; on Israel, 78; as leading party, 7–8, 23, 27–29, 84; military relations with, 79–80; November 2002 election win, 244, 246–49, 251–56; and political Islam, 71–74, 252–53; since September 11, 81–82; U.S. relations with, 24, 25, 29–30, 81, 247

Albright, Madeleine, 218

Amnesties for politically motivated offenses, 103

Amnesty International, 103, 226

Ankara Social Research Center survey on Middle East conflict, 154–56

Ankara University and teaching of religion, 63, 64

Annan, Kofi, 15, 27. See also Annan Plan for Cyprus

Annan Plan for Cyprus, 183–87; Belgian model, 15, 186–87, 203; evolution of, 184–86; failure of, 26; negotiations on, 28, 202–04; tabling of, 199; and U.S. role in Cyprus situation, 200, 201

Anti-Americanism, 19, 111, 150–53, 154

Anti-Semitism, 77–79. See also Israel

Anti-statism, 69

Arinç, Bülent, 255

Armenian genocide issue, 226, 227, 229

Armenia, Turkish relations with, 131–32

Arms embargo on Turkey, 112, 151, 157–58, 185, 213, 223, 227

Army. See Military

Ash, Timothy Garton, 146

Asian crisis, 42

Atatürk, 61–62, 88. See also Kemalism

Atatürk Law, 64

Ateş, Atilla, 122

Aydinlar Ocagi (Intellectuals Hearth), 65

Azerbaijan, Turkish relations with, 131

Aziz, Tarik, 219

Bagdad Pact of 1955, 113

Bahçeli, Devlet, 96

Bakü-Ceyhan pipeline, 116–17, 119, 131

Balkan countries, Turkish relations with, 140, 210

Banking Regulatory and Supervisory Authority (BRSA), 45, 48, 49

Banking sector, 35, 36, 37–38, 45, 48, 50, 53; reform of, 54–55, 58

Barkey, Henri, 182

Bases in Turkey: DECA renegotiation, 114, 117; in Gulf War, 115; Turkish control over, 111; U.S. building of airfields, 112–13; U.S. dependence on, 209–10; U.S. use of in war on Iraq, 19, 118

Bayar, Mehmet Ali, 7, 73

Baykal, Deniz, 70

Belgian model for government of Cyprus, 15, 186–87, 203

bin Laden, Osama, 82, 113, 127. See also Terrorism

Boyner, Cem, 7

Bush (G.W.) administration: on Central Asian republics and Turkey, 210; economic aid for Turkey, 232; Iraqi action and security issues, 164, 231, 244; position on Cyprus, 201, 203; reluctance to criticize Turkey, 24; on strategic partnership with Turkey, 22, 236; support of EU admission for Turkey, 29–30, 139, 169, 171. See also U.S.-Turkey relations

Büyükanit, Yasar, 149

Caliphate, abolition of, 62

Çandar, Cengiz, 221

Capital account transactions, liberalization of, 37–38

Carter administration, 113

Çelik, Feridun, 94–95

Cem, Ismail: on Cyprus, 125, 180, 193, 194, 202; on Iraqi relations, 122; on Kurdish problem, 95; leader of New Turkey Party, 73; resignation of, 181; on September 11, 147

Central Asian republics, 131–34, 140, 210

Centre for European Policy Studies, 186, 198

Chechens, 133

Cheney, Dick, 123

China, 226

CHP. See Republican People's Party (CHP)

Christian missionaries, 76

Christopher, Warren, 112

Çiller, Tansu, 96, 116, 122, 123, 220

Clerides, Glafcos, 15, 173, 187

Clinton administration, 23–24, 44, 158, 213–23; on Central Asian republics and Turkey, 210; harmonious relationship at end of term, 230–31; Iraq policy, 216–20; support of EU admission for Turkey, 169–70

Coalition governments: AK Party and CHP as possibility, 73; end of, 23; three-party coalition in 1999, 96; U.S. relations with, 24; weak economic position of, 43, 58. See also Ecevit government

Cold war, 220

Communism: Islam as weapon against, 65, 113

Congress, U.S., views on Turkey, 225–27

Constitutional amendments as steps toward EU admission, 45, 103

Constitution of 1961, 64
Corruption in government, 6, 51
Customs union with EU, 117,
    119, 130, 189, 194, 215;
    Turkish termination of, 240
Cyprus, 173–205; background,
    176–77; Belgian model for
    government of, 15, 186–87,
    203; confidence-building
    measures to move toward set-
    tlement, 205; EU position on,
    182–83, 194–98; Greek
    attempt to annex, 111;
    Johnson letter preventing
    Turkish action in 1964, 110,
    151; majority-minority con-
    cepts, elimination of, 191–92;
    priority of situation, 177–79;
    and reconciliation between
    Greece and Turkey, 175,
    180–82; settlement needed for
    Turkey's EU membership, 13,
    28, 95, 126, 136–37, 174, 178,
    182–83, 194–98; significance
    of situation, 136, 174–75;
    south-east European agenda
    in, 175–76; stakes of strategy
    on, 179–83; Turkish military
    views on, 123; and Turkish
    policymaking, 125; United
    Nations role in, 15, 173, 174,
    183–87; U.S. leadership and
    interests in, 2–3, 16, 24–25,
    26, 110, 175, 199–205, 224,
    237. See also EU membership
    (proposed for Cyprus);
    Greek-Cypriots; Turkish-
    Cypriots
Cyprus as Lighthouse of the East
    Mediterranean: Shaping EU
    Accession and Re-unification
    Together (Centre for European
    Policy Studies), 186, 198

Death penalty reform, 11, 75, 84,
    93, 102, 103, 122, 178, 245
Decisionmaking process in
    Turkish foreign policy, 119–27
Defense and Economic
    Cooperation Agreement
    (DECA), 114, 117
DEHAP (the Democratic People's
    Party), 12
D-8 project, 70, 221, 254
Demirel, Suleyman: anarchy
    under, 112; and Kurdish prob-
    lem, 95; longevity of, 7; on
    military role, 121, 123; on
    OPC, 115; poppy cultivation
    under, 111
Democracy, Labor and Human
    Rights, Bureau of, 225
Democratic Left Party (DSP), 90, 125
Democrat Party (DP), 64, 73
Denktash, Rauf: demanding sov-
    ereignty for Turkish Cyprus,
    189; leadership role of,
    190–91; role in settlement of
    Cyprus situation, 15, 16, 18,
    173, 184; terminology used by
    in vision of settlement,
    191–92; and Turkish policy-
    making, 13, 126, 196
Dervis, Kemal: appointment to
    run economy, 54, 147; effec-
    tiveness of, 7; IMF funding,
    role in, 6
Drug trafficking, 111
DYP. See True Path Party (Dogru
    Yol Partisi)

Earthquake and economic condi-
    tions, 44
Ecevit, Bulent: health problems
    of, 5; leadership failure of, 7;
    on Palestinian-Israeli situa-
    tion, 130, 155, 227;

Washington visit by, 109, 234.
See also Ecevit government
Ecevit government: as bridge
between Christain and Islamic
worlds, 128; as coalition government, 5; coordinating with
military views, 122; on
Cyprus, 14–15, 111, 125, 193;
fall of, 3, 4; foreign policy of,
124; on Iraq and U.S. desire to
topple Saddam, 164–65, 168,
219, 234–35; and proposed
EU membership, 3; and
Provide Comfort Operation of
U.S., 116; Soviet sympathies
of, 112
Economic instability, 1–2, 31–60;
AK Party's focus on, 29, 248,
255; and Asian crisis, 42;
attempts at stability in 1970s,
34; Bush administration's
position on aid, 232; causes of
crisis, 53; and early elections
in 2002, 60; EU admission
affected by, 2, 5, 13, 57, 134;
February 2001 crisis situation,
1, 51–54; future challenges,
6–7, 25, 57–60; government
spending, 6, 32, 38–43; history
of, 33; IMF program, 35,
46–49, 54–56, 248; IMF's preconditions for support, 2,
44–45; November 2000 crisis
situation, 1, 49–51; Özal's era,
35–36; and political climate
currently, 58; and political liberalization, 36–38; post-
February 2001 program,
54–56; post-September 11
finances, 56; "reform fatigue,"
48, 60; and Russian crisis,
42–43; standby arrangement
of 1985, 36; standby arrange-

ment of 2002, 56–57; U.S.
compensation for losses due
to Iraqi military action, 168,
234; U.S. support for IMF program, 20, 26, 119, 138, 147,
214, 244
Educational institutions. *See*
Schools; *specific institution*
Elections in Turkey as of 2002, 3,
235; results of, 7–8, 246–49,
251–56. *See also* AK Party
Elekdağ, Sükrü, 95
Embargo, 116, 165, 214. *See also*
Arms embargo on Turkey
Erbakan, Necmettin: AK Party's
break from, 71; compared to
Erdoğan, 254; critical of West,
81; foreign policies of, 221,
247; and Iraqi relations, 219;
on majority parties, 70; mistakes of, 23, 80, 221; "National
Vision" of, 67, 72; and
November 2002 election
results, 251; and political
Islamists, 9, 10; political parties of, 67; as prime minister,
68, 69; on religious youth's
role, 66; removal as prime
minister, 70, 153; secularists'
reaction to, 70; SP Party's view
of, 82; on Zionism, 77, 78
Erdem, Tarhan, 253
Erdoğan, Recip Tayyip: on AK
Party, 9, 72, 73; on anti-
Semitism and Israel, 78–79;
ban from official political role,
73, 74, 221–22, 244, 249; on
Cyprus, 15, 27, 28, 182, 194;
on dictatorial regimes, 81; on
EU admission, 82; on future
changes, 27, 28; international
relations of, 254, 255; military
relations with, 79–80; on

Palestinian situation, 81; public distrust of, 10; role of, 10, 28; on U.S. attack on Iraq, 82; U.S. relations with, 24, 222. *See also* AK Party

Erim, Nihat, 111

Erkaya, Güven, 70

EU membership (proposed for Cyprus): agreement by two Cypriot communities to enter as one, 174; Ecevit government position on, 14–15; effect on Turkey, 3, 127, 189; Turkish-Cypriots' refusal to negotiate, 176–77, 194–95; U.S. position on, 237

EU membership (proposed for Turkey), 12–18, 134–37, 139–42; acceptance scenario, 141–42, 242–43; AK Party support for, 82–83; announcement at EU Helsinki summit, 44, 86, 99, 101, 134, 176, 230; anti-EU sentiment in Turkey, 13, 239–40; Copenhagen requirements for, 11, 13–14, 18, 28, 79, 100–01, 245; and Cyprus situation, 13, 28, 95, 126, 136, 174, 178, 182–83, 194–98; and Ecevit government, 3; economic crisis's effect on, 2, 5, 13, 57; effect on U.S.-Turkish relations, 141–42, 168–71, 242–43; Erdoğan's desire for, 28; impediments to, 5, 17, 215; and Kurdish problem, 11–12, 91, 100–02; military views on, 135, 168; national plan created for, 101–03; political conditionality of, 25, 99–104; rejection scenario, 17, 134, 139–41, 168, 182–83, 241–42;

SP Party support for, 82; Turkish public opinion on, 13, 103, 135; Turkish rejection of, 239–40; U.S. support for, 17, 26, 29, 169–71, 214–16, 236–37, 245–46

European Union (EU): *acquis communitaire,* adoption required by members, 101, 178; customs union agreement, 117, 119, 130, 189, 194, 215, 240; Kurds relocated in, 88, 106; PKK listed as terrorist organization by, 105, 150; position on Cyprus, 189, 195–98; Turkish military's view of, 162; Turkish policy on, 125–26, 134–37; view of Turkey if EU accession rejected, 141; view of Turkish military's role in government, 9, 134–35

Evren, Kenan, 123

Exchange rate, 36–38, 45–47, 50–57

February 28 as important date for Islamists, 71, 79

Felicity Party (Saadet Partisi), 9; anti-Israel, 78; election of November 2002 results, 247; on EU admission, 82; founding of, 71; and Kurdish problem, 76; and military, 79; post-September 11, 81–82; as representative of political Islam, 72, 84; role if AK Party banned, 74; on U.S. attack on Iraq, 82

Foreign exchange rate. *See* Exchange rate

Foreign policy of Turkey, 4, 109–43; decisionmaking

process, 119–27; former Soviet Union nations, 131–34; Middle East position, 129–31; National Security Council (NSC) role, 119–20, 135, 162, 165; new challenges, 127–37; position in world as of September 11, 127–29. See also EU membership (proposed for Turkey); U.S.-Turkey relations; specific countries

Former Soviet nations, Turkish relations with, 131–34

Franks, Tommy, 164

Free expression rights, 8, 93, 102, 103, 213

Fundamentalist Islam. See Political Islam

Georgia, Turkish relations with, 131

Germany, 161–62, 196

Gordon, Philip, 182

Gore, Al, 116

Government spending, 6, 32, 36–37, 38–43

Great Britain, 111

Greece-Turkey relations, 44, 180–82; Erdoğan's approach to, 254; Turkish public's views on, 154; U.S. views on, 111. See also Cyprus

Greek-Cypriots, 137, 187–90; EU admission of, 174, 177; link to mainland Greeks, 188–90; views on UN efforts, 185

Green Line. See Cyprus

Gül, Abdullah, 72, 78, 247, 254

Gulf War, 114–15, 159–60, 165

Gürel, Sükrü Sina, 125

HADEP (the People's Democratic Party), 11, 76, 94–99, 107

Hamas, 81

Hat Law (1925), 62

Headscarf as political issue, 73, 74, 76, 79, 84

Helms, Jesse, 227

Hisarciklioglu, Rifat, 166

Holbrooke, Richard, 207

Human rights: as EU admission criteria, 100, 103; in Turkish Cyprus, 190; and U.S.-Turkey relations, 220–23, 224

Hussein, Saddam. See Iraq

Iakovos (Archbishop of America), 114

Imia/Kardak crisis (1996), 180, 181

Income levels, 5; and economic collapse, 52; wage increases, 36–37

Inflation. See Economic instability

Inönü, Ismet, 110

Institute of Islamic Research, 63

International Monetary Fund (IMF): aid to Turkey from, 2; economic program for Turkey, 6–7, 35, 46–49, 54–56; preconditions for aid to Turkey from, 2, 44–45; standby arrangement (2002), 56–57; standby arrangement of 1985, 36; supplement to standby arrangement (2000), 50; U.S. support for continued IMF funding, 20, 26, 119, 138, 147, 214, 244

Iran: Islamic revolution in, 66; and Kurdish problem, 85, 87; Turkish relations with, 117, 122, 123, 129, 154, 162, 210; U.S. policy on, 216, 235

Iraq: and Cyprus situation, 201–02; and Kurdish problem,

85, 87, 88, 90, 96–97, 115, 218;
postwar status of Iraq, 20–21,
25–26, 139; Turkish relations
with, 129, 154, 165; UN
approval as prerequisite to
action against, 165; UN sanctions against, 217, 219; UN
weapons inspections, 216–17;
U.S.-Turkish relationship in
terms of, 2, 18–21, 25–26,
114–15, 138–39, 163, 164–68,
216–20, 233, 244, 248. *See also*
Gulf War; Kurdish state
Islamist movement. *See* Political
Islam
Islamist Welfare Party. *See*
Welfare Party
Israel: as enemy of Islamism, 67,
77–79; Turkish relations with,
114, 129–31, 140, 146, 154–55,
226–27

Johnson, Lyndon, 110, 151
Justice and Development Party.
See AK Party
Justice Party (Adalet Partisi), 65,
110

KADEK. *See* Kurdistan Freedom
and Democracy Congress
Kakarcali, Bulent, 182
Kazan, Şevket, 78
Kemalism, 62, 64, 88, 136
Kilinç, Tuncer, 162, 166, 239
Kıvrıkoğlu, Hüseyin, 79, 123,
136, 156, 166
Koh, Harold, 225
Korean conflict, 110
Kramer, Heinz, 211, 228
Kurdi, Said-i, 64
Kurdish language: ban on, 86;
campaign for use in education
and media, 98; military views

on, 121–22; permitted use in
education and media, 8, 11,
86, 93, 96, 98, 102, 103, 245
Kurdish state: AK Party's acquies-
cence to, 248; building of,
after disintegration of Iraq, 11,
20, 26, 138, 233–34; effect on
Turkish Kurds, 97; and political Islam, 76; U.S. intention to
build after Iraq war, 116, 165,
217; U.S. opposition to after
Iraq war, 244
Kurdistan Freedom and
Democracy Congress
(KADEK), 92, 233
Kurdistan National Liberation
Front (ERNK), 92
Kurdistan Popular Liberation
Army (ARGK), 92
Kurdistan Workers' Party. *See*
PKK (Kurdistan Labor Party)
Kurds, 11–12, 85–107; background of problem, 86–89;
death toll in political struggle,
85; as EU membership issue,
11–12, 91, 100–02; future of,
106–07, 234; Islamists' views
on, 64, 67, 74–76; policy
reform on, 96–99; and political Islam, 74–76; political
party of, 11–12, 94–99; representation lacking in new government, 95; settlement
sentiments, 95; size of constituency, 87; U.S. views on,
115–16, 212, 218, 220, 234. *See
also* Iraq; Kurdish state; PKK
(Kurdistan Labor Party)
Kutan, Recai, 72, 82
Kyprianou, Spyros, 184, 201

Language reforms. *See* Kurdish
language

Lausanne Treaty of 1923, 137
Lesser, Ian, 128, 238
Liberalization process. *See*
  Reform legislation
Liberal voters, 84
License transfer agreements, 45
Lobbying in U.S., 118, 130, 158,
  225–26, 235; Greek-
  Americans on Cyprus, 185;
  Jewish-Americans as pro-
  Turkey, 226–27

Makarios, Archbishop, 111, 184
Makovsky, Alan, 221
Media, 124–25. *See also* Kurdish
  language
Mehmet, Dervish, 63
Menemen Olayi, 63
MHP (Milliyetçi Hareket Partisi).
  See Nationalist Action Party
Middle East: Turkey as example
  to other countries, 210, 236,
  255; Turkish position in, 113,
  129–31, 242; U.S. influence in,
  238. *See also* Palestinian
  Israeli issue; *specific countries*
Military: arms purchases from
  Israel, 130, 156; EU in eyes of,
  162; and EU membership, 79,
  135, 136, 239; foreign policy
  role, 121, 228–30; Germany in
  eyes of, 161–62; intervention
  in northern Iraq, 20–21; Iraqi
  war waged by U.S., involvement in, 245; and Kurdish language use, 121–22; in Office
  of Prime Minister, 122; participation with U.S. and allies in
  recent conflicts, 210; and
  political Islam, 10, 79–80;
  political role of, 8, 70, 212,
  228–30; pro-Americanism of
  Turkish military, 160–63; U.S.

in eyes of, 18, 110, 157–63;
  "The Viewpoint of Turkish
  Civilian and Military
  Intelligentsia in Historical
  Perspective," 162–63. *See also*
  Military rule
Military rule: constitution under,
  64; and economic situation,
  35; and Islam, 66, 68, 71; and
  Kurds, 88; and U.S.-Turkish
  relations, 221
Milli Gazette, 77, 78
Minorities, repression of, 64,
  88–89, 100, 101. *See also*
  Kurds
Monetary policy, 36
Motherland Party, 125, 193, 255

Nagorno-Karabakh dispute, 131
Nationalist Action Party, 13, 66,
  71, 90, 125; opposition to
  reforms, 136
Nationalist Movement Party
  (Milliyetçi Hareket Partisi). *See*
  Nationalist Action Party
Nationalist Turkish Students
  Association, 66, 72
National Order Party (Milli Nizam
  Partisi), 64–65, 66, 67
National Review article on
  Turkish-Israeli relations, 155
National Salvation Party (Milli
  Selamet Partisi), 67
National Vision, 67, 72, 81
NATO. *See* North Atlantic Treaty
  Organization
New Turkey Party (Yeni Türkiye
  Partisi), 73
NGOs, human rights, 226. *See*
  also Human rights
North Atlantic Treaty
  Organization (NATO), 65, 104,
  110, 117, 133, 142, 157; chang-

ing nature of, 238; and Cyprus
situation, 175, 200, 204; and
Turkey's commitment to, 210
Nursi, Said-i, 64

Öcalan, Abdullah, 89–94; death
penalty for, 11, 75, 103; Greek
assistance to, 180, 218; public
opinion on, 96; pursuit and
capture of, 86, 117, 118, 218,
219, 230. *See also* PKK
(Kurdistan Labor Party)
Öcalan, Osman, 105–06
Official religion, abolition of, 62
Oil-drilling rights, dispute with
Greece, 181
O'Neill, Paul, 232
Operation Northern Watch, 217,
219
Operation Provide Comfort
(OPC), 115–16, 217, 219
Organization for Security and Cooperation in Europe (OSCE),
44, 133
Özal, Turgut: Cyprus strategy of,
180, 193; economic situation
under, 35–36, 37, 112; elections of, 35, 36, 113; foreign
policy of, 121, 123, 241; poli-
cies of, 113–14, 150; on strate-
gic relationship with U.S., 22,
113–14, 145, 150, 211
Özilhan, Tuncay, 165–66

Palestinian Israeli issue, 81, 130;
Turkish public's views on,
154–56, 227. *See also* Israel
Pantelides, Leonidas, 203
Papandreou, Andreas, 180
Parris, Mark R., 207
Peace Corps, 111
People's Democratic Party. *See*
HADEP

Pipeline construction, 116–17,
119, 131, 133, 214
PKK (Kurdistan Labor Party),
11–12, 89–94; ceasefire, 86,
90; defeat of, 220; development of, 89; Eighth Party
Congress, 92; EU admission of
Turkey supported by, 91;
European views of, 105; fighting Turkish government, 20,
89, 117; goals of, 93; Islamic
symbols used by, 74; KADEK
as successor to, 92, 233; reaction to EU's listing as terrorist
organization, 105–06, 136,
150; Seventh Party Congress,
91–92; U.S. position on, 211,
218, 244
Political and economic history,
33
Political Islam, 4, 9–10, 61–84;
and AK Party, 71–74, 252–53;
and army relations, 79–80;
and European Union, 82–83;
evaluation of development of,
10, 68–69; and February 28
coup, 69–71; ideology of, 66,
69–83; isolation policy's effect
on, 63; Israel as enemy of,
77–79; and Kurdish problem,
67, 74–76; and modernization
of Turkey, 61–63; multiparty
democracy and, 64–66;
phases of, 61–69; post-1980
military rule, 66–68; post-
September 11, 81–82, 152–53;
secular-adaptive vs. reactionary-conflictive type, 65;
setback to agenda of, 9–10;
size of Sunni-conservative
electorate, 83–84; as source of
anti-Americanism, 151–52;
uneducated poor as base of,

69; U.S.-Turkish relations affected by, 211, 221
Political parties, 7–9. *See also* Religious parties; *specific parties*
Poppy cultivation, 111
Powell, Colin, 201, 231
Provide Comfort, 115–16, 217
Public opinion: on Erdoğan, 10; on EU admission, 13, 103, 135, 168–69, 239–40; on international relations, 153–54; on Iraqi action by U.S., 235; on Israeli-Palestinian conflict, 154–56; on Kurdish nationalism, 96

Radical Islam. *See* Political Islam
RAND study on strategic relationship, 237
Reform legislation, 4, 11, 102–03, 107, 178, 245; for EU membership, under Copenhagen requirements, 11, 13–14, 25, 28, 134; free expression rights, 8, 93, 102, 103. *See also* Death penalty reform; Kurdish language
Religion, department of, 62
Religious parties: creation of, 63; and military, 8
Republican administrations in U.S., 118, 231
Republican People's Party (CHP): Dervis's effect on, 7; and November 2002 election results, 252; possible coalition with AK Party, 73; as substitute for AK Party, 74
Rogers Agreement, 119
Russian crisis and Turkish economy, 42–43
Russian-Turkish relations, 133–34, 140, 162

Saadet Party. *See* Felicity Party (Saadet Partisi)
Sanberk, Özdem, 147–48, 170
Saudi Arabia, 129, 132, 234
Savings Deposit Insurance Fund (SDIF), 45, 53, 55
Schools: reopening of religious schools, 64, 65; switch from religious to secular, 62. *See also* Kurdish language
Secularism. *See* Kemalism
September 11: and AK Party, 81–82; anti-Americanism after, 150–53; effect on U.S.-Turkish relations, 2, 104, 145–72, 208, 232–37; and EU relations with Turkey, 104–06; European views of, 105; foreign policy of Turkey as of, 127–29; and SP Party, 81–82; Turkish views of, 127, 146–50; as U.S.-Israeli plot, 82. *See also* Terrorism
Sezer, Ahmet Necdet, 122, 165
Sharon, Ariel, 131
Social security law, 45
Soros, George, 240
SP. *See* Felicity Party (Saadet Partisi)
Spirit of Davos (reconciliation effort over Cyprus), 180
State Department, U.S., view of Turkey, 223–25
State Economic Enterprises (SEEs), 35, 39, 46
Stoiber, Edmund, 196
Sufi sect, 64
Syria: Turkish relations with, 129, 154, 228; U.S. policy on, 235; warned not to harbor Öcalan, 117, 122–23

Talbott, Strobe, 212, 222
Taşgetrin, Ahmet, 76

Taxation, 37
Terrorism: PKK as terrorist organization, 105–06, 136, 149–50, 161; Turkey's cooperation in counterterrorism, 2, 81, 104, 127, 233; U.S. war against, 233–35. *See also* September 11
Textile industry. *See* Embargo
Toker, Metin, 110
Torumtay, Necip, 115
Trade, 35; with Armenia, 131–32; free-trade agreement with U.S., 240; in Middle East, 129; "suitcase trade" with Russia, 42, 133; and UN sanctions on Iraq, 217, 219; U.S. relations over, 114, 117, 138, 216. *See also* Embargo
Trafficking in persons report, 224
True Path Party (Dogru Yol Partisi), 68, 71, 96, 211, 244; AK Party as successor to, 255; opposition to reforms, 136
Truman Doctrine, 110
Turkey's Transformation and American Policy (Abramowitz), 164
Turkish Airlines, 48
Turkish Industrialists and Businessmen Association (TUSIAD), 126, 140, 165, 169
Turkish-Cypriots, 190–94; "Common Vision" document calling for settlement, 191; EU need to address concerns of, 197–98; independence as Turkish Republic of Northern Cyprus, 191; link to mainland Turkey, 193–94; majority-minority concepts, elimination of, 191–92; refusal to negotiate for EU accession, 176–77, 194–95;

UN resolutions and, 184–85, 190
Turkish Economic and Social Studies Foundation, 187
Türkmen, Ilter, 119
Türk Ocaklari (Turkish Janissary Corps), 65
Türk Telekom, 48

Unemployment, 58
United Nations: Cyprus, role in, 15, 173, 174, 183–87, 201; Iraq arms inspections, 216; Iraq campaign, approval for, 165; Iraq sanctions, 217, 219; peacekeeping missions and Turkish participation, 128. *See also* Annan Plan for Cyprus
U.S.-Turkey Joint Economic Council, 138
U.S.-Turkey relations, 4, 109–43, 207–49; as alternative to EU membership, 14, 26, 139, 169; ambiguity of, 153–56, 208; compensation for Turkish losses due to Iraqi military action, 168; Congress's views on, 225–27; decisionmaking process on in U.S., 223–30; and democratization, 220–23; designation of Turkey as major emerging market, 214; future of, 21–27, 137–39, 171–72; and human rights, 220–23; human rights issues, 220–23, 224; and Iraq, 2, 18–21, 164–68, 216–20; and Kurdish problem, 115–16; military aid from U.S., 157–58; military views of, 18, 110, 157–63; objectives of U.S., 209–13; policy recommendations, 243–46; post-Iraq war relations, 20–21; post-

September 11 relations, 2, 104,
145–72, 208, 232–37; pre-
September 11 relations, 230–32;
pro-Americanism of Turkish
military, 160–63; recent status
of, 110–19; strategic partnership, 2, 17, 22, 27, 118, 224,
236, 237–43; U.S. executive
branch's views on, 223–25. *See
also* Anti-Americanism; Bases
in Turkey; Bush (G.W.) administration; Clinton administration; Cyprus; EU membership
(proposed for Turkey)

Vassiliou, George, 184
Verheugen, Guenter, 198

Vietnam War, 151
Virtue Party (Fazilet Partisi), 67,
71, 72, 78

Wages. *See* Income levels
Water, 130
Welfare Party, 9, 67, 68, 71, 153,
211, 244, 252
Wolfowitz, Paul, 19, 113, 166–68,
169, 170, 235, 238
World Bank, 35, 50

Yilmaz, Mesut, 123–24, 143, 193,
222, 230

Zionism, opposition to, 65,
77–79. *See also* Israel

ABOUT THE CONTRIBUTORS

MORTON ABRAMOWITZ is a senior fellow at The Century Foundation. He was assistant secretary of state for intelligence and research (1985–89) and ambassador to Turkey (1989–91). He also was president of the Carnegie Endowment for International Peace (1991–97). He is the author of numerous articles on a wide range of foreign policy issues and editor of *Turkey's Transformation and American Policy* (The Century Foundation Press, 2000).

HENRI J. BARKEY is the Bernard L. and Bertha F. Cohen Professor of International Relations at Lehigh University, specializing in the international relations and domestic politics of Turkey and the Middle East. From 1998 to 2000 he served on the State Department's Policy Planning Staff. He is the author (with Graham E. Fuller) of *Turkey's Kurdish Question* (Rowman and Littlefield, 1998).

CENGIZ ÇANDAR is one of Turkey's leading political columnists and has worked for many major newspapers. He was special adviser to President Turgut Özal (1991–93) and is a founding member of the New Democracy Movement in Turkey. He was a public policy scholar at the Woodrow Wilson International Center in Washington, D.C., and a senior fellow at the U.S. Institute of Peace. He is the author of six books in Turkish, mainly on Middle East politics.

OMER CELIK is a columnist for the *Star* newspaper (Istanbul). He was elected to parliament in November 2002. He serves as chief political adviser to the chairman of the AK Party.

YALİM ERALP is a former Turkish ambassador to India and to the Organization for Security and Cooperation in Europe. In 1978–79 he was director of the U.S.–Turkish Security Relations Desk. From 1979 to 1983 he was first counselor and later deputy chief of mission of the

Turkish Embassy in Washington, D.C. From 1984 to 1987 he served as spokesman of the foreign ministry and from 1987 to 1991 as ambassador in India. From 1991 to 1996 he was adviser first to Prime Minister Mesut Yilmaz and later to Prime Minister Tansu Çiller while serving as director general of NATO affairs. From 1996 to 2000 he served as permanent representative of Turkey to the OSCE in Vienna. He is now a freelance writer and commentator for CNNTURK.

ERCAN KUMCU is the vice chairman of Tekfenbank, a former vice governor of the Central Bank of Turkey (1988–93), and a prominent Turkish columnist.

PHILIP ROBINS is a university lecturer specializing in the politics of the Middle East at the University of Oxford and a fellow of St. Antony's College. He also is the director of the university's Programme on Contemporary Turkey. He is the author of *Suits and Uniforms: Turkish Foreign Policy since the Cold War* (Hurst/University of Washington Press, forthcoming).

M. JAMES WILKINSON had an active role in U.S.-Greek-Turkish affairs as deputy assistant secretary of state for Europe and U.S. special Cyprus coordinator (1985–89). He also was engaged in Cyprus issues at the UN as deputy U.S. representative to the Security Council with the rank of ambassador (1989–90). He consulted (1996–98) for the Carnegie Commission on Preventing Deadly Conflict, which published his report on the area in June 1998.